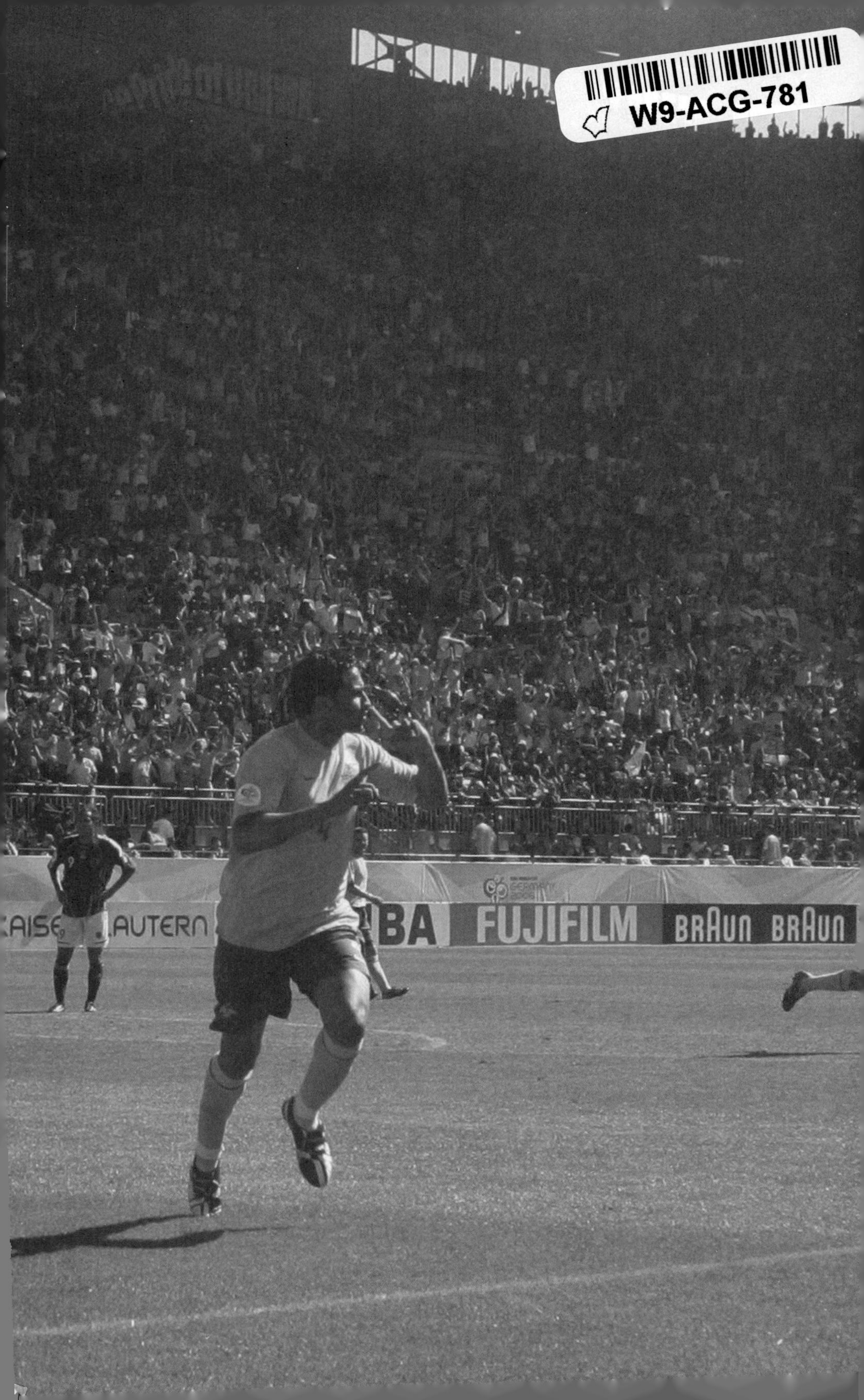
FUJIFILM
BRAUN BRAUN

LEGACY

TIM CAHILL
LEGACY

HarperCollins*Publishers*

In memory of
Faataualofa Tuato
Born 3 April 1932, died 27 May 2005

The backbone of our family

The strongest person in my life, along with
my mother Sisifo Tuato Cahill

Taught me everything about my culture,
heritage and beliefs

And the most important lesson of all:
family over everything

I learned that courage was not the absence of fear, but the triumph over it. The brave man is not he who does not feel afraid, but he who conquers that fear.

Nelson Mandela

CONTENTS

FOREWORD

I'LL NEVER FORGET THE DAY I decided to sign Tim Cahill. Not simply because I was sure I'd spotted a fantastic raw talent. It was quite a day all round. It was 2 May 2002. In my last season in charge of Preston we'd been searching around for players of ability and seen Millwall a couple of times. This energetic, pugnacious Aussie in midfield stood out.

My first transfer market as Everton manager was about to open and, having seen Tim about the championship a couple of times, I persuaded chairman Bill Kenwright that we should go together to watch Millwall against Birmingham in the second leg of the play-off semi-final. I mentioned to Bill that we'd be looking at a couple of guys, including Steven Reid, but, privately, my main attention was going to be on this Aussie fella.

Bill picked me up in his old Jag and we drove down to the New Den in South London. I've seen some atmospheres in my time as a player and coach, but this was fearsome, let me tell you. Tight streets, low bridges, both sets of fans with a reputation for being a bit feisty; in fact, there was horrible rioting and fighting associated with this tie, and as we drove past the supporters in this elegant old motor they were thumping and banging on the roof and the windows. We had to want to be there.

Millwall lost 0–1 in the last seconds and thus missed the chance of going to the final in Cardiff. Tim hit the bar with one of what would become his trademark headers with Everton. Immediately after the game, as we drove north, I told Bill that we had to have this guy. What stood out to the naked eye was that he was tremendously effective in both boxes: defensively able and usually the first to head clear, but also with the hunger, ambition and engine to be up in the opposition penalty area quickly afterwards looking to do danger.

Right then, he brought to mind a guy I'd always admired – John Wark. John would often outscore the strikers at his club because he had this fantastic ability to time when he arrived in and around the box and the means to finish the physical work he'd put in to get there. I was sure that this Cahill fella was one from that production line.

When we finally got him to our offices for a meeting with me and the chairman something else happened. His personality knocked our socks off. Not only was I very impressed by this guy in whom I was about to invest a lot of faith and a lot of hope, but Bill was bowled over too. What oozed out of him was not only resolute self-belief but great character. To this day

Tim has the ability to charm people, to make them like him or believe in him. In truth, he's a very likeable guy who conducts himself well.

This won't surprise you, but I'd mark him down as easily one of the two or three players who most helped me change Everton, one of the best signings I've ever made. He's seen, I think, as a major Premier League footballer, but the fact that he came from the lower leagues to the very top and not only managed to bridge that gap with considerable ease but also help rebuild the fortunes and reputation of a leading Premier club is a terrific testimony to his personal and footballing talents.

Beyond his immense character, I'd pinpoint two things about Tim. Obviously the first is his world-class aerial ability. He's among the best ever. But we'll come back to that. The other is that he has this great tendency to 'appear' when he's most needed. Big games where a win is vital, a match where things are going against you, a draw turned into a single-goal win – Tim was the fella you'd always count on. Any manager – more importantly, any fan – will tell you that they treasure a player like that. Priceless.

We got a pretty quick return on our investment if you look at his first-season performance and his debut goal. That header past David James for an away win at Manchester City, just seconds before Tim was sent off, will live as long in the memory as the day we decided to buy him.

Whether he was scoring or not, what was an absolute constant throughout his years for us was that Tim was a real man in training. He trained as hard as he played, and my advice to younger players is to copy that. Train as you mean to play: compete, work, give everything and match day will not only see you perform better but win more. That's what Tim always gave: 100 per cent, every day.

Physically he'd compete with you, mentally he'd look for ways to outsmart other players or find their weak points. Both in training and in matches, he'd leave a bit on you in the challenge if that's what he felt was important in order to win. He never, ever hid.

Saying all that, what I guess most people will talk about is his remarkable leap. We often tried to figure out what were the elements behind it. He's not got particularly massive thighs or calf muscles, and what we concluded was that it was a mix of innate timing, hunger to win the ball in all situations and the fact that he was very, very lean. With his extremely low body fat, he was light – as well toned as he was muscularly. Mix all that and getting above bigger men to head the ball becomes both feasible and a great art.

But I want to add to that perception: it's one thing to get to the ball, quite another what you do with it. Tim was an absolutely phenomenal header of the ball. Once he got up, he was in a class of his own, whether heading it away from danger or putting it where a keeper couldn't reach it.

Thanks for all those headers, Tim. One other little thing that people often forget is that it takes bravery. You had that in buckets.

However, I'll dare to lift the lid on another side of you. When we completed the medical to sign this promising midfielder from Millwall, it was a massive, massive relief to Tim because of a nasty cruciate ligament injury he'd had about a year previously. Footballers sweat over medicals and deals can break down. So when he got the news that he'd passed with flying colours there were some tears of relief and happiness. I liked that. I saw it as determination and ambition and a need to push upwards to bigger challenges. Raw desire to win exhibits itself in different ways.

Tim leaving Everton was a terrible wrench for me. He'd been so much a fundamental part of what we'd constructed at Goodison. But we knew there would be a moment when he needed a change and going to the New York Red Bulls was a great move for him. I wasn't in the least surprised that he proved himself important there too. I suspect he became really popular in New York, just as he was with Everton fans. In China he's been scoring frequently since he moved to Shanghai and I think his career will, once again, find another level there.

Tim's international career with Australia was always something of a difficulty for us when he was at Everton. Usually it meant travel to the other side of the world and international games midweek – not ideal for a Premier League star who's a vital component in a hard-working team. Yet he'd always get himself back in time, by hook or by crook, no matter what the distance, no matter how inconvenient the travel, no matter how severe the jet lag or lack of sleep. He fought like a tiger to make sure he could star for his country *and* help Everton win.

He's been just immense for Australia, I think. His goal in the 2014 World Cup against the Netherlands was the best in the tournament. Some achievement that!

As a football nation Australia has continued to grow in importance and a big part of that has come from Tim and what he's done for the country. Talent and personality. He and Harry Kewell, in particular, have been the standard bearers. Top European players. His legacy for Everton and for Australia will be that of quality, hunger, achievement and popularity. Of goals, thrills, fun, competitiveness and ambition. That will live on in the memory for a long, long time.

Tim joined me on the pitch when I said my own goodbyes at Everton and I was surrounded by some really special players – it was good of him to make that journey for me. I thought it was very fitting. In fact I was grateful and delighted.

Vital to me from the beginning, there with me at the end.

Thanks for everything, Tim. It's been emotional.

David Moyes
September 2015

LEGACY

PART 01

BEGINNING THE DREAM

FEARLESS

I CAN'T REMEMBER A TIME when I wasn't dreaming of football.

I grew up in Sydney, in a football-loving home. My dad, a Londoner by birth, was fanatical about all things related to the game. From the time I was three or four years old, I didn't need to play with toys. I was perfectly happy with something round that could be kicked.

Funnily enough, during my first competitive football match, I found myself scared out of my wits. We played Under-5s for a team called the Balmain Police Tigers. My brother Sean was five years old. I was four. I remember the match so clearly. I wore an orange kit with black shorts and orange socks. And when I ran out onto the pitch, I immediately started crying. The pitch was muddy, the other kids looked big and intimidating, and I didn't want to get my kit dirty. But every time I tried to run off, my parents pushed me back from the touchline.

The kids on the team laughed at me. All the adults on the touchline did too, thinking it was cute, I suppose. But I wasn't laughing. Tears kept streaming down my cheeks.

Maybe I wasn't quite ready to play with the older boys, but it was like how a lot of kids learn to swim. You're thrown in the water, you splash around, then dog-paddle over to the side of the pool—no adult is really going to let you sink—and that's how you learn the lesson.

After that miserable first half, I realized I wasn't going to be trampled. I touched the ball a few times and got into the flow of the game. I didn't go after the ball so much as the ball was kicked against me by the other boys.

I was too frightened to be making any actual passes, let alone take a shot. But even that cold, muddy ball hitting my thighs and shins taught me something. The fear of what you *imagine* is often the worst part. With every ball that came to me, I learned I could withstand the impact, the surprising sting of the ball.

Touch by touch, I started to get better. As frightening as that first match was, my nervousness faded away—my passion for football began to grow.

*

My mum's from a small village in Samoa. She grew up on a plantation that raised livestock and grew crops like taro and bananas. It was a simple life, and I don't think she ever, in her wildest dreams, imagined she'd get married and live one day in a big city like Sydney, let alone have four Australian-born children.

My father left England by boat in search of a new life. He ended up stopping off in Samoa, doing some fishing, met my mum, Sissy, fell in love, and then had to steal her off the island before my Samoan grandfather could catch him. My dad and mum went on a massive adventure to Australia—and, from what I always heard as a boy, it was pretty hard times back then. Both worked long hours, crashing at friends' places, until they could afford to rent their first home. When I speak to my mum, even to this day, I can hear in her voice how tough her life has been. Talk about a risk! She left behind the only world she knew, in that simple but happy village—Tufuiopa, Apia—where her father and grandfather were both chiefs, to start a family in Australia.

I have an older sister, Dorothy—we all call her Opa—an older brother, Sean, and then I came along in December 1979. We never had much money or security. We would rent a place for six or eight months, then pack up and move. It seemed like we were always hopping from one new neighbourhood and new bedroom to another, where we'd do it all over again.

Constantly moving homes had its difficulties, but the reason was always in the back of my mind—my parents were working hard to put food on the table and make our lives better, whatever it took.

I'm sure it was stressful and anxious at times for my mum and dad, but for me there was always an escape: football.

My dad always watched the big English league matches, the FA Cups and the European Cups. I can remember it from when I was as young as three years old. Even at that age, I understood the passion for the game, if not all the rules and finer points.

West Ham United had been my father's club and those allegiances never leave you, as I would later see myself in my years playing for Millwall and Everton. My father grew up in Rainham, Essex, where his dad, my grandfather, had played for the Rainham Working Men's Club. He had been on the verge of getting signed for Colchester when he broke his leg badly, which ended his career. Dad often talked about his being coached by guys like the centre-back Charlie Hurley, from County Cork in Ireland, who ended up playing for Millwall and then had a long career as a top defender at Sunderland.

I remember being a tiny kid, waking up at silly hours of the morning because I could hear loud cheering in the lounge room, or could see flickering lights from the hallway—even hear the sound of the football being kicked—and I'd sneak out of my bedroom and not let my dad see me, just hide for the first fifteen minutes, until he'd finally notice and allow me to sit with him and watch the match.

Even though I had school the next day, Dad would let me miss sleep to watch all the highlights we could from England. Rarely were West Ham games shown in Australia, but we'd see the biggest clubs, like Manchester United, Arsenal, Liverpool and Chelsea, in what was then called the First Division (the Premier

League didn't come into existence until 1992 when I was already a teenager).

We'd also watch a lot of continental football, especially Italian teams. AC Milan playing Juventus—that was a big Italian league match I remember well. One of the most powerful experiences of my life was seeing that "golden age" Milan team made up of so many gifted players—greats like Marco van Basten, Ruud Gullit, Paolo Maldini.

Dad would also let me watch World Cup games into the early hours of the morning. I'd be too excited to sleep. As a kid, I remember dreaming of one day playing professionally. But I realized that was such a long shot.

By this point my kid brother Chris had been born and part of my realization was that with the size of our family—three boys and a sister—there was no way my parents would ever be able to meet the costs involved. Even at that age, I somehow understood that making it as a professional footballer wasn't only about talent. Or even willpower. Maybe it was something Dad had said in passing, but I knew that money was often the biggest obstacle to getting the opportunity to play at the highest levels of the sport.

*

I kept watching big European and English matches on TV with my dad, playing in the back garden, in the hallway with my brothers, even in the tight spaces of the bedroom.

Everywhere I walked, I was basically kicking a football. In the bedroom, Sean and I used to kick the ball off the walls. The rule was you got one touch to volley it to the bunk beds. We'd take turns: five shots each from a fair distance. When we'd hear my mum walking down the hallway we'd instantly stop—"Sean and Tim, what are you up to?" My brother would rush to sit at the desk, I'd hop on the bed and pretend to be reading a book, because, like mothers everywhere, she didn't want us banging a football off the walls or the bedroom furniture.

Sharing that time with my older brother was crucial. Despite the age difference, my father always had us placed in the same teams. Sean's typical of big brothers, but especially of Samoan big brothers. He was always looking after me, protecting me, giving me little pointers and tricks. If some kid on the opposing team came in hard on a challenge and fouled me, well, Sean made sure that kid would never kick me again. Deep down, Sean has the kindest nature, but he could be a tough guy on the pitch—especially when it came to watching out for me.

By the time I reached eight or nine years old, my skills had improved a lot. I think that came from always playing in a higher age group. That was my mum and dad's influence. Survival of the fittest, I suppose. If I was going to be the youngest and smallest boy on the field, forced to hold my own against larger, stronger opponents, my technique and confidence had to improve. I knew early on that I would have to be quicker, learn faster and outsmart the boys I played against. I couldn't out-jump or out-muscle anyone, but I saw pretty soon that I might be able to out-think them.

Never in my entire youth football career did I play in my own age group. Part of it was logistics, too. Our parents were so busy working that Sean and I had to train on the same schedule. We couldn't go to different pitches, have different pick-up times. It would be a huge inconvenience and cost Mum and Dad more in petrol.

*

We often say in a Samoan family that you've got to have a head like a coconut. Playing football or rugby in the back garden, you get more than a few knocks and kicks to the head. It's just part of growing up. And Samoans are known for being rough and tumble. With us—with all islanders, really—when you have a fight at home, the kid who cries first is the one who gets the parental smack. That's just the Samoan culture. Boys aren't coddled much; they're taught to hold their own, take a few knocks and get on with it.

Of course this meant I was always getting the smack, because there was no chance I was ever beating my older brother Sean, let alone some of my Samoan cousins—hulking guys twice my size, some of whom went on to play professional rugby.

Sean and I would often get into tussles. We'd stand there toe to toe, he'd be looking down into my eyes, I'd be looking up into his, defiant, and he'd always say, "Don't let fear hold you back. If you want a shot at the title, I'm here."

He'd say it with a smile, because he knew no matter how angry I got, how much I fought, I could never put him down.

"Don't let fear hold you back, bro!"

I'd stare at him with anger, then charge him like a little bull. It was like hitting a brick wall—BOOM!—and I'd pop up and run at him again.

We moved beyond those years, but Sean's words always stuck with me. To this day it's something Sean and I still share—more than an in-joke, it's a brotherly bond. No matter where I'm playing—in England or New York or Shanghai, or representing the national team in World Cups—I'll get a text from him, out of the blue, with those same words:

Don't let fear hold you back.

*

After Balmain Tigers, my next club was Marrickville Red Devils. Marrickville was a community that simply loved football. Every weekend was like a carnival, with the different languages and cultures, the foods, smells and flags of so many diverse nations. Nowhere do you see the melting pot of Australia as clearly as in the faces of the families who are passionate about football.

I soon made a lot of great friends in Marrickville and, now that I had more technical skills, football actually became *fun*. I was no longer the frightened four-year-old who had to be shoved onto the pitch. In the ebb and flow of the match, I found my release. I wasn't afraid to take on other players, dribbling, feinting and using the simple art of the one-two with the other midfielders and forwards.

Marrickville Red Devils holds a special place in my heart because it was where I scored my first header. I can still see it unfolding vividly in my mind—like a slow-motion movie. We'd won a corner. The ball was whipped in from the right, I timed my jump, keeping my eyes wide open. Three defenders around me flinched and shrugged at the ball. I climbed above them, saw my chance and took it. I headed it, clean on the forehead, directing it exactly where I'd intended—with power—into the goal.

When the net bulged, when my team-mates swarmed me and cheered, my confidence soared. I remember turning, even as the ball flew past the keeper, to see people on the touchlines—my mum and dad and some of the other adults—already screaming.

It's a big deal in a young footballer's life when he scores his first header. We'd all scored goals with tap-ins or well-timed strikes, but leaping and directing a header with power was a more advanced skill.

Over the years, it's become something of a signature for me. Five of the first six goals I scored for the Australian national team came from headers. People have said that I head a ball the way most other players kick it. That's largely because when I see that cross come in, I'm fearless. Players often head the ball with reservation: they tuck their head in, flinch and squint— you even see this among some professionals. What that means, in effect, is that they're letting the ball take *control*. You can see they don't truly *want* to head it. With me, it's the opposite.

Once I understood how to do it properly, I fell in love with heading. It felt, for some reason, very Samoan. Being fearless, athletic and powerful with your head is not something everyone has the ability to do on the pitch and I soon saw that as an avenue to success.

Confidence breeds more confidence. There was a natural progression from that moment; I started scoring a lot of headers regularly. My dad's often said that even as a youth player I probably scored a good fifty or sixty per cent of my goals with my head. Crosses from the wing, free kicks and especially corners—I'd found I had a knack for leaping and getting good contact on the ball with my forehead. Still, at that age, I didn't have much power in my shot, though I always had excellent timing: catching the ball as it bounced and volleying it over the goalkeeper's head. We were still all relatively short kids, so lobbing over the net-minder was an effective way to score.

With the Red Devils, my vision, technique and ability to head the ball made me stand out, despite being a year younger than anyone else in the squad. And the more I scored with my head, the more I would train and train at heading. Some weeks, I spent hours just trying to perfect the angling and generate more power with my contact.

I see this change in confidence a lot in the youth academies I run in Australia, and it comes down to the basics. You have to take kids through the art of heading slowly, step by step, from square one, because sticking your head in the path of a flying object goes against common sense! To do it well you have to keep your eyes wide open and your mouth shut. You can't be passive and let the ball hit the crown, but actually have to attack it with your forehead.

Now I teach my own son Cruz, who's still only three—just as I've taught my sons Kyah and Shae and my daughter Sienna: "Head the ball the way Daddy does. Open your eyes, make clean contact!" I can already see the confidence growing in Cruz. When you breed that self-assuredness in a young kid, it makes it easier for them to do *anything*. Getting that parental encouragement and the first sense of confidence only snowballs and you inevitably get better.

I'm a firm believer that kids don't truly find themselves until they experience that first moment of confidence. For me it came when I scored that first header for Marrickville Red Devils.

*

In the midst of all my outdoor team commitments, I started regularly playing indoor soccer, also known as *futsal*. Playing indoor soccer was important in my technical development because the spaces are tighter, the action quicker, and it requires a player to develop a greater sense of touch and ball control.

We played for a team called Banshee Knights. Our team identity was Irish but our close-knit group of friends—Ian Frenkel, Filimon Filippou, Vince Hansimikali and Nick

Pizzano—were from loads of backgrounds. The name Banshee Knights was my father's idea. Dad's of Irish descent and loved those screaming banshees of Celtic legend. We wore the green and white with black shorts.

We were all talented individuals, and as a team we were fierce. We played in a lot of big competitions. Once we even travelled to Canberra for a tournament, though we lost in the finals to a team led by Nick and Leo Carle, two South American brothers who were also fantastically gifted indoor players. Despite that loss we continued to be known as the underdog team that seemed to do well on big occasions.

*

When I'm asked about my mentality as a footballer—what drives me so hard on and off the park—I always say it was seeing my parents get up at the crack of dawn, 5:30 a.m., to go to work. Mum always had two jobs: working at various hotels early in the day, then a second job at Streets Ice Cream factory that she would finish by 6 p.m. My dad got up early, too, to drive her to work—he'd suffered an injury on his job, but he became the best house-dad. He did all the cleaning, cooking, all the running around with the four of us kids—probably one of the hardest jobs in the world.

My family wasn't well-off—my brothers, sister and I were never in a position to spend money frivolously with our mates, because that would affect the household budget. I was constantly aware of how hard both my mum and dad worked just to make ends meet.

Even at a young age I worried about how much my mum pushed herself: how many hours she worked, the lack of sleep, just to make sure we had the necessities like school books and school uniforms—not to mention those extras for football.

By the time I was ten years old, I fully understood and respected what my parents did to support our passion for the game. I understood how expensive it was for new boots and kit, plus the registration fees for clubs. I knew the sacrifices my parents were making. It wasn't a hobby, even at that age, to join a club and play in tournaments. Football was a *commitment* and a major financial sacrifice for my family.

Often, I heard my mum get up in the morning and, just before she left, I'd hop out of bed and say goodbye to her because I knew I wouldn't see her until very late that evening. Those memories left a mental scar that has stayed with me for life. Even at four years old I knew that life for my parents was a constant struggle.

After my indoor football games, we'd drive to a small Greek gyros shop in Marrickville. We'd go there on Thursday night, excited because it was our one treat for the week. I'd order a beef gyros with lettuce, onions and barbecue sauce, and many times my mum wouldn't order: "No, I'm okay—I don't want anything."

I'd eat only half, handing the rest to my mum, saying, "Sorry, I'm full." She's a very astute woman, but to this day she probably doesn't know that I understood the reason she didn't order anything was because, first and foremost, she was always looking out for us.

And even now, regardless of how much I'm earning as a footballer, she hasn't changed. Whenever we go to a restaurant in Australia, my mother will pick the cheapest item on the menu. I'll smile and say, "Mum, go ahead, order *whatever.*" But it doesn't matter—she's still as economical as she was when I was a kid.

REACHING HIGHER

THE NEXT LEVEL UP IN my youth career was when I joined Lakemba Soccer Club and was selected to play for Canterbury Reps. Now I'd joined an elite group of boys. One of my best mates, even to this day, Anthony Panzarino, was to become a massive influence on my development. Anthony and I hit it off immediately and were soon inseparable. We played together for both Lakemba and the Reps. Canterbury had more than a dozen club teams; if you'd done well at your club, you'd receive a call up, but only one or two players from each club got the honour.

Only a few players from Lakemba were selected. Making it to Canterbury Reps was a pretty big deal; this was no longer football as recreation. If you made the team you'd travel all around Australia. We were ten and eleven years old, the age when we were starting to find ourselves as footballers, and travelling with Canterbury opened the world to us.

I remember during our Lakemba and Canterbury Representative days it seemed like we *never* stopped playing football. If we weren't in class—or sleeping—we had a ball at our feet. I'd go round to Anthony's house, kicking the ball with him for an hour before training, shooting and passing against the wall or along the side of his garage.

Anthony and I both had long hair down the back of our necks like so many of the great Italian and Latin American players in those days. We were trying to look like Redondo, the brilliant Argentine midfielder; just about everything else we did was an imitation of the big-time professional footballers: the way they walked, their mannerisms we'd seen on the TV, right down to how they wore their kit.

At home, Anthony's dad, Mick Panzarino, always watched Italian league matches. Anthony's mum, Beatrice, would put out a huge spread of food. His dad would sit at the head of the table and we'd feast on fresh-baked Italian bread, salads, pastas, meatballs and imported mozzarella, while watching those matches from Italy on the TV in the living room.

I used to love going to the Panzarinos', especially after training when we were always ravenous. I'd never tasted better food in my life.

Anthony and I didn't have one single day in the week when we weren't playing football. Talk about a time commitment: there were loads of driving and logistical arrangements for our parents. During the indoor season our schedules were packed. Lakemba matches on Saturday, Canterbury Reps on

Sunday, indoor matches with the Banshee Knights on Thursday afternoon.

Add in practices for all those teams and there was really not a single day of the week when I wasn't either in training or playing a competitive match. Football consumed my entire life, but I didn't *want* anything else. I didn't want to hang out and do what the other kids from school were doing. And, outside of games and practices, Anthony and I would put in hours training on our own at his place. Looking back on it now, it's obvious we were little machines who were completely in love with the game.

By this time in our lives we were getting a reputation as an elite group, and I was lucky to be among such skilled young players. My parents still have a clipping from one of the Sydney papers that referred to us as "the Maradonas of tomorrow". For a kid my age, at that time, there was no higher compliment.

Such a *fantastic* age, too. We had so much energy, jumping fences, meeting up after school. My mates and I would quickly ring each other after school and go to the park with my brothers Sean and Chris. We'd play three v. three. I remember getting into punch-ups because one team had lost 1–0 or 2–3 or some such foolishness—I mean, we took those kickabouts *that* seriously. We'd fight over who scored, or who fouled whom. Whether it should be a throw-in or a corner kick—any little thing. Then we'd run home to our own houses. And the next day—it didn't matter that we'd fought the day before—we'd ring each other up and do it all over again.

Those are priceless childhood memories. I could never stand losing at anything. Not with my brothers, not with my mates. Just wasn't acceptable. Years later, funnily enough, when I was playing for Everton, I'd find myself having a similarly competitive friendship with one of the most gifted footballers of the Premier League, the Spaniard Mikel Arteta.

Some days Anthony's dad would take us to training, other days it would be my dad's turn. But no matter who was driving there was no small talk: these were serious football lessons. The whole way to training, our dads would talk tactics and strategy: how we were going to play and link up together as midfielders. If it was a game day, the talk would be more motivational—"How badly do you want to win, boys?"—right down to the level of asking us if our boots were clean. It's those details that show your level of passion, pride and commitment to the sport.

When it came to football both our dads knew what they were talking about. With my father, it was bred in the bone: that hard-core working-class Londoner's love of the game. With Anthony's father, there was more Italian flair, but he was equally passionate.

Anthony and I usually huffed and puffed and muttered under our breath: "Bloody hell, our dads don't know nothing ..." But I can see now how much they did know, and how deeply they affected our lives.

I can still hear Anthony's father's voice as we'd drive to the Lakemba training sessions.

"Anthony, you need to shoot more—you're taking too long on the ball" or "Anthony, you need to get the ball wide to the wing, so Tim can meet the cross. And you both need to link better together."

Anthony and I formed a solid partnership on the pitch. We both played in midfield. Sometimes I'd play slightly in front of him. We each had our strengths. He had a really powerful shot. I had strong heading ability and vision.

Still, I was a long way from a finished article at that age. Some of the other kids had better shots, great touch and control of the ball. At that stage in our lives, I often played with kids who were more polished and technical. I wasn't discouraged if I saw one of my mates, or one of my brothers, had a better shot, though I'd sometimes shake my head in amazement when he'd strike a precise volley into the back of the net. If anything, my admiration for that skill fuelled my own ambition. It inspired me to improve my own shooting. I'd find myself studying everything my mates did to generate that same power.

By the time I was playing with Lakemba and Canterbury Reps, my dad's expectations for me had grown. He'd always been this way, but, as I got older, he kept raising the bar and the scrutiny got more intense.

Back when we lived in Annandale, Dad would take all three of us brothers—Sean, Chris and me—down to the park at the back of Johnson Street for training. These weren't casual kickabouts: he had us looking like little professionals, running through cones, doing sprints against each other, various triangle passing drills. He'd also make us work hard on our heading. He kept a ball inside a net-bag, hooked to the branch of a tree. Talk about an *old-school* trick. You rarely see anyone practising headers that way anymore. Each one of us in turn would run as fast as we could, leap up and head the ball, learning how to make good contact and get proper direction. And we'd *better* get it right, or Dad would make us do it over and over again.

Because he always stressed the importance of being two-footed, Dad would sometimes have us take the boot off our stronger-kicking leg—in my case the right—and have us shoot only left-footed. It's a simple technique but a highly effective one.

Dad would also regularly take videos of my matches and then show them to me on the TV at home, focussing not on what I'd done well, but on what I could improve.

"Look, Tim, I know you scored three goals but you could have had four." He used to stress that I needed to develop more power in my legs. He would also tell me that I was arriving in the box too early. He would freeze-frame the video and show me. "Look, here: if you'd held up your run a bit, see how much better positioned you'd be for the open cross?"

My dad was an instinctive motivator. He was never one for patting you on the back. No hugs after matches. And I'd never—or very rarely—hear him say, "Well done, son, you were terrific out there today."

Still, I'd occasionally catch him, when I'd scored a nice goal—a well-timed header or difficult volley—and there'd be a momentary flash of pride. A glance that expressed words he'd never say, just for a second in his eyes.

That was priceless to me. Even as a kid, that's all you need: to catch that fraction of a second of pride in your father's eyes. I never needed anything more than that. The fact that he withheld praise, I think, prevented me from becoming complacent. He gave me enough praise to keep me going—and held back enough to keep me hungry.

In fact, I think my parents' tough motivational style, more than anything else, is what made me into a top-flight footballer. So many times after a match, when I'd done alright on the pitch, I'd get in the car and my mum would take the sandal off her foot and smack me on the back of the head—not to hurt or anything, just chiding me, because that's the Samoan way of doing things. My dad, meanwhile, was peppering me with his criticisms: "Why are you smiling, son? You could've won 5–0 instead of 5–3. Why weren't you tracking back from the midfield? Helping out the back four? Letting in those late goals is nothing to be proud of."

The funny thing was, when my parents said something similar to my brothers Sean and Chris, their response would be to nod and shrug: *Yeah, so what? Not bothered.* Yet each of my brothers in his own way was very gifted. Sean was an incredible goalkeeper and Chris, five years younger than me, was technically superb. My dad has often said that Chris had better footballing attributes than I did at his age. He was the more complete player, with better skills and a more developed body.

Where my brothers would shrug off our father's critique of our playing, I'd go home and dwell on it. *Yeah, you know, Dad's right*, I'd say to myself. *If only I'd taken a better touch, and simply passed the ball into the net, instead of trying to smash it—two feet wide of the post! I missed that chance—* missed *it ...*

It would actually keep me awake at night, obsessing over the littlest mistakes my dad had scolded me for in some regular Under-10 or Under-11 game. It didn't matter that I'd scored. I'd lie there angry at myself for the ones I hadn't put in the back of the net. If a missed opportunity had meant a draw instead of a win, because I'd made the decision to go for power rather than simply pass the ball into the net, I'd beat myself up over it. I know that sounds ludicrously perfectionist for a kid of ten, but you've got to have that kind of drive to succeed in football. My commitment and passion were on a different level from either of my brothers'— and to this day, no one in the family knows exactly why.

I wasn't a normal kid. I'm the first to admit it. I was definitely not *normal*. I was so obsessed with football that when I got up in the morning, the first thing I did was look at my boots, making sure they were clean and spotless. Not a speck of dirt or a grass stain better be on them. They had to look brand new. I had various official team kits. I especially loved the Manchester United kits—the green and yellow away shirt and the classic red home kit with the tie-up front. I'd make sure they were all hung up, clean and neat in the closet, looking just like they were in a shop window.

Before I left for school, I'd have my Lakemba or Canterbury Reps kit all laid out for when I got home, knowing I'd have after-school training. Boots spotless, shin pads perfect, my socks neatly laid out across the bed. When it was time to leave I had my trainers on, my boot bag ready, my water bottle filled— my parents didn't have to do a thing. I already had that focussed mind-set of a full-time footballer.

At a very young age I was self-disciplined and an extreme perfectionist. I can't recall a time when I wasn't this way: my brother Sean used to tease me about it. He still does, because I'm known as the one of the three boys who can't stand clutter, disorganization or anything out of order in my home or with my clothes.

I realize now, in hindsight, that in the six or seven years since I'd started playing football, a combination of my perfectionist personality, good role models, opportunities to play—even my mum's Samoan whacks with her sandal and my dad's post-match analysis—all of it turned a passion for the game of football into an obsession that would soon consume my life.

GOLDEN BICYCLES AND OLYMPIC DREAMS

FOOTBALL BECAME MY WHOLE WORLD. I fell hopelessly in love with the game. The only friends I had were my footballing friends. I had mates at school, but we didn't get together after school. I really didn't have a spare minute. I was so engrossed in the game that I watched it and trained every day. More importantly, I was learning to *respect* the game.

At the age of seven, my dad took me to meet a key figure, a man who was to play a pivotal role in transforming my game. His name was Johnny Doyle. Johnny Doyle was the local guru of football, a former player turned coach, who was known for bringing out the best in players though private clinics and lessons.

Before we even met, my dad told me about Johnny Doyle's past: born in Ireland, he came to Australia and played professionally at centre-forward for various teams like

South Sydney Croatia, Pan Hellenic, APIA Leichhardt and Canterbury-Marrickville Olympic. He'd even been called up for the Australian national team in 1970. After his playing days he became a coach at a high level for football teams in Australia.

Johnny had the build of a classic No. 9—the strong centre-forward. A big dominating presence. He also had a schoolteacher's mentality. He was a mathematics teacher at Kingsgrove North High School, where I would be enrolled a few years later.

I started doing sessions with Johnny Doyle at the age of seven and continued until I was fifteen. Meeting him for the first time, I was excited but nervous. Here was this coach who'd made dozens of good players into great ones. And, according to my dad, there were even some players who used to train with Johnny Doyle right before they went overseas to trial with professional clubs.

That was my dream. Somehow getting an overseas trial. Johnny was like the finishing act: the master trainer before any kid—any good Sydney-based player—jetted overseas. My dad's opinion, at least, was that the only way I was going to make it as a professional footballer was under the tutelage of Johnny Doyle.

He held his lessons on the little home pitch of St George Football Club. Simple clubhouse, locker room, three pitches. We used to park the car, jump over a little fence, then walk down this pathway to where Johnny Doyle would be waiting with his sack of footballs and his equipment. We'd do private lessons, just me individually, but also small group sessions of two or three. Those were usually with my brother Sean, and with a young player named David James who in later years would become one of my closest mates.

Straightaway, I saw that Johnny was a different style of coach from any I'd met before: he stressed close ball control, quick touches, two-footed shooting—a more European or Latin American style of technical football. He changed my entire sense of touch and way of striking the ball.

But the most important characteristic of Johnny Doyle's style was *belief*. He took my game to the next level because he believed in me. Long before anyone else, he saw that I might really have a future in the sport. He recognized the intangibles: the drive, the fire, the passion. He saw that I loved football more than anything in the world besides my family. Some coaches just didn't see it. They couldn't look past my size.

Johnny Doyle used endless repetition to develop my close-control skills. There are no shortcuts: loads of touches. Left foot, right foot. Left foot, right foot. Over and over and over.

At training, we used to shoot against a brick wall. There was a small green door in the centre of the wall. We all called it the "magic door". Hitting it meant you'd won a "golden bicycle". Nothing fancy about these drills. Just a brick wall, a green door, and I'd shoot from fifteen or twenty metres out. We'd practise kicking against the wall over and over again, aiming for the green door.

Johnny Doyle's objective was to make me two-footed. The drill was two touches with your left foot, pass, hit the wall, two touches, pass, and hit the wall again. Ideally you could take the touch—kill the ball completely—strike it cleanly and hit the green door, then Johnny would say you'd won a golden bicycle. If you could take the touch and hit the green with your left foot, you'd earn two golden bicycles.

A golden bicycle—man, it felt like you'd achieved something. It felt like scoring a goal in a competitive match. It was good fun, but if you were doing it with two other players there was added pressure.

Johnny Doyle would always tell me to concentrate on what I was good at: whether that was heading or my vision. To play to my strengths. As a kid, I could play in the middle and find a through-pass other players didn't see. I always had a good sense of space and peripheral vision on the pitch.

We also worked for hours on all aspects of heading. People often say I've simply got an uncanny ability to jump, but it's much more complex than that. If someone tests you and says, "Jump, Tim!" to touch the chalk line at the top of the wall, that's a vastly different skill from jumping and heading a ball. The art of heading is leaping and being able to *adjust* to the ball mid-flight. Frequently, you'll leap and, as the ball is making its cross, the spin on it will change its trajectory. It'll dip, the wind will drop it; you'll have to recalibrate your jump; not so high, bend over more. Heading well takes a combination of vertical leap, anticipation, intuition *and* a healthy dose of improvisation.

Here's an example: take an in-swinging ball from the left. Most likely this will have been kicked by the left foot of the sender, causing it to curl into you. You don't want to head an in-curling ball too hard because you have both the ball itself *and* the spin to account for. You need to let the ball touch your head and convert that natural power and spin of the cross into a directed header. If you try to make too much contact, you're guaranteed to sky that ball right over the crossbar. You'll have zero control. The objective is to use the force of the cross, meet the ball and *gently*, with control, angle it on target.

Teaching me this lesson, Doyle would say, "You don't need power on it, Timmy. Just say good morning to the ball."

It's a phrase of Johnny's that I still remember—and teach in my youth academies to this day: *Say good morning to the ball.*

Johnny Doyle taught emotions and attitudes as much as technical ability, physical drills, tactics and strategies on the pitch. He was the kind of football tutor who took on kids who'd been rejected for a variety of reasons, who could work with kids who didn't even need physical training but needed only mental strengthening.

That was often my problem as a kid—I lacked the mental skills that are often crucial in determining the outcome of a match. Few men I've ever met in football truly understand the psychological side of the game the way Johnny Doyle did.

If I'd had a match with my club team and been tentative about shooting, Johnny would help me get inside my own thought processes.

"Tim," he'd say, "why didn't you take the shot? What were you afraid of? You know you can hit that green door. You hit that five times out of seven—with your right foot and your left. Now picture yourself doing it in a game. What's the difference? The only difference is that there's more people around you, there's an atmosphere that you need to block out."

Johnny Doyle understood that there was no way you can achieve success, maybe even greatness as an athlete—or anything in life, really—if you're not mentally tough.

"Hit the door, Tim," he'd say. "It's a fraction of the size of a real goal. Maybe one-fifth of a proper goal. Now take that small area and hit it every single time with power."

I took the confidence that came from earning Johnny Doyle's golden bicycles and transferred it to my competitive match play.

And, in later years, whenever I was out on the pitch, I still aimed for Johnny Doyle's green door. The sense of inner pride, earning that golden bicycle, was immense. When I hit that green door with my left foot, it felt as big as if I'd scored a goal for Australia in the World Cup.

*

It used to be in Australia that football was known as the sport of immigrants. Football—or "soccer" as it's still generally called—wasn't seen as a *real* Australian sport in the same way that cricket and rugby union were, even though we've produced world-class Australian footballers for decades.

This was already changing quite bit when I was a kid in the 1980s, but traditionally the sport hierarchy remained: cricket, rugby league, and Australian rules football.

They've been the dominant sports in the country and to this day remain the most popular. Football was seen as a game that had "flown here" with the immigrants.

This led to some ugliness over the years, and I heard about it even as a youth player. Some of the kids' fathers who grew up in Australia would talk about how the sport used to be referred to as *wogball*.

Wog is a derogatory term for the immigrant Europeans—Greeks, Italians, Croatians, Serbians, Latin Americans—who were seen as the only people who played and enjoyed the sport. Fortunately, you almost never hear anyone in Australia calling it *wogball* any more.

Even in my youngest playing days, I got thrown into that ethnic melting pot. Sydney Olympic Football Club played a huge part in my development. They were known throughout Sydney as *the* Greek team. Everything associated with the club was Greek. They had some other nationalities playing in the squad, but for the supporters, the hard-core fan-base, everything was Greek: the blue and white flags, the food eaten at the matches, the songs sung in the stands. It was a club run by Greeks, backed by Greeks, with a flavour straight out of Athens. First known as the Pan Hellenic Football Club, established in 1957 in Sydney by Greek immigrants, the team soon became one of the mainstays of the National Soccer League (NSL).

Sydney Olympic's main rivals were the Marconi Stallions, an Italian club to the core. Everywhere you looked in their stadium you'd see the tricolour flag of Italy—green, white and red. Men sported the Marconi Stallion jerseys and sometimes the famous *Azzurri* shirt of the Italian national team. In fact, Christian Vieri, the great Italian striker—tied for first as Italy's record World Cup goal-scorer, along with Roberto Baggio and Paolo Rossi—lived in Sydney when he was younger and played for the Marconi Stallions.

Sydney Olympic had a well-run youth system with Under-12, Under-13, Under-14 teams, all the way up to the reserves and the first team, which competed in the NSL. All the best kids who lived close by me wanted to trial at Olympic. If you lived closer to Marconi, you trialled there. Some youth players who lived in my area felt Marconi was the better club. It was often a matter of heated debate among us kids.

The first step to becoming part of the Olympic "family" was to get invited to trials. I first made it at age eleven, playing with my brother Sean in the Under-12s. Again, my dad felt I was always ready to play up an age, but it meant I was always the smallest kid on the pitch.

When you got selected, your parents would get a letter, then you'd go round to the Sydney Olympic clubhouse and collect the tracksuits and your kit. I remember how much pride I felt in that tracksuit: cobalt-blue and white with the Olympic crest. Alongside my replica Manchester United kits, kept immaculate in my bedroom, I now added my own Sydney Olympic kit and tracksuit.

The training sessions had an air of intense competition. The place was jammed. Dads parked in all different corners of the ground, wherever they could find a spot, and each kid had to bring his own football. From the moment you arrived, fathers would have their kids stretching, kicking the ball against the back wall, practising heading.

My brother Sean and I were always together, so we'd start straightaway passing the ball back and forth, juggling, heading it. I would keep my tracksuit on as if I was warming up for the big-time professional leagues. I'd do my stretching and warm-ups, and once it was time for training I'd strip off my tracksuit bottoms, then my top, and sprint out as if it was the start of a match. That's how serious I was at that young age and it was no different for the kids from Greek backgrounds. Sydney Olympic was the pinnacle; it was the highest level of football they could ever envisage playing.

The key was to impress the coaches. There was never a moment to slack off. Every drill, every touch, every pass, shot and dribble was scrutinized. Sydney Olympic had one youth coach, George Psaroudis, who had a lot of faith in my brother Sean as a goalkeeper. Some people said I'd only made the team because Sean was so good at that position. In fact, I think it was Coach Psaroudis who first said to Sean, "Don't let fear hold you back," but my brother took that phrase and made it his own.

This made every weekend a trial game for me. I was under the microscope. But I found my rhythm, was strong and creative in midfield, and made an impact pretty quickly for my club. People would start saying on the touchline: "Well, done. Young Tim Cahill's played well."

I started scoring a lot of goals for Olympic. If you were a youth player and you made it into the starting eleven of Sydney Olympic, Marconi Stallions or Sydney United, you were on the radar as a top prospect. No guarantees of course, but you could sense you might be on the road to making it as a professional in the NSL.

One of the best things about being in the Under-12 team was that I got a job being a ball boy for Sydney Olympic first team. There was an incredible atmosphere at every home match. In the stands behind me, the chanting would come in waves. *Olympic! Olympic!* It would start slow, then grow faster, with clapping in the rhythm to those syllables:

"Ohhhh-*lymmm*-pic!"

When the home team scored, the grounds erupted as if it was a match in Europe. Throughout the match, I'd fetch balls for the first-team players for throw-ins and corner kicks, sprinting up and down the touchline, thinking, *One day I'm going to play for Olympic, in the first team, and maybe if I'm lucky I'll score boatloads of goals for them.*

It was an incredibly family-friendly atmosphere. Tons of kids in the stands with their parents. During the matches you could buy authentic Greek food like souvlakis and gyros.

You could get bags of peanuts or pumpkin seeds—in fact, this brilliant little guy named Andrea—everyone called him "Mr Olympic"—would shout out the words in Greek, and the ground would be littered everywhere with discarded shells. Another guy sold DVDs of Olympic matches but also of the big clubs back home in the Greek national league.

Being the half-Samoan, half-English kid, I didn't have a natural niche, didn't fit into the typical ethnic divisions, but being part of Olympic, it didn't matter; I soon became known as an "adopted Greek". The fans and the parents of the other kids in the youth squads all talked to me in a mixture of Greek and their heavily accented English, and it got to the point that I understood some of it and could even get by with a few phrases.

Australian football has changed a lot since then. The A-League is the only thing many younger fans know today, but, for me, the old NSL was my highest aspiration. My dream was to make it into the starting eleven of Olympic and have those Greek fans waving blue and white flags and screaming when I'd score.

But even though you're wearing the Olympic colours and crest as a youth player, it's still a massive dream—a huge long shot—that you're ever going to play for the starting eleven in the Olympic men's squad.

I played with some top players at Sydney Olympic—really exceptionally talented young guys. There were players who never fulfilled the potential of that talent because of the various paths they chose. Some got a serious injury. Some met a girl and had a kid. Or the needs of family called on them to step up and work full time rather than pursuing their dream of football. And then there were those who had the talent and the drive but lacked some other advantage—they often didn't have that one good role model in their life who believed in them.

Others, however, just didn't have the discipline. They chose going out, having a party lifestyle, rather than the regimen of daily training. It's a hard truth: reaching the pinnacle of anything requires not only talent, and good fortune, but also a single-mindedness towards those things you *can* control—if you're disciplined enough.

It's nearly impossible to have this combination of advantages and personal qualities, but today I tell the kids in the youth football academies I run in Australia that what matters, if you really want it, is that you devote yourself to those things you can influence. Give yourself over to your passion. Take every opportunity presented to you.

At Olympic I came up through the ranks, part of a tremendous youth system, much like the system used by Barcelona or Manchester United to develop the talent of the youngest schoolboys in their academies. I was fortunate enough to have great opportunities—and I *took* them.

LESSONS FROM SAMOA

WHEN I WAS FOURTEEN I made a trip back to Samoa that turned out to be one of the best—and most complicated—experiences of my young life.

I'd been to Samoa at a young age; we'd go there long enough to get a taste for the culture and lifestyle and, most importantly, our family heritage. It was crucial in helping us kids understand where we'd come from.

Then, sadly, my grandmother became very ill. At the same time, I'd been called up to play for Samoa as a youth international. Both Sean and I were selected for an Under-20 tournament team, Sean, of course, as the goalkeeper. I was picked as a midfielder though I was still six years under the cut-off age and doubted I'd see much playing time.

I vividly remember the family discussing it over the kitchen table. Football, was in fact, secondary: the biggest thing for Sean and me was going to seeing my grandmother—we could make certain she was being cared for by the local doctors and my Samoan family.

We're from a tiny village in Samoa called Tufuiopa, right on the water. It's the village where all my maternal family were born and raised. We had a small family house situated on a bit of land. The typical home in Samoa is called a *fale*, an open dwelling with a concrete base, some mats, four big poles and a roof. But if it rained—and the afternoon storms were often fierce—the rain would lash in through the sides. The *fale* is where they have village meetings, traditional ceremonies, feasts, as well as prayer for church on Sunday. It's the centre for communal life in that tiny village.

This visit to Samoa was different from the ones I'd made as a kid, trips I could hardly remember. Now, for the first time, my brother and I were fully immersed in our Samoan heritage and culture. In the mornings we bathed in a watering hole right across the road from where my grandmother lived. One side of the hole was for cleaning your clothes and the other side was for washing yourself. It was the strangest thing for a couple of kids from the suburbs of Sydney to look down and see a fish swimming at your feet as you're soaping yourself up.

Bathing that way is just an integral part of Samoan culture. No one bats an eye; you go down and have a wash in the local watering hole. Right next to you are other families bathing and also the local women are doing the laundry.

The Under-20 team prepped in Samoa for three weeks before leaving for Fiji. When Sean and I weren't training, we spent loads of time with my grandmother and we did it rough. We enjoyed mucking in, cleaning up, helping with the cooking—all while running back and forth from training. Living just the way most Samoans live their daily lives.

We got so immersed in the culture that whenever we weren't in our football kits we'd wear the national dress. The men wear a lava-lava—a type of simple sarong, often brightly coloured and with beautiful patterns. Sean and I would walk around the village in the lava-lava with no T-shirt, sometimes in flip-flops, sometimes barefoot, to and from the watering hole, looking exactly like the locals.

*

My brother and I were there for football but, in truth, rugby is the important sport for most Samoans. Many of my own cousins became quite successful playing at both the club and the international level. It's unreal the amount of talent that comes out of Samoa—a lot of it ends up in Australia in rugby league, or in New Zealand for rugby union and in New Zealand's national team, the All-Blacks. In American Samoa, there's also been an explosion of academies to discover talented youths to take to the USA to play in the National Football League. That's largely due to the success in the States of islanders like Troy Polamalu, who grew up in California but is of Samoan descent.

We got to know our extended family, all these rugby-playing uncles and cousins, most of whom had that typical Samoan male build: huge and powerful, which made me feel even smaller than I already did. There's something in the Samoan genes—yes, the men are strong and big-boned, but they also tend to be quick and athletic. I never could sort out if it's a combination of the diet and the outdoor lifestyle, but clearly there is also something in the Samoan DNA. You can see it as you stroll around the island, predominantly in the younger men: they're basically naturally built athletes.

Not every Samoan male is big and agile, but many are. They've had generations of natural training. It's often said that the only tool a Samoan man needs is a machete: to cut the grass, to slash open a coconut, even chop down a tree.

Because my grandmother was so ill, Sean and I would wake at 5:30 a.m., fetch water for tea, then walk down to the bakery, which opened at 6 a.m., to get hot bread. We used to have this delicious New Zealand butter spread really thick on the toasted bread, with a cup of hot tea, and if you were lucky maybe some baked beans or spaghetti from a can. That was considered a special treat.

Normally, when you go into camp as an international, you think you'll stay in a hotel, get tracksuits, proper kits. Not in Samoa. When we went to meet the staff and the players—a few of whom had flown in from New Zealand—we realized most were locals and were dirt-poor. Some of the boys had no football boots, or if they did, the boots were in horrible condition, not even the correct size for their feet.

The training pitches were awful—the grass was very high, the field was lumpy, the goalposts were wonky. The quality of the play was poor and the organization was disjointed. Once we put all the boys together, you could see what a mixed bag we had on our hands: some were above-average footballers, but some had mostly played rugby, so they had some stamina but minimal technique. You could see from the outset we were unlikely to be bringing home any silverware from Fiji.

Still, for me, that camp was a brilliant experience. Not for the footballing but for the cultural values I learned—the traditional way of life; feeling myself, for one of the first times in my life, to be truly a Samoan. When we ate, we cooked collectively as a team, mostly foods from the plantation like taro and pork, though sometimes we'd whip up some chop suey. The players would cook together, and then we'd all sit on the floor cross-legged and eat in the *fale*.

It was basic, but it was also so *real*. This was more than just playing football. As part of the process of building our bond as a team, we'd say a prayer before and after every game. This prayer, called the *Toa Samoa*, is a spiritual expression in the form of a song, a profound symbol of the country and people. We'd clap at the same time—passionate, aggressive, singing the *Toa Samoa* in harmony. It's not exactly like the *haka* in New Zealand rugby, but there's a similarity: you'd better sing it with everything you've got, because it's seen as much more than an anthem.

My parents helped gather funds to send over all new kits and football boots. In fact, Sean and I brought over three suitcases between us and came home with virtually nothing in them. We ended up giving all our clothes away. Did we really need them? We had so much more than these island kids. We figured they'd appreciate jeans or trainers or jumpers more than us.

We used to jog together as a team, someone sitting on the back of the ute, singing a Samoan song, egging us on, and we'd run that way, three or four miles, to get to training. Some boys had holes in their shoes, a couple were actually running barefoot, while my brother and I wore perfect new trainers from Australia.

*

At the end of a month in Samoa, we went to Fiji and didn't perform well at all in the Under-20 tournament—lost every single match, in fact, and I played for only a handful of minutes, coming on as a substitute late in a game that was already a lost cause.

Little did I realize the impact those few minutes would have later in my life. No one had a crystal ball when I was fourteen. No one knew that I was going to become a professional; no one knew I'd go to England and learn my trade. And certainly no one could have imagined that I might someday be called up to represent my country and that those few moments on the pitch in one game for Samoa would become a huge legal complication for me.

Despite the trouble it caused, I have absolutely no regrets about living there and playing for Samoa. On the contrary, it changed my whole outlook on life.

In Samoa, they grow up with virtually nothing: sun, sand, the plantation, a few livestock—it's so bare-bones and simple. Virtually everyone visiting Samoa looks at these islanders and feels sorry for them. I did, myself, the first time I saw my family and their friends in Samoa.

But my mind-set changed. Today I don't feel the least bit sorry for them. Why? Because they're *happy*. Imagine being in Samoa, living in a *fale* with just four poles holding up the roof, where everyone you love sleeps together, eats together, gathers for family meetings. Imagine having nothing more than the sand, sea, food and family—all the essential things in life. What more do you really need?

In fact, now that I'm thirty-five and have had a successful career, have travelled the world, I can tell you: in general, those kids in Samoa—and most of the adults, too—are happier than a lot of millionaires in Sydney or Melbourne, London or New York, who live in mansions or penthouse apartments and drive luxury cars to the fanciest shopping malls.

The Samoan life is simple, it's true, but they're content. They don't need the things we have; they haven't grown soft and dependent on our culture of excess. They're happy with the lifestyle that revolves around freedom and nature and love of one's family.

That trip with my brother Sean to be with our grandmother was one of the greatest eye-openers for me. It helped me learn what's really important—that life can be simple, without any luxuries, but still filled with satisfaction and fulfilment.

BEATING THE ODDS

THE BIGGEST STRIKE AGAINST ME at that age—and another reason I was often told I wasn't being *realistic* about my dreams of being a professional footballer in England—was that I was still very small. In high school, I was only 165 cm tall and weighed only 55 kilos.

Some of the stars of the global game, whose pictures I clipped out of glossy magazines and pinned up on my wall, weren't much bigger. The two Brazilian strikers of the 1994 World Cup—Bebeto and Romario—had pride of place on my wall and were hardly giants. Romario had a stockier build, but on the pitch Bebeto was so slight he looked like a teenager who'd stolen his father's shorts for the game—and yet in that 1994 World Cup he was a superstar. He routinely beat defenders, had incredible touch, laid effortless passes for Romario, and together they formed the most beautiful strike partnership.

I was well aware that in the Australian mind-set of that time, I was nowhere near the height and weight and strength of a professional athlete—a striker who could outleap 183-cm tall central defenders to gain purchase on a header inside the penalty box. Australian coaches were scouting for the classic "target man" forward—a big No. 9 who could play with his back to goal in the mould of Gary Lineker or Marco van Basten.

I wasn't that kid, but one of the brilliant things about football is that your skills, technique and passion can counterbalance your opponent's advantages in size and strength. Picture Maradona famously dribbling through the entire England defence in the 1986 World Cup—a masterpiece of close control, change of pace, feinting and balance—to score that match winner voted the "Greatest Goal of the Century".

To this day, people debate why football under-performs at the international level in certain countries—England is a prime example—and whether an emphasis on physical strength over technical skills at the youth development level is to blame. It's a complex question, and I don't claim to have all the answers. But I do know that when I was growing up, I played with quite a few smaller South American kids—gifted athletes with phenomenal touch and dribbling skills—who didn't succeed in the Australian system. They quit football because they were told they were too small. It just wasn't in fashion to favour technique over physique.

Fast-forward a couple decades and it's almost inconceivable how much the game has changed. Nowadays some of the best players in the world are only 165 cm, 168 cm or 170 cm tall. Guys like Messi, Xavi, Tevez—some of the most talented players in the game. But had they been in Australia in my schoolboy days, players as short as Tevez or Messi, or as slight as David Silva, would surely have been told they were too small and not strong enough to make it. In my opinion, a kid's size—or lack of size—should never be seen as an impediment to success at the highest levels of football.

*

Even at a young age I was aware that my size could be seen as a disadvantage, but I was determined that it would never stand in my way. By high school, I'd managed to gain a reputation as a top-club player; I also started to shine in school sport. I played in the Primary Schools Sports Association league. Then there came a chance to play for the representative school district team called Metropolitan East. This was a public school select team, in the same way that Canterbury Reps was a clubs' select team.

Playing for Metropolitan East was a significant milestone in my development. The squad was drawn from dozens of schools—Canterbury, Eastern Suburbs and St George—but only one kid per school was chosen. Even though my talent was still a bit raw, being selected was a recognition of my hard work.

We played in an intense competition in Sutherland, in south Sydney, right next to Cronulla Oval, ten games going on at once against other district select squads.

On days like that, you try to keep your wits about you on the pitch, but it's such a nervous moment—you know if you do well you could potentially be selected to represent your state: the whole of New South Wales.

We spent the entire day playing matches. Even at that age, I planned everything in my mind, hyper-analysing, trying to anticipate how to shape my performance.

What did I need to do to stand out in a tournament like this, where there were so many good midfielders? Did I need to score goals? Did I need to be unselfish and more creative? Should I allow myself a few minutes of dribbling, bossing the play, or immediately lay-off a clever through-pass?

One thing I knew: I *had to* impress. Youth football is a series of tests and trials, of potential opportunities and life-changing matches and tournaments, and I knew this was one of my first big chances to break through.

After hours of pounding, intense action, I found myself sitting at the end of the tournament with hundreds of other kids, cross-legged on one of the pitches. All our parents were there as well and all the coaches in their light-blue tracksuits, every one of them with a clipboard: "When we call your name, please come forward. You've been selected for the preliminary squad for the New South Wales PSSA Team."

Various players would get called out, they'd stand—the adults would cheer.

I'd already done the calculations: I figured there were so many matches going on simultaneously, the odds were that the coaches had seen at least four or five highly skilled midfielders who were taller and stronger than me. I told myself I'd better accept that I wouldn't be called.

A few of the lads from my representative squad had been chosen for their district teams and had played in the same tournament. Some of them had already been called and as their names were read, they stood up confidently, striding forward to form a line behind the coaches. They had an air that told me they'd known all along that they were head and shoulders better than the rest of us. It wasn't cockiness; it was just confidence in their abilities.

Then one of the coaches read out: "Metropolitan East. Tim Cahill ..."

My eyes shot open wide, I jumped to my feet and half-ran toward the rest of the guys who'd formed up in the queue behind the coaches. I had worked so hard for this, I was nearly in tears.

Some of the guys selected were on a different planet. They were the best physical specimens, not just from our local schools or New South Wales, but in all of Australia. They were fast and strong. Some were enormous for that age: they looked like men with full moustaches, dark hair over their legs and arms, muscles like they were eighteen or nineteen years old.

We have team photos of that NSW select squad—I look like a *baby* compared to some of them. We had one striker in the NSW team whose body was so well developed that when midfielders kicked the ball over the top to him, he'd burst onto it like an Olympic sprinter. He terrorised defenders, thundering down on them with that pace and his legs churning.

The NSW team was in great form and we ended up winning the entire tournament. And yet, for some of those well-built kids, that select team was the pinnacle of their careers. Many of them stopped developing at fifteen or sixteen years old and never went further in football than that NSW representative team.

It's a lesson I learned only in hindsight: nothing is ever predetermined. It's a constant reminder to work hard, stay focussed and never believe that your future is assured.

*

My obsession with football was so complete at that age that it felt as if I went from game to practice to trial, to another team and another tournament, and back again. By this point Sydney Olympic was home; I'd been there five years. I'd learned Greek, made great friends, become part of the culture. Now, after my experience with the NSW select team, I dreamed of making Olympic's first team and playing for them in the NSL.

The way the system worked, each year—regardless of how many years you'd played in the youth teams—you had to try out again. In my fifth year, I went to trial for the Olympic youth team, but despite my best efforts, I was not selected.

When he asked why, my dad was told by one of the coaches, "Tim's too small and not fast enough."

"Yeah?" my dad said. "Alright—we'll see ..."

As it sank in, I realized that the coaches had essentially determined that I would never shine in the NSL, so they decided to drop me and develop younger team players they felt had more potential.

I don't want to fault the coaches completely. It could have been the case that at fourteen I was still too undeveloped physically, but all I knew at the time was that, emotionally, I was crushed.

All my mates played in the team. I knew I was getting better every year; I knew I was giving my all in every match and in every training session. I knew I was progressing, but with their rejection I felt as if everything I had worked for was being closed off to me.

My dad remained upbeat. He said we'd just hit a bump in the road and we'd continue the private training with Johnny Doyle. But it kept echoing in my mind: *Too small. Not strong enough. Not fast enough ...*

I said to my dad, "There's got to be somewhere I can go to get stronger."

My parents did some looking around, then decided to send me to the Institute of Sport in Lidcombe. The institute is a world-class facility, set up to test athletes in every facet of their ability: speed, reaction time, vertical jump. I did a fifty-metre run; they timed it, but also made a video so we could review my form. They taught me how to jump more explosively and, for the first time, I had nutritionists analysing my diet. I was looking for a reason—some scientific explanation—as to why the hell I didn't get picked for Sydney Olympic.

It may have been nothing more than bad luck, but I'm not a big believer in blaming things on luck—good or bad. To this day I often say, "Luck is great, but if I want to be lucky I'll go buy a lottery ticket." If things don't go your way, sometimes you have to do everything in your power to put yourself back in the position of achieving your goals.

My failure to make the next level at Sydney Olympic filled me with doubt, had me believing, rightly or wrongly, that perhaps I wasn't ready, that perhaps what the coaches were saying was true—I wasn't tall enough, strong enough or fast enough.

After completing the initial assessment at the institute, I was given a program to rework my body mechanics. "We're going to change the way you run," one of the instructors told me.

They replayed the video of me, showing me how my arms flew out too wide, how my thigh movement could be improved. They had me change my running style by keeping my arms and legs in tight, close to my body, moving like a track-and-field sprinter: right-knee left-arm, left-knee right-arm.

In reality, you don't need blazing speed over distance to be a top footballer. Very rarely in open play are you covering fifty metres of the pitch at a full sprint. You only need to have explosive pace in those first ten or fifteen metres.

That's where the scientific analysis of my running paid dividends. Being quicker off the mark helped me beat my opponents and put me in position to receive a pass.

Changing my running style didn't come easily, but by working tirelessly on my coordination and rhythm, I made my running style more complete.

My parents bought a small trampoline, which the instructors told me I should put in my bedroom, in front of the mirror, so I could watch myself. They recommended this as a way to study my form, running until I was out of breath. I also did lunges and sit-ups and push-ups and box-jumps—the basics of plyometrics.

I went a bit crazy with it, I suppose. I did this same bloody routine every day until I was drenched in sweat. I can be an extremist when I'm trying to improve something and I reckon my friends and brothers, maybe even my parents, were looking at me saying, "Timmy's finally gone round the bend." While other kids were off doing what normal teenagers do after school—watching TV, hanging out at shopping centres—I was working out in the bedroom, sweat pouring off me.

At the institute, they shot more video and we analysed it. I returned home and kept working on my form, kept telling myself, "I'm going to be a machine." The institute, the plyometrics, the trampoline workout—they all helped.

But I still needed to play football. Since I couldn't play for Sydney Olympic, we had to find a club that would take me. My dad found yet another Greek club, Belmore Hercules, which played two divisions lower.

Belmore Hercules is not quite as well known as Sydney Olympic, but it is still a proud club, founded in 1971. My dad and I went to Belmore for the trial and I told them I'd been playing for five years for Sydney Olympic. A few of the players and staff recognized me.

By now, to be honest, Olympic's rejection was a massive blow to my confidence, but it was also a reality check. I said to myself, "If you make it through trials, you're playing here, in a lower division, because this is your proper level."

Luckily, I was selected. Once again, I was much younger than all the other players. At Hercules, there were Under-18s, Under-21s and then the adult first team—and at the age of fifteen I was by far the youngest kid in the Under-18s.

My dad volunteered as one of the assistant managers, which I found a bit uncomfortable. I'd seen it plenty of times where one of the coaches was a parent of a kid in the team. People would snicker when the kid was named captain or played all ninety minutes just because his dad was on the touchline with a clipboard and a whistle. I didn't want anyone thinking I'd made the starting squad because my dad was pulling strings. It was in fact quite the opposite, since my dad didn't volunteer until I'd already been selected at trials. In the end, it didn't matter—I knew that my work rate and quality on the pitch would speak for itself.

Sean was our starting goalkeeper; I played as an attacking-midfielder, sometimes as an outright striker. It was one of the best footballing seasons I ever had. I started scoring a lot of goals, then after one particularly good match with the Under-

18s, I was called in by the coach. "Tim, if you're not too worn out, I think we should play you in the Under-21s as well."

I wanted the opportunity and played with both the Under-18s and the Under-21s. The season roared along until I suddenly found myself on a goal record and my name, for the first time, started appearing in the local press. The Greek papers were writing about me. The local Sydney sports writers were noticing me.

And again, a lot of what had got me noticed was my heading: 'Cahill jumps like a kangaroo.'

I had never stopped training in how to head the ball, and would still practise with my dad, with Johnny Doyle and with friends. Those explosive jumping drills, squats, and lunges I'd been doing in my bedroom had made my natural leaping ability all that much more powerful. Even at less than 167 cm in height, I was often able to jump higher than defenders who were over 183 cm tall. It was due to a combination of factors: vertical leap, timing and desire. No one was going to out-leap me or out-muscle me as I planted my head on that cross.

John Xipolitas was the first-team coach for Belmore Hercules. They had some big players from the NSL who'd come to play for Belmore's first team during the off-season, because it was their old club. I played in one Under-18s game and was gearing up to play for the Under-21s when Coach Xipolitas said to me in his heavy Greek accent: "Tim, you won't play with the Under-21s today."

"What do you mean?"

"Today I want you to play in first team."

The Hercules' first team played at Belmore Oval, right across the road from Canterbury Boys School. Everyone—all the fans and the families of the players—sat on the hill or stood behind the clubhouse and huddled around the souvlaki stand. It was a big deal on the weekends for the Hercules faithful to gather at Belmore Oval for the first-team matches.

To this day, I'm still the youngest player ever to lace his boots for the Belmore first team. I was a small fifteen-year-old, playing with grown men. At one point, late in the match, the coach waved me on as a substitute at a set-piece. I ran on just as one of our midfielders was about to take a corner. The way the play unfolded, it took me straight back to my days with Marrickville Red Devils—the first time I'd ever scored in a match with my head.

The ball came over from the right, I jumped with three other defenders—men who were much bigger than me. I managed to climb out of the pack: not using vertical leap, but proper timing of my run.

There was no *luck* involved. I saw the ball, knew I was going to get my head on it but now the quality of the contact was the most important thing. Eyes wide open, I opened my body up a bit, my right shoulder squared, then I headed it down, aiming for the bottom right corner. The grass was a little wet, and I turned and watched as the ball skipped past the goalkeeper, billowing the net.

I was swarmed by my team-mates! Even the other team—after the match—came over to congratulate me on the quality of the header that won us the league.

I was named top scorer in the league that year: thirty goals in all competitions for all three teams—Under-18s, Under-21s and first team—the most goals ever scored in a season for Belmore Hercules.

I'd been cut by Sydney Olympic for the Under-18s squad—wasn't considered good enough—but I could start for the first team of Belmore Hercules, albeit two divisions below, and win the championship and the overall scoring record.

That was one of my proudest moments growing up as a footballer in Australia. I had spent that entire season trying to recover from being dropped by Sydney Olympic, but I made something of the setback. I had scored big goals practically every week for Hercules with the Under-18s and Under-21s, and now I'd come on in a big match to score the winner with the first team.

At Hercules, I blossomed and found my niche. In the end, being dropped by Sydney Olympic might have been the best thing that could have happened to me.

PART
02

NO ONE LIKES US, WE DON'T CARE

SACRIFICES

THROUGHOUT MY HIGH SCHOOL YEARS at Kingsgrove North I continued playing high-level football—now for Sydney United, a club as heavily influenced by its Croatian culture as Sydney Olympic was by its Greek origins.

Though I ended up staying less than a full season, Sydney United was another stepping stone, a club with a rich history where I had a chance to play with some fantastic youth talent like Joel Griffiths and David James—my old mate from the Johnny Doyle private training lesson. Phil Pavela, our coach, really believed in me, could see that I had potential even if I still needed some polish. That'd been the story of my life with some coaches: they either saw the future player I could become or they didn't. Sydney United played at Edensor Park—a beautiful 12,000-seat stadium—against all the big teams like Marconi and Olympic. Coach Pavela gave me a lot of playing time with the Under-21s, pushed me hard in training, but also helped me a lot off the park, becoming close with my family.

Then one day, midway through Year 11, I got home from school and something was different in the house.

"Have a seat, Tim," my dad said. "We need to have a chat."

I put my things down and joined my parents at the kitchen table.

"I've made a few calls to England," my father began.

Now I glanced at my mum and I could see she was upset. She'd been crying a few minutes earlier. I lost track of what my father was saying. Anytime my mum's upset, I'm upset.

"... In any event, we think you're ready," Dad said. "We've got an opportunity to send you to England and we think it's the right time ..."

"What? England?"

"You're just sixteen," my mum said. "You have to tell us— is this something you really want to do?"

I sat there, silently mulling it over.

"It's not going to be easy," she continued. "You're not going to be at home. You're going to be ..."

"Where will I live?"

"You'll be staying with Mum's relatives," Dad said.

"Glen and Lindsey," Mum said. "The Stanleys."

I remembered seeing a photograph or two, but I really had no connection besides recognizing their names.

I asked what club I would have a trial with. What my dad said came as a bit of a shock.

"You don't have an official trial as yet, but don't worry about that. I'll be working out the details. If we can get you a trial—and it's still a big *if*—you're going to have to wait in England. Nothing's guaranteed, Tim. We don't even know if you'll get a trial this year, so you may have to enrol in school. But you'll need to be over there if and when we get that call."

My dad had already made calls to a man named Allen Batsford. He'd been the manager of Wimbledon and was now a talent scout for Nottingham Forest. I didn't understand the details fully, but Allen Batsford had a relationship with the Millwall youth team as well. Dad had also been in touch with another guy named Bob Pearson, who at the time was the chief scout for Millwall Football Club.

Once I heard those names—Millwall and Nottingham Forest—I was sold on the idea. Just to have a shot at a trial for a professional football club in England was enough for me.

"But listen to me, Tim," Mum said. "You're the only one who can say if you're ready to do it."

"Ready to go off and live with Mum's relatives all on your own?" Dad said. "Do you understand what that'll mean?"

"Yeah, I understand," I said, though I really hadn't a clue.

Maybe my dad saw the uncertainty in my face, because he said: "There's another route, you know. You can stay here, live at home, finish up your schooling and play in Australia."

I thought about that—about not making it with Sydney Olympic, dropping to a lower division to prove what I could do with Belmore Hercules. That was a tough battle, and even though things were now going well for me at Sydney United, I sensed that having a career as a professional footballer at home—given the tastes of the Australian system at the time for strikers and attacking-midfielders who looked a lot different from me—just wasn't going to happen.

"I'll never make it here, Dad. I won't get a chance to play in Australia. I want to go to England and at least give it a go."

My mum had a few more tears in her eyes.

"Tim, listen to me," she said. "It's gonna be tough. You'll be on your own."

I turned and said to her, "I know it's going to be tough. But if you're telling me you've got a ticket for me to go to England, I'm saying I'm ready."

"You're going to be living in the middle of nowhere, you're not going to have much money," Dad added. "Pretty much the clothes on your back, not much else. And you're going to have to wait for your trial, assuming Allen or Bob can even get you one."

"I don't care, Dad. I just want the chance."

I understood at least some of the sacrifices I'd be making—less so the many sacrifices my mum and dad had already made, and would continue to make.

Suddenly, a hand was on my shoulder. I turned and saw Sean.

"Bloody hell—you ready, Tim?"

There was such pride in his voice.

"Yeah, I'm ready," I said. But looking up at Sean, I felt suddenly conflicted; I was thinking about Sean's own football career.

In the preceding year, Sean had made one of the biggest sacrifices of anyone. Mum and Dad were prepared to take out a loan to finance my trip to England for a trial, but to allow me to continue my studies at Kingsgrove North and to keep playing football, Sean had left school to work as a mechanic and was bringing in money to help pay the household bills.

He didn't complain, never said a word. He just went to work, contributing every week to help my parents cover rent and bills. Some of those bills were to support my dream of being a professional footballer.

Now, as a result of his sacrifice, I had an opportunity to go overseas—and he didn't. I felt such mixed emotions, because I was trying to put myself in Sean's shoes.

Why was I being given the chance and not him?

It's not in Sean's nature to be envious and resentful. He's a true Samoan older brother—very protective—and he wanted me to succeed for the overall pride of the family.

All of this churned around in my brain at the kitchen table. He didn't realize it at the time—and probably doesn't know to this day that I ever thought about what that decision meant for him—but I did. It wasn't that Sean wasn't a *good* enough footballer to get the chance at the professional level. It was that in our Samoan family, culture and tradition meant that, as the oldest son, he had to make the hard sacrifice, so that I could have a chance at going the distance.

Sean was a hell of a goalkeeper and I knew he was good enough to warrant a trial. Could he have played in the English leagues, even made it up to the Premiership someday?

In hindsight, I can only say *maybe*—because so many factors come into play that are really beyond one's control, one's own ability and drive. Who would have had the better outcome between us? It's an impossible question to answer, and I don't think my dad ever made that calculation.

The truth was that the answer at that moment was the same for both of us. We were in it together. Could we make it? Were we good enough?

In the end, it was me who got the opportunity to go to England for trial and Sean who stayed in Sydney, going to work every day.

*

Thoughts about the sacrifices my family made have never left my mind. In fact, my career is built on the shoulders of loads of folks—my earliest coaches, Johnny Doyle, Mum and Dad, of course—but also my big brother, Sean. In the weeks before the trip, I remember going to bed at night and lying there with my eyes open for hours, thinking about Sean not getting a trial and me getting one. I'd think about my mum and dad taking out a loan to finance the trip. Tossing from side to side.

What if I didn't make it? What if I didn't even get the call for a trial? Nothing was guaranteed, Dad said ...

My brain raced for hours with these sorts of worries. There were nights when, by 3 a.m., rather than feeling that the chance to go to England was a big break—and an opportunity to make the Cahill family proud—I felt enormous pressure. If I didn't do everything just perfectly, we'd all be embarrassed ... and Mum and Dad would be paying off some massive debt. Worse, I'd have screwed up *everyone's* life, not just my own.

*

The time finally came to go to England. I'd done my intensive last weeks of one-on-one training with Johnny Doyle and everyone was in agreement: I was as prepared as I was ever going to be. On the day I had set aside to say my goodbyes to everyone at Kingsgrove North, I went looking for Rebecca Greenfield. She wasn't my girlfriend—just a real cool mate. We often talked about our dreams and aspirations, what we'd both do when we were adults.

"What do you reckon you'll do when you get older?" Bek would ask.

"Reckon I'll play football."

"No," she'd laugh. "To make money, Tim. As a career."

"I'll play football. That's how I'll make my living."

At that, Bek would almost double over with laughter.

"Can't you ever be serious for once? What do you think you'll really do?"

"Most likely in England. Yeah, I'm going to be a professional footballer in England."

It had been like this for years, since Bexley North Public School. It had always been the same answer.

"What are you going to be when you grow up, Timmy?"

"Professional footballer."

In fact, in my career studies course in Kingsgrove North, we'd been required to choose subjects and write them on a sheet of paper. Some were mandatory, of course: maths, English, science, history. I wrote down my electives as French, Italian, and Spanish. I remember the teacher's reaction when she read that list.

"French?" she said.

"Just in case I play football in France."

"And Italian?"

"In case I play in Italy."

"And Spanish in case you play in Spain?" She was laughing at me now.

"That's right. In case I end up playing in Spain."

Later, that teacher took me aside.

"Come on, Tim, you can't keep thinking like this."

"Like what?"

"With this tunnel vision that you're *only* going to be a footballer."

"Why not?"

"Tim, there's nothing wrong with having a Plan B."

"Why do I need a Plan B?"

"Because things don't always follow a script. It's fine to dream of being a footballer, but you should have another career choice, a fall-back plan."

I nodded, but I really didn't care what she was saying. She thought I was being a smart-arse—when in fact I was only being honest. I'm sure somewhere, jotted down in red ink in a teacher's notebook in Kingsgrove North is the assessment:

Timothy Cahill—unrealistic. Has his mind set on being a professional footballer.

On that final day of school at Kingsgrove North, I finally found Rebecca.

"Bek, I don't know if I'll see you again for a long while. I'm leaving in a week."

"What are you on about, Tim?"

"I'm leaving school today," I said. "It's my last full day. Next week I'm flying to England."

"For what?'

"I'm going to be a professional footballer."

Again she thought I was clowning around, but then she saw the changed look in my eyes.

"Well, good luck, Tim. Hope you make it."

I told her that early that day, I'd tried to ring her at her house to give her the news and spoken briefly to her great-grandfather, Lou. He was originally from London, a massive Tottenham supporter. When I told him I was leaving for England, hoping to get a trial at Millwall, Lou was so enthusiastic. "Millwall—great club," he said. "I hope you make the team, son. If you can play at Millwall, you can play anywhere." That was a powerful statement and it stuck with me for years.

I could never have imagined the life I'd later have with Rebecca. She was someone I had a strong connection with through high school. But looking back, I suppose it was already the kind of bond that would later become the basis for something deeper.

I completed my goodbyes and, unlike Rebecca, most of my teachers and schoolmates met my news with eye-rolling and a bit of sarcasm. To be fair, a few did wish me well at chasing my dream, even if deep down they thought it was a long shot.

Like my career studies teacher, a few of the staff cautioned me to be balanced.

"You're a good player, Tim," one teacher told me, "but make sure you keep up with school work." As if to say: it'll likely not work out for you, chasing this footballer's dream—so please, son, have something to fall back on.

I didn't have a fall-back plan, because I had no intention of falling back.

ENGLAND

I WAS STILL A CHILD when I made the trip to England in late-1997. I remember saying a tearful goodbye to my parents at the airport, but I was also filled with excitement.

I'd never been on a flight alone, even a short one within Australia. My trips to Samoa had always been with Sean or Mum and Dad. During that long flight from Sydney to London, I had no idea how to occupy myself, given all the excitement I felt. I watched movie after movie after movie. Between films, I read football magazines about the Premiership. I read the statistics of every team and player from the First Division and Second Division, trying to memorize the details as if I had to pass an examination upon my arrival in London.

Halfway through the flight, in the middle of watching *Meet Joe Black*, my mind started racing again. I wasn't even in England and I was already feeling homesick. I suppose it was only now beginning to sink in—the massive leap into the unknown I was about to make.

When the plane landed at Heathrow, Glen and Lindsey Stanley were there to meet me. They were so welcoming that not even for an instant did I feel like a stranger. Glen immediately treated me like a son—gave me a big powerful hug—and straightaway I felt his warmth. Lindsey's from New Zealand, a Kiwi girl—just brilliant. We drove to their home in Dartford and met their kids: the boys Ben, Michael and Sam, and their youngest, daughter Olivia.

Everyone who knows me can tell you I'm never happier than when I'm surrounded by a bunch of kids. That's another very Samoan trait. Throw five kids in a room with me, and a baby in my lap, and that's when I'm most relaxed. Had the Stanley kids been older than me, who knows? Perhaps I might have felt a bit ill at ease—but now, in this house with three boys and a girl all various ages, and all younger than me—yes, I felt right at home.

The Stanleys lived in a three-storey terrace house. Space was pretty tight already, with two parents and four kids—now five, including me. There was a small kitchen and lounge room, a sliver of a backyard. I shared a room with the boys—double bunk beds—and Olivia had her own room.

Soon as I sorted things out, I called my mum and dad. I couldn't have sounded happier, and I remember hearing the relief in my mum's voice.

"Yeah, I'm running around with the kids," I said. "No

worries, Mum. Glen and Lindsey are fantastic, they've welcomed me with open arms ..."

Looking back on it, I can see how lucky I was to be in that Samoan atmosphere, in that communal island-style environment. There was never a moment of isolation. Breakfast, lunch and dinner, we were together. It was a bit like being in camp on Samoa during the build-up to the tournament in Fiji, where we all ate together and helped out with the cleaning up and doing the chores.

Finally, after a day or two settling in, I made the call to Allen Batsford, the former Wimbledon manager, whom my dad had been talking to about coordinating my trials.

"Heard good things about you already, Tim," Allen said when I rang him. "Just give me some time. Could take weeks, could take months, but we'll get you sorted."

Months? Months sounded like an eternity to me—I was so eager to get on with things—but I'd been well warned by my dad that nothing was guaranteed. I hoped for a trial with a professional club, but things had to run their course, in their own time.

I'd come so early, it wasn't even pre-season yet for the professional clubs. That was over a month away, so what was I going to do? I needed to stay fit.

The Stanleys, like a lot of Samoans, were a big rugby family. Glenn's brother, Joe Stanley, is a legend in New Zealand rugby and is also known as Smokin' Joe. He was the centre in the All-Blacks side that won the Rugby World Cup in 1987. He and his brothers and cousins are sometimes called the "Stanley Rugby Clan", which includes Joe and Jeremy Stanley. Michael, Ben and Sam all played for the local youth rugby team. In fact, all three boys would go on to have distinguished careers playing rugby at youth, club and international levels.

When I'd go out to watch them play with their local rugby clubs, it didn't take long to catch the bug. No way was I going out and getting into a scrum with some of those giants, but I decided to join the touch-rugby team.

Touch rugby—it's mainly known in Australia as "touch football"—is a variation of rugby with six rather than fifteen players. Its rules are similar to standard rugby league, minus the scrums and hard tackling. As soon as you're tagged with two hands you stop running and put the ball on the ground just as if you'd been tackled.

I joined up for touch rugby as part of my fitness regimen. Being so much older than the Stanley kids, I ended up playing with Glenn on the adult touch team, and soon made some friends. We'd all hang out in the pub, muddy and sweaty, after running around the pitch for a couple hours.

For the first time in my life, I wasn't in school during the academic year, so when the Stanley kids left in the morning, I'd wake up with them, eat my breakfast and get to it. No way was I going to sit about the house reading magazines or watching TV. My dad always told me that being a professional footballer was a job—no different from being a bricklayer, teacher or doctor. I had to treat my training as serious work. I'd get my football, head out to the local park—about a five-minute jog—lace up my boots, juggle the ball, do some laps, then some sprints. I'd pretty much follow the set routine I'd followed since my assessment by the Institute of Sport.

I felt like Dartford was in the middle of nowhere. While everyone my age was off at school, there I was alone in that little park running wind sprints and juggling the ball and taking practice free kicks.

Truth be told, it was miserable. Coming from Sydney's hot climate, my first weeks in England seemed so bloody cold. Many days the skies were completely grey or filled with a cold, lashing rain. It made me realize how lucky I'd been growing up in a city like Sydney, with its green landscape and beaches.

It was more than cold—the atmosphere of that season and the park itself felt almost eerie. The park was immense—it had eight training pitches—but none of them were in use in the middle of a work and school day. I was completely alone out there, and sometimes I'd get this otherworldly feeling, picturing what I must have looked like to a plane passing overhead: a solitary figure practising football, lost in a sea of green.

Day after day, that was my routine. Even to the housewives and postmen in the neighbourhood, I must have seemed mad.

I can tell you, if it had gone on much longer, I would have been.

I realized how important it was for me to have more in my life than solitary training. I needed to be part of a community. I was doing what I had to do, yes, but it was vital for me to have the Stanley kids, as well as Glenn and Lindsey and my new mates on Glenn's adult touch-rugby team.

After six weeks, football pre-season started in earnest, and at last I got a phone call from Allen Batsford.

"Lad, it's time," Allen said. "You ready? Can't promise you anything but let's have a look at you."

Allen made a phone call to Bob Pearson, the head scout of Millwall at that time. Because I was so nervous that day, I wore the socks and shorts of two different clubs, and my favourite Manchester United jersey—such a *crazy* look. I was a ball of energy.

I got picked up to meet Allen and Bob for the first time face to face.

"Son, nice to finally meet you, what've you been up to?" Bob asked.

I described my daily regimen of training solo, jogging down to the park, even some of the more advanced exercises I'd learned back home at the Institute of Sport in Sydney. And keeping up my cardio fitness with the touch-rugby league.

That was all well and good, but they both wanted to know about my footballing. When was the last time I'd played in a match?

"I suppose it's been … well, nearly three months ago."

"You think you're fit for trial?" Bob asked, looking a bit concerned.

"I'm fit," I said. "I can run all day. I've been training hard. No doubt in my mind I'm match-fit."

"Alright then. We're going to take you to the training facilities in Bromley, throw you in with a few of the new boys. Some of the older boys as well. You'll have a run around. We'll see where you're at."

It seemed all very matter-of-fact to them, but for me this was one of the biggest mornings of my life. I knew my future—at least whatever career I might have as a professional footballer—was dependent on what I did in the next sixty or ninety minutes. What they'd casually called a *run around* ...

*

Millwall's home is the famous South London stadium known as the Den. But the Millwall first team, reserves, youth team and academy all trained at a facility six-and-a-half miles further south, in Bromley, right near Beckenham Place Park.

As we drove up that first time, I saw it was a beautiful area: there was a glade up the road, a nice shopping centre, and little well-kept family homes across the street on Calmont Road. The training ground itself had four or five pitches in use and clubhouses, with one whole side fenced in by the car park, the other side open to the forest behind us.

I'm not going to sugar-coat it. The first morning of my trial was bloody scary.

Here I was—an unknown face, some teenager from Australia. Why on earth were these English kids going to give me a chance, trying to take one of their spots?

I knew that on the park I could play to the best of my ability, but if the other lads wanted to make me look bad, it was easy enough to do. Just don't pass me the ball properly or send in a high cross for a header that no one could reach. Trust me, skilled players can make *any* other player look bad. A trial is entirely cutthroat. It wasn't in their interests to help me make the team—a Samoan-Aussie kid they'd never set eyes on before.

Straightaway when I met the boys, I knew my instincts were spot-on. Nothing was ever said verbally—just pleasantries like "all right, nice to meet you lads"—but you could see the fire in their eyes. I'd come to take their jobs. I was a threat. The only way I could stay in England was to sign a professional contract with Millwall. And if I was lucky enough to sign a contract with Millwall, of course, it meant one of them would *not* be signing.

I can still picture myself in the Bromley changing room— my bag with everything in it perfectly neat, the way I'd been my whole life since I was a four-year-old back in Sydney. I can see myself lacing up my boots, pulling up my socks, zipping up my tracksuit.

The first person I met in the changing room was another young kid named Paul Ifill. Paul had been brought down by Bob Pearson for a trial just like me.

Paul was of Bajan-English background—his family is originally from Barbados—a few months older than me, born in Brighton. Despite the competition between us, Paul and I immediately made a connection. Maybe it was me being a

Samoan-Australian, and him being Bajan—we both felt like outsiders. Or maybe it was Bob Pearson who threw us together in the changing room, knowing we'd help each other out. In any event, we just clicked.

It certainly wasn't that way with the other guys there for the trial. During the first training, I remember feeling like every five-metre pass was a bullet, designed to bounce off my shin guards. And with every ball I touched, I felt like I was under such scrutiny from the coaches. The pressure was immense; I was breathing too hard while I was running around—almost like I was gasping. I was match-fit, and as strong as I was ever going to be. No, it was all just nervous energy. Adrenaline overload. In some parts of that first training session, I was almost too out of breath to perform.

My mind raced just as much as my heart—with thoughts of my mum and dad, or Johnny Doyle, or that endless flight over from Australia. With every passing minute I knew I was at risk of making a cock-up of the trial.

Then I got my thoughts under control and focussed on the task at hand. These guys were young, but they were professionals—contracted to Millwall—and everything they did was harder and quicker and better than any football experience I'd had back home, be it Belmore Hercules or Sydney Olympic. Everything felt like it moved at such speed! I had barely finished one drill when I had to turn around and get right into another. By the time I had finished one sprint, I was on the starting line again. Non-stop whistles blowing, coaches shouting—never a moment to think or pause. It was full-on: run, turn, pass, shoot, move, turn, pass, shoot, control, run ...

That night I went home to Bob's house. I was staying with him for the trials and I kept rewinding the whole training session as if it was a film, telling myself I could have played so much better. It put me straight back in the car with my mum and dad when I was ten years old, never hearing about what I'd done well—just Mum's sandal to the back of the head and Dad hammering me on the stuff I should have done better. *You could have had six goals instead of three. You could have played a better ball forward in that first counterattack after half-time.* Only difference was this was my own voice being ultra-critical.

That was a piss-weak pass, Tim! What were you thinking? The left side of midfield was wide open ...

I lay there on the bunk, calves pinging, thighs cramping, every muscle and sinew and tendon feeling overstretched, worn out, pushed to its limit.

I lay there in the tub in a Radox bath, then ate my post-training pasta, then rang my mum and dad.

"How you getting on?" Mum asked.

"It's bloody hard," I said, "I could have done better."

"You'll be fine, son," Dad said. "Keep going. You'll do better tomorrow."

Next day: same routine, but even harder. But as time went on I began to notice I became accustomed to the pace, the intensity, the level of competition. No longer was my mind racing. I was barely nervous now. I'd grown calmer under pressure.

By the end of the fourth day the nerves had settled and, in certain drills, I began to shine. My strongest showing involved a sequence run with the midfielder. I'd pass the ball, he'd send it back; we'd start a forward run to designated positions. My partner would ping the ball out to the right and as he'd make his run, darting to the near post, I'd cross it over to him, dashing to the back post, and he'd finish with a cross to me.

This was my game. During this one particular drill, everything I touched went in the net. A header, a half-volley, a volley, a side-foot finish while I was falling off balance. You have days like that as a player, when it feels like you can't miss.

There were miscues, too, of course. During that same drill, when it was my turn to ping the ball out to my partner, I made an awful, soft safety pass. The ball lofted so high everyone laughed.

"You want to put any more *snow* on that?"

Under that kind of pressure your mistakes can begin to feed on each other. Mental nerves become physical tightening. Fear of failure affects every move.

Mental toughness can bring you back in line, but it takes time to develop. Luckily, even though I had so much to learn, I had at least developed enough mental strength to get my head back into the game.

The connection I'd formed with Paul Ifill was part of why I felt increasingly confident during that trial. In warm-ups and the actual training drills, we'd pass the ball back and forth, shouting out encouragement: "Well done" or "Keep going, mate!" It created a spirit of partnership between us—mutual support rather than cutthroat competition. It strengthened us both, made us better—much stronger than if one of us had decided it was every man for himself.

Changing out of our kit after a day on the pitch, Paul and I would talk about the rigours of making it through the trial, being offered contracts, and playing at the Den, in the first team.

"Paul, what if we made the team together?"

"Yeah, wouldn't that be brilliant, Tim?"

Paul's friendship and our wishful thinking were a huge boost to my confidence during those days. It gave me something beyond just willpower that I could draw on.

This was another important lesson for me. It's always best to have allies. I was actually a better player if I was united with and felt the support of my team-mates. Whatever you want to call it—camaraderie, I suppose—it brought out something in my play that was impossible to access if I felt I was alone in the competition, just me against everyone else.

THE LION'S DEN

THE INTENSITY OF THE MILLWALL trials never let up. Day after day, the coaching staff put us through the same gruelling paces. We'd arrive, have breakfast with the lads, then three hours' training; lunch. Then a second hard training session in the afternoon.

At that age—sixteen or seventeen—most boys have never been through anything like Millwall's trial program. You're simply not used to training at that intensity every single day. The result is that you feel like you're constantly repairing your body—stretching, baths, massages. You also feel—and see—massive changes happening to your physique and to your playing form. You tap into a strength you never knew you had.

I remained a seventeen-year-old in spirit—raw and so full of enthusiasm. There I was, changing my body and mind through the long hours of trials, then at the end of the day I couldn't wait to put on whatever was clean of my Millwall kit so I could wear it out in public. I used to swing by the Lakeside shopping centre in Dartford, dressed like I was on my way to Millwall training, just so I could show my pride.

Having those official kits was one of the best things about being on trial for Millwall. There were two kits: light blue and dark blue. I loved the dark blue with the proper number, the lion crest and the sponsor's logo. I also had a jumper and shorts, T-shirt, tracksuit bottoms. And I didn't just wear them at home; I actually slept in them. No word of a lie. I'd wash them, dry them and sleep in them.

That gear made me feel like a real footballer. In my whole time trialling for Millwall, there wasn't a day I didn't wear some item of clothing with that famous lion crest.

*

After several weeks at the trials, I learned that Bob and Allen had rung my parents and told them I was doing well. Then it came time to sit down with Bob, chief scout for the club, and with Allen, who by now acted as my advisor—the same way an agent would in a professional contract negotiation.

"Son, you've been excellent," Bob began. "Of course, there are still quite a few things you need to work on. We'll iron out all those specifics. But the long and the short of it is, we're going to offer you a contract."

He didn't say anything about money. No figures at all. No salary in pounds; no duration in months or years. Simply that they were prepared to sign me to a contract.

And the tears immediately welled in my eyes.

"Thank you, Bob."

I must have said that six or seven times in succession.

Money was the last of my concerns at that moment. Bob could have offered me two Australian dollars—roughly a pound a week—and I'd have taken it.

"You need to speak to your parents, Tim. We've already given your dad the details. The deal's going to be £250 a week and your digs paid."

Today that sounds like such a modest amount of money, but I was overjoyed just to be a professional footballer. In a short few minutes I'd hugged them, shed a few more tears of joy, then burst out laughing.

I rode high on the news and a few days later was called back for a follow-up meeting with Allen. To my surprise, he told me there was a Premier League team that wanted to sign me to a contract.

"Premier League?"

He nodded. "We've had an offer from a First Division team as well."

I was confused. How could a First Division and Premiership team want to offer me contracts when I hadn't been to trial with them? I saw the Millwall offer as a bird in the hand and had no desire to risk losing it. I didn't want to hear anymore.

"Millwall's offered me a contract. This is all I've ever wanted since I was five years old."

Allen explained the various options, the pros and cons. Millwall, being in the Second Division, could only offer a limited amount of money for a young, untested player like me. Their coffers were limited. The offer from the Premiership came from Nottingham Forest, the club with whom Allen had a longstanding relationship. He told me Forest could offer double the Millwall offer: £500 per week and digs paid. The other contract offer was from Queens Park Rangers (QPR), a First-Division club—£350 a week, digs paid.

I learned that football scouting is all about longstanding relationships and operated largely by word of mouth: *this Australian kid's got talent, a bit raw, needs work, but passionate.* Allen had informal scouting relationships with multiple clubs, so without even doing a formal trial with QPR or Forest, I'd had offers from them.

Now I had a critical decision to make and I was barely old enough to make it on my own. Contracts from clubs in the Premiership, First Division and Second Division! How was I to sort this out?

Though I was a teenager, I was savvy enough as a footballer to know my place, to know my proper level. I remember both Allen and my mum saying I should weigh the options and consider taking the Premiership. But money remained one of the least important factors for me.

"Mum," I said, "I can't forget where I've come from. Millwall's the club that gave me the trial."

I didn't use the word, but I knew if I left Millwall after they'd made an offer, it would feel to me like I'd *betrayed* them. I'd been granted the opportunity to train and be fully scouted by Millwall; to turn around and jump at an offer from a higher division club, for more money—it seemed awfully mercenary to me. I told my mum this.

"Tim," she said, "your heart's given you the answer. It's Millwall then. That's the club for you."

I took a few days to mull it over. Despite the fact that no one tried to influence my decision, the expectation was that I'd probably take the higher-valued contract, the higher-profile club, and sign with Nottingham Forest in the Premier League. Finally, I got back to Allen and Bob.

"Yeah, I've decided. I want to sign with Millwall," I told them.

It's true that I'm loyal—at least that's what I hope my family and friends would tell you. I'm also a realist. I knew those other clubs weren't my level.

Maybe being honest about my level reflects my Samoan heritage or my modest Australian upbringing. I try never to kid myself about my true knowledge, ability or potential. At that point in my development, those clubs were far beyond my level of play. I was talented but raw, and I knew I was nowhere near the finished article. I wouldn't have cared if the offer had come from Manchester United, AC Milan or Real Madrid—it was laughable to think I was ready to play among the top professionals in the world, to play week-in, week-out against men gifted enough to represent their nations in the World Cup. I had enough belief to think I would get there *someday*—but at the age of seventeen I knew it was still years away.

I also knew that to play above my level might be disastrous. One season spent sitting mostly on the bench and getting injured playing in the reserves could have ended my career before it even started.

In the process of deciding, I was very methodical, asking myself serious questions and forcing myself to give honest answers.

Was I ready to play in the Premiership with Nottingham Forest? Against the very top professionals in the UK? Would I have even started a match? Was I ready to play in the First Division with Queens Park Rangers?

Not a chance.

Was I ready to play in the Second Division, with Millwall, where I could work hard and learn my trade?

Perfect.

Choosing Millwall meant I could start my career as a professional footballer at a level that was appropriate. After I made the decision, no one argued with me, despite having their own opinions about what would have been best for me. We all agreed that the goal was for me to fulfil my potential.

*

The week I signed the Millwall contract was the same week I moved in with a couple of Irish players near the training facility in Southeast London. There was an Irish flag on the wall. Every night they played traditional Irish songs like "Black is the Colour"—and pretty soon I could sing all the words. I still know them by heart.

It was a hard transition from the communal family life with Glen and Lindsey and the Stanley kids. On my weekends off, I would take the Tube back to the Stanleys' place in Dartford, my home away from home. But the rest of the time my roommates and I were pretty much in each other's faces all day—on the football pitch and in the clubhouse; then home to hang out, eat together and sleep in the same digs. It was awkward at first because I didn't know them well enough to joke or ask them to change the channel after watching *Match of the Day* on BBC. No one had his own space—no one had any privacy.

The Irish boys were often homesick, too. We all missed our families. Speaking to my parents and brothers became the one bright spot socially—but it was very infrequent. A phone call to Australia could eat up my entire week's wages, and this was obviously long before FaceTime or Skype or texting. I would buy pre-paid phone cards and ring any chance I got—sometime from those old-fashioned red London phone boxes. I'd sort out the time difference and figure the best time to have a conversation with them that didn't wake them in the middle of the night.

Starting with Millwall was a tough spell emotionally, for all of us. I was growing into a man's body, but inside I was still a pretty fragile kid. A few nights I cried myself to sleep—the Irish boys couldn't hear me—and I'd be wondering if I'd have been better off playing in Australia for a few more years until I was more mature, and then trying to come to England.

*

But whenever I felt homesick, I had a sure-fire way to snap out of it. I told myself that tomorrow morning I was putting on my Millwall tracksuit and then off to work as a professional footballer.

That did it every time. Every day I was thrilled to go to the training ground and find my kit all laid out for me in the clubhouse—just like a proper member of the first team. Shirt, shorts, socks, boots.

Tradition ran deep within the Millwall system. You were reminded of that every time you looked at the team crest, known as the *lion rampant*, with the date of the club's foundation in bold: 1885. I learned the club actually started as Millwall Rovers, but the traditions handed down from generations of footballers remained largely unchanged.

One tradition is for youth-team members to be apprenticed to a designated first-team player. Even though I'd signed a contract with the club, I was still learning my trade. That involved learning from men who'd been playing professionally for years.

I was assigned to Kim Grant, a Ghanaian international striker who'd come to Millwall on loan from Luton Town in September 1997.

Kim was friendly, but all business. One of my roles was to wash his boots after training every day.

"Don't get any water inside the boots," Kim used to tell me. "Not even a drop. Make sure you wash them carefully."

They were a great pair of boots—he had a fairly small foot—and I can see them clearly, even now: red with a white stripe. I took care of them as if they were the crown jewels. I cleaned them so well that they were spotless after every training session, and I never got a splatter of water inside. I even managed to wash the exterior without getting any water on his laces. I did that job as if my entire footballing career depended on it. By the time I was done, those boots looked like they'd just come out of a High Street shop.

Grant was a big signing for Millwall. He'd been brought in to be a top goal-scorer, though when I was apprenticed to him he wasn't on the hottest streak. In two seasons at Millwall Grant had fifty-eight appearances and scored eight goals, and ended up going on loan to Notts County during the 1998–99 season. Still, to be apprenticed to Kim Grant was a big deal to me. He was a professional footballer who'd been capped by his country. I took a lot of pride in my role as his apprentice.

There were other chores we were expected to do as well. After each training session for the first team, we apprentices would have to clean the whole grounds. We'd do it in rotation, some players cleaning toilets, others cleaning the showers, some sweeping up, others mopping. One squad had to take care of the gym—wipe down the machines and organize the free weights—while another tidied up the physio room.

This sort of thing rarely goes on in football now, but in 1997, there in the southeast of London, I was part of something special, traditions that went back to my grandfather's—or maybe even my great-grandfather's—generation.

Making the youth players—even the contracted ones—responsible for the grounds was a brilliant idea because it instilled pride in the club. Millwall FC wasn't just about having that lion and '1885' on the crest of your tracksuit. It was also about pride in the team, in the institution itself.

If my assigned job was cleaning the toilets, I cleaned them *properly*. Rubber gloves, brush, down on my hands and knees. If I was washing sinks, I gave them the same level of attention. No half-arsed jobs. If any single one of us didn't do our jobs properly, we were all made to stay until the job met with the coach's approval. It instilled a sense of camaraderie in us—and work ethic—but it also gave us the sense that we were a team in which complacency would never be accepted. There was a level of excellence expected at Millwall in all aspects of membership of the team—including our role as youth apprentices.

I didn't care whether it was toilet duty or something else. I just did it. The test of the youth team was to muck in. If you didn't muck in, if you went against the grain, you were finished. We all learned it, and learned it well: that the first lesson of Millwall was to become part of Millwall—not just to wear the jersey, but to wear it with pride.

*

Playing for English managers and coaches was quite a shock after Australia. I had had some good coaches in Sydney, of course—and guys like Johnny Doyle definitely knew football. But the training at Millwall, every single day, was far more intense than anything I'd encountered at home. In spite of us being a Second Division club, from a pass to a shot to a set piece, the quality was higher. We had three coaches on the pitch at once, shouting at us, correcting everything we did. And the fitness regimen was relentless. We were run ragged every day.

But I soon saw how much I loved the roughness, the physicality, of this new life. Training in the wet, slide-tackling in the mud—there was no way to escape without bruises and knocks and other minor injuries. But nothing fazed me and I soon earned a reputation as a tough kid. Not a hard man; certainly not looking for problems on the pitch. Just a kid who trained with passion and was a fierce competitor. I went in full steam on every challenge, clattering, fighting for every ball. As I progressed as a Millwall player, I earned more than my fair share of fouls and cautions from the refs.

All that aggressive play came from the fact that I was determined never to miss a chance, never to slack off in any session—and I definitely didn't want any of the staff, or my team-mates, to think I was soft. If you got a knock on the knee or had a strained hamstring, no one was going to force you to play through the pain. I suppose you could have sat out a training session. But I never did. It would have taken a compound fracture in my leg to get me off the pitch.

My goal—from which I never wavered—was to get spotted in the youth team, get called up to the reserves, then get my chance with the first team. I saw reaching that goal meant no lingering in the physio room, complaining about aches and pains. I swore I would never get a reputation as a whinger, someone not ready to play through the hard physicality of the sport.

*

We played all our matches at the training centre, but in our apprentice role to the older players we went to Millwall's ground. That's where we cleaned up and also where we watched the first team play. On weekends the entire youth team would go to watch the first team play, every one of us dreaming that might be us in a few months—maybe a year.

The veteran supporters call the grounds "the *New* Den", because they still think of the club's original stadium, on the Isle of Dogs, as "the Den". The new Den is in South Bermondsey and has a capacity of just over 20,000. It's bordered by four massive stands and all around it are hung blue banners. I'd never seen anything like it. The grounds are almost directly adjacent to the railway line between London Bridge and New Cross Gate. With the train tracks right above, you can watch the Millwall fans streaming down the stairs from the train in full song. South Bermondsey is a rough section of south-east London, but it perfectly suited the team.

The Millwall fans reputation was … let's call them extremely *passionate*. There's a fearlessness about them. It's in their blood. They're on a different planet when it comes to supporting the team. When they sing their famous anthem, "Let 'Em All Come Down to the Den", it gives you the shivers.

All I kept repeating to Bob Pearson and Paul Ifill during my first visit to the park was my sense of awe. "Can you imagine playing here? Can you imagine making it onto the first team and scoring a goal in front of these fans?"

Bob started laughing. "Why not, son?" he said. "Anything's possible, isn't it?"

*

One of the best parts of signing with Millwall was that the club had, as one of its first-team starters, another Australian— Lucas Neill. Lucas and I trained together and later became close mates. Lucas had played for Millwall since 1995 and was well established in English football. He also represented Australia at the international level. I was still a nobody—a baby-faced kid from Sydney trying to make it into the first team. Lucas took me under his wing, spent a lot of time talking to me, and gave me the confidence to believe that I had a chance to make it at Millwall.

There was one particular training game that defined me as a Millwall player. I'd been playing well with the youth team and reserves, and I got a chance to start training regularly with the first team. During the training game, a cross came in to me, I got a touch, shot and forced the keeper to make a great save, punching the ball over the bar. I nearly scored and won us a corner kick.

We set up for the corner, coming in from the right. I was primed. This was my kind of moment. Throughout my career, a lot of my best goals would be scored from crosses or corners swinging in from the right which I met with my head.

The corner sailed in, I jumped, positioning myself and timing it perfectly. The ball was an in-swinger and I was about to make contact with my forehead when—BOOM!—elbow, knee and feet all clattering into me at once with great force, and I was completely taken out in mid-air. I hit the ground hard.

I got up, dazed, muddy, the whole scene fuzzy.

"What the hell was that?" I shouted.

It was clearly a foul, but it was a training match and normally you don't expect to get knocked nearly unconscious by a team-mate. I blinked, trying to figure out who had just bowled me over. I found myself looking straight into the pale blue eyes of the centre-back Keith Stevens.

Rhino.

Rhino Stevens was one of the most respected—and feared—Millwall stars of his day. He was a true Millwall legend. Ironically, he now lives in Australia and remains one of my closest mates, but, on that day, I didn't know Rhino Stevens from Adam. I just knew he wasn't a footballer to mess with.

Stevens could play centre-back, or right-back, or even sometimes defensive-midfielder. He was a hard man, but smart: he ended up being the Millwall player-manager, because his tactical understanding of the game was so sharp. In the early 1980s, when I was still a kid running around the parks of Sydney, Rhino Stevens was already a Millwall starter and a fixture with the club.

As I stood there on the pitch, looking at him, Rhino didn't glower at me. In fact, he simply smiled. I turned around to the coach, arms outstretched, because the play had continued with no whistle blown.

"Fuck! What happened there? That's a foul!"

"Play on, lad!"

I realized what had happened. Rhino took me out of the play on the corner because he knew I was a danger. Because on the previous touch, I'd nearly scored. Rhino was sending me a message: *Watch your back, lad. This is Millwall. We don't easily concede goals.*

I dusted myself off and jumped back into the mix.

About ten minutes later, in comes another curling cross. It's a high ball from the right, sixty-forty in my favour. I think I can get good contact with my head. But now here comes Rhino Stevens again, charging in, full tilt. I realize why his team-mates call him Rhino—this guy goes through anything.

I'm airborne, but instead of heading the ball or taking the hit from Rhino's body, I decide to take him out as he's trying to do the same to me. He's the larger man, but I have momentum, and I connect with him on the side hard enough to hurt. There is nothing clean about the challenge: the ball sails overhead as my elbow and knee make good contact.

Okay, you've had your go. Message received. Now here's a message for you.

I beat him to the punch. Had it not been a training game— if this was a regulation match—I'd have been cautioned by the referee, if not booked outright. What I didn't understand at the time was that no one *ever* went after Rhino. No one took him completely out of the play with a hard challenge like that.

Rhino lay on the ground, staring up at me.

Bloody hell, Cahill. Now what have you done? It's Rhino Stevens. He's going to kill you.

Rhino hoisted himself to his feet, grabbed me by the shoulders, and I got a good stare into those pale blue eyes again. I was ready for anything, a tongue-lashing—or worse. But Rhino, to my surprise, smiled.

"Well done, son. Get on with it."

Behind me, the coach shouted: "Play on!"

Rhino had taken it on the chin and I'd learned a big lesson about being a Millwall lion: give as good as you get. Don't be afraid to go hard and take risks. Rather than being annoyed that some kid had clattered him, it was as if Rhino had said, "All right, lad, you're on your way to earning some respect around here."

That one challenge was the big moment of my early days at Millwall. From that day forward, Rhino always looked after me on and off the pitch. Just in that momentary shoulder-grab, he'd given me his blessing.

SAMOAN FIRE

AFTER A YEAR I WAS ready to make my professional debut with Millwall, having been called up from the youth level. Rhino Stevens was now our player-manager. The date was 2 May 1998, and I was a substitute in the first team. We were playing at home against Bournemouth. Rhino told me to be ready, that I'd get into the match at some point.

I stood on the touchline, warming up, next to my team-mate Steven Reid. Rhino started yelling: "Where the hell are your studs, Cahill?"

With football boots, you have moulded plastic or aluminium studs of different lengths. I prefer moulded boots, but the gaffer wanted me to wear the screw-in studs.

If I'd asked why, I knew how he would have answered: "Because we're *Millwall*! That's why!"

The value of screw-in studs is that you get more grip in the turf and you can turn better. The *unstated* reason is that when you go into a tackle, studs are far more intimidating. Getting clattered with plastic moulds versus aluminium studs—well, you can work out the difference for yourself.

I put on the studs and raced onto the pitch. For months at Millwall I had played like a kid possessed. Every training session, every game, felt like it was my last. I knew this was where I was meant to be and it showed in my play. I was eighteen years old in that game against Bournemouth. We ended up losing 2–1, but by that point I had learned something invaluable: I'd learned to play with freedom.

*

It was during these early days in the first team that I started to feel the "Samoan warrior" side of me coming out. Since then, I've always described myself that way, both as a footballer and as a man. I don't have the physical size of some of my rugby-playing cousins, but I have the spirit of a warrior. I don't hold back and I always try to play without fear.

Ask guys who've played against me. If there's a challenge on the pitch, when they see Tim Cahill coming in, they know that nine times out of ten I'm not going to pull out. And you can always see, if only for a brief moment, when the other guy is coming into the tackle with fear. I'd see it in his eyes and use that to my advantage. I'd throw myself in with feet, body or head—whatever it takes. I'm a battler and I learned how to be one at Millwall.

That warrior mentality was—and is—something I carry into my role as a husband, as a son, and as a provider for my family. When Rhino Stevens and Alan McLeary took over the managerial jobs under Bob Pearson, it wasn't long before I was called into the office. I'd been offered another contract and we were in negotiations.

Rhino said, "What are you looking for, son?"

"I just want to sign—get what's fair—so I can send money back to Australia."

I explained about paying back my parents for all they'd invested in me over the years.

Rhino nodded. "We'll make sure we take care of you."

He knew what I was after. He also knew I was committed to Millwall. Rhino went in to bat for me with Bob, to make sure I was properly taken care of.

I got the contract and signed immediately. I told both Bob and Allen that I wouldn't let them down.

The £5,000 signing-on fee converted, at that time, to A$14,500. I sent it all straight home and put it toward repaying my brother and parents. Then we made a first-ever deposit on a house. That was a big milestone for our family. The days of renting were over. It was a house my parents were to live in for years. Today, my sister and her family live there.

I'll never forget Rhino for helping negotiate that bonus, which went so far to help my family back home. Rhino and I had mutual respect—we still do. We've had it since that first day we clattered into each other.

At that point in my early career I was making £1,000 a month, digs paid, and I sent just under half of that home to Australia. It felt like nothing, given all my family had sacrificed for me, but it was important for me to do it.

"Don't worry, Tim, you don't have to send anything this week," Mum would say. "Just look after yourself, make sure you'll have enough."

But sending part of my Millwall pay cheque back to my parents in Sydney was another way I was stepping up—feeling less like a teenager and more like a man.

*

It is the Millwall fans in the stands who make the Den so intimidating. On match days they're out in force, emptying from the train station in a river of blue jerseys. Working-class guys who were born and raised on the matches of Millwall Football Club. Tough, tattooed football fans who love to fight, who sing the team's anthem from the stands, thousands-strong:

No one likes us, no one likes us!
No one likes us, we don't care!
We are Millwall, super Millwall
We are Millwall, from the Den!

The singing stops—there's some clapping and cheering, followed by a deafening chant:

Mill-wallllllll!

Mill-wallllll!

Mill-wallllll!

Mill-walllll!

No player who faced Millwall ever wanted to play at the Den. Some players who played *for* Millwall didn't want to play at the Den.

For me, the Den was a test of character. To put up with that noise, the expectations of the fans, the pressure of failure. To this day I often repeat those words I first heard from Rebecca's great-grandfather, Lou: "If you can play at Millwall, you can play anywhere."

A lot of teams play pranks, but with Millwall, there were no *half* measures. You'd come back to the changing room after a match and find that all your clothes had been cut up with a pair of scissors. Or your clothes would be in a pile—on fire. You'd have to stamp it out quickly, as the rest of the boys just stood there and laughed.

The Millwall players have the same culture as the fans. Some might find that ludicrous. I found it brilliant. You can't buy that kind of chemistry and camaraderie. If you can fit in at that club—and not every player could—it made playing there the greatest experience you can imagine.

DOWN BUT NEVER OUT

THROUGHOUT MY EARLY DAYS AT Millwall, my old classmate Rebecca Greenfield and I had continued to write to each other. No texting back in the late-1990s—handwritten letters. Then she decided to come on holiday to England with a friend. We caught up in London and had a few laughs, but it was only when I got my first bad injury that we really connected on a deeper level.

As an eighteen-year-old, you never think you're going to get injured. You feel like you're invincible. But then, at the start of the second season, I broke my fifth metatarsal. It seemed so innocuous—all I did was play a ball across my body but, as I made the kick, I rolled my foot.

Instantly, I felt something snap. The X-ray left no doubt.

"Afraid it's broken, lad."

"Broken?"

"Fifth metatarsal fracture."

They put a pin in my foot, then secured my foot in a heavy boot. For an entire month I was ordered to keep my weight off it, using crutches and being extremely careful how I walked. This was no minor setback. It meant a minimum of three months' recovery, and months more of rehabilitation and physiotherapy to make sure the bone was fully healed.

I didn't think it was a big deal, but for years I have had recurring problems with that fifth metatarsal. Because it was still so early in my Millwall career, the biggest factor for me about being injured was that I was missing crucial training and matches.

It made me homesick and I wondered if it might be best to go back to Sydney and spend time with my family during rehabilitation. It was a pretty tough time. There came a point where I even questioned if I wanted to continue with professional football.

That's one of the major obstacles you face when you're injured. It affects you emotionally, especially your self-confidence. It just drains you. Any significant injury means you can't play and can't train, so you're left wondering if you want to go back on the pitch and try again—whether it's all worth it.

For me, being thousands of miles from Australia, the injury meant I couldn't just call on my mum or dad or spend time with family. I was in a heavy black boot and had no choice but to wait for it to heal. I'd sit there on the bench and watch the boys play.

As a young athlete, you never factor injuries into your plan. Who in the world wants to be a professional footballer and thinks injuries will be part of the equation? That, in fact, just when you're getting started, you'll break a bone in your foot?

I did end up flying back to Australia to spend time with my family during my rehabilitation, and there was one upside, at least. It brought me a lot closer to Rebecca. We had always been good friends, but now we talked to each other pretty much every day.

Unfortunately during my stay in Sydney, her great-grandfather's health took a grave turn and he was in hospital. Lou was so in love with the game of football and was always asking Bek about me. I wanted to go and see him and tell him personally about playing my first season at the Den. He was in intensive care, and we went and had a long visit. When it was time to leave, Lou said to me, "Whatever you do, Tim, look after Rebecca." I said, "Of course I will." Shortly after we left the hospital, Lou died. Bek was in tears, and I was comforting her—and it was one of those moments when we both realized how strong and intimate our friendship had become.

I had never been able to commit to a relationship because football had always come first. Bek and I still weren't really going out, but something clicked in me when I realized I would have to leave Australia again.

When I was fit, I got back to England, back to my playing season, but we were writing letters every day, running up huge phone bills, making mix-tape cassettes for each other—just those early stages of falling in love.

After months of long-distance communication, I finally rang her up.

"Enough is enough," I said. "Look, Bek, why don't you just come over?"

"And stay where?"

"With me—in digs."

She flew straight over. It was brilliant. At the time I was staying in digs with Debbie and Chris Grey. They were a fantastic couple, native South Londoners and diehard Millwall fans. They regularly took in young players like me and treated us as if we were members of their family. Debbie was a care-worker and Chris was a tradesman. We'd sit in their front lounge room and watch *Eastenders* together; we'd have Sunday roasts and parties. They were massive Millwall supporters; every home match was like a family affair. Chris and his brother Tony would also come to our away games, travelling up and down the country. But one thing about Debbie and Chris that I'll never forget was the way they accepted Rebecca into their home as if she was family, too.

After a few months we decided to get our own place. I was the professional footballer—supposedly on the road to this glamorous life—but when Bek first came to England she found a job as a travel agent and was soon earning more money than I was.

By now I was starting my third year at Millwall and I decided to buy an apartment—a lovely place in Bromley, close to the training ground. It was the biggest financial decision of my life to date. It was £80,000 and, truthfully, I couldn't afford it. I could cover the mortgage, but Bek worked nine-to-five every day, sometimes on the weekends, too, and she paid all the other bills and bought all the groceries.

Bek was never a fan of football when we were kids in Australia. She didn't give a damn about football, actually. But if she wasn't working, she'd come to the Millwall matches. She grew to love the game. Looking back on it, I don't think she had much *choice* ...

What made our relationship work is the fact that we were best mates first. She understood my priorities. At the start of my career, I loved football more than I loved her, and she knew it. She knew I would never forget the sacrifices my family had made to give me a chance at living my dream. Bek knew I wasn't going to let my personal life overtake my need to fulfil my dream—my family's dream—of me making it as a professional footballer.

I just had tunnel vision.

But things changed drastically when, one afternoon after training with Millwall, I came back to the flat and Bek was crying.

I thought, *Oh shit, what have I done now?*

"Don't know how to tell you this, Tim. I'm pregnant."

She thought I'd be disappointed. She knows me: beyond football, the only women in my life had been my mum, grandmother and sister.

But disappointed? What? I was buzzing. I kissed Bek and hugged her to bits.

My whole life I've loved being around kids. I love babies, could always put my little brother and younger cousins to sleep, was always a good baby-sitter.

My son Kyah was born in 1999 and I hadn't a clue what it meant. I was learning it all on the go, making all kinds of young-dad mistakes, all the while being a full-time footballer. When you have a newborn baby in a small place, it's tough on any couple. But when you have a kid *and* you're a professional footballer, and you don't sleep seven or eight hours a night, your playing suffers. You almost can't function on the pitch. Bek and I were lucky if we got four hours' sleep because Kyah had colic.

Those were really trying months. And then we had yet another injury to contend with—which threw our lives into further turmoil.

＊

My anterior cruciate ligament (ACL) injury, like the break in my foot, came about through another freak accident. During training, I went to pass the ball from my right foot and my knee just gave way. It was a totally routine motion I'd done thousands of times in my playing career. I hobbled off the pitch and was told I'd damaged my ACL. I would have to have surgery, go through the rehabilitation again, and miss yet more months of playing time.

But this is when I turned into a machine—all due to a chance meeting with Sir Alex Ferguson.

While I was injured I went to a Blackburn Rovers game with Graeme Souness, the Scotland international and former captain of Liverpool; at half-time, Graeme took me to meet Ferguson.

Sir Alex looked down at my knee brace and said, "I see you've done your knee."

"Yeah, tore up the ACL."

"Do you know Roy Keane?" he asked.

I'd never met Manchester United's captain Roy Keane personally, but most everyone who followed Premier League football respected the fierceness with which the Irish international played at midfield for the Red Devils.

Sir Alex then told me how hard Keane had worked to rebuild his knee after his own ACL tear. Keane got his treatment and rehabilitation in the morning, again in the afternoon, and continued working on the knee at home. I nodded as Sir Alex explained how Keane had basically worked and willed himself back to recovery. Our chat was brief and ended with him wishing me well.

"Stay on top of that, Tim. Make sure you look after it."

After that conversation with Sir Alex, his advice about Roy Keane never left my mind. I'd go to the clubhouse in the morning and after my shower work with the physio, Gerry Docherty.

The doctors tell you after the surgery: "Make sure you get the knee straight, get the flex back into in it."

I couldn't run but in the gym I did endless sets of push-ups, sit-ups, dips. I turned into the Millwall gym rat. I did everything

I couldn't do on the park in that gym. I put on muscle weight, got much stronger and fitter, even though I'd done my knee.

One day I remember Bek came home and found me sitting in our new flat. She saw me squeezing my knee down into the floor with a towel underneath it. Tensing my VMO—that's the vastus medialis oblique part of the quadriceps muscle—for hours at a time. I strengthened it so much that, in fact, if you look at my two knees today you can't even tell which VMO I injured.

For many players, tearing your ACL can mark the end of your career. I was lucky.

The key was hard work—in rehabilitation, in the weight room, doing my own towel technique at home. All things considered, I made a surprisingly quick recovery. The physios and the gaffer were shocked by how quickly I was back to training. I was back in full form in six months. I went out there smashing with that Samoan warrior spirit, playing as hard as ever for Millwall.

I remember one match we played against Scunthorpe United. The knee was feeling good and I went into a challenge with force. The Scunthorpe defender slid in, both feet up, studs showing. This properly sliced me up. I got up and tried to play, only to find there was a massive hole in my leg. I was strong enough to walk off the pitch without assistance. The doctor gave me an injection to numb the pain, washed my wound and sewed me up. It took twenty stitches inside and out to close that hole. But I was soon playing again as if nothing had happened.

*

In spite of the two serious injuries, my time with Millwall had gone better than I could have hoped. Once he'd become player-manager, Rhino played me every single game. Even when I was off form, struggling with certain aspects of my game, he played me. He did it because he believed in me. That's something I've never forgotten.

"You need to play games," Rhino said. "You need to get as many under your belt as possible. It's the only way you learn your trade."

We had such a terrific group of players in that team, men like David Livermore. He played to the left of me in the midfield, I played in the centre, and to the right of me was Steven Reid. Up front on the left was my close mate Paul Ifill, then Richard Sadlier and Neil Harris, at centre-forward, leading the line.

We had some team, especially for a Second Division club whose fans proudly chanted: "No one likes us, we don't care". We had built up some hope in Millwall. Yeah, there was hope in those stands that we might have what it took to claw our way into the First Division.

On the pitch, in the Den, we knew it was up to us to prove the Millwall fans right.

THE CUP RUN

THE PINNACLE OF MY MILLWALL career was our FA Cup run of 2004. The FA Cup is unique in sports—certainly in the UK—in that you frequently have Cinderella teams from the lower divisions—even non-league teams sometimes—facing off against the big boys like Chelsea, Manchester United and Arsenal, and perhaps even stealing a game.

Every few years there's some club that no one rates that makes a great run. It was Millwall's turn in 2004. Neil Harris was on fire. We were all on fire, but Harris in particular. Neil was our star striker who, after a brief spell at Cambridge City, had become a fixture with the Lions. He would ultimately end up being Millwall's all-time record goal-scorer, with 125 league goals and 138 in all competitions, then go on to serve as manager for the club.

I remember during that 2004 cup run we were staying at some fancy hotel up north prior to the match against Tranmere.

You'd think we'd be in our beds the night before—or at least quietly preparing for the match. Hardly.

We were larking about in the hallway, having a laugh, and I can't recall who started the nonsense, but suddenly all the boys were throwing apples at each other. If you played for Millwall, this was perfectly normal. Suddenly, we were chucking apples at our team-mates in a fancy hotel hallway.

As I was running away from a chucked apple, someone slammed a door and it hit me in the eye, cutting open my eyebrow.

It was a deep cut, bleeding quite a bit. Straightaway, all the boys turned serious.

"Shit! What do we do?"

I said, "Into the shower. I'll put a towel on it. I'll say I slipped and cut my head."

We ran into the bathroom and wrapped the towel round my head—someone even snapped a picture—while one of the other guys fetched the team doctor.

In minutes, the boss found out what had happened.

"You were pissing about!" he yelled.

"No, Tim slipped and cut his eye in the shower!"

That was our story and we stuck to it. A butterfly stitch stopped the bleeding and kept the cut from forming a bad scar.

There was no question about whether I was going to play and there was no way a deep cut, even stitches, was going to affect my heading the ball. At Millwall, you played with injuries all the time. You played with one leg if you had to.

*

Against Tranmere at Prenton Park, we had a cracker of a match. I scored after just eleven minutes when Danny Dichio sent me a clever flick. It wasn't the most technical of my goals, but it was one of the most memorable: I controlled it well in the penalty area and steered it perfectly into the net. Five minutes later Danny passed to Neil Harris who scored with a left-footed volley.

The win meant Millwall would be playing in their first FA Cup semi-final in sixty-seven years.

A fantastic photo appeared in the next day's newspapers: Neil Harris and me with our arms around each other. You can see my eye all swollen and stitched up. To this day, the thought of that chucked apple and the door slicing me wide open makes me laugh. At Millwall, on and off the park, football was insane fun. It was like being a schoolboy again.

*

The FA Cup semi-final, played at Old Trafford against Sunderland on 4 April 2004, is still regarded as the biggest match in Millwall club history. A win meant Millwall would be in the FA Cup final for the first time in 119 years.

The night before the match, as I lay in bed in a hotel in Manchester, I thought back to my childhood bedroom in Sydney, with my posters of footballers. One of my dreams, of course, was to play professionally. Given my obsession with all things Manchester United, another of my dreams was to play someday at Old Trafford. I could barely fall asleep realizing I'd accomplished one goal and was on the verge of achieving a second.

I got to start in that semi-final at Old Trafford and the most beautiful thing about it was that Paul Ifill was there on the pitch starting with me as well. The same kid I'd met that first day of the trials, with our shared daydream of making it together into the first team as professionals. And here we were warming up on that gorgeous Old Trafford pitch, pinging passes back and forth to one another.

No one really expected much of Millwall in that match— mostly because we hadn't been this far in an FA Cup before. Most experts picked Sunderland to win and on paper Sunderland were probably the superior team. But we had fire. Dennis Wise and Ray Wilkins, during that whole cup run, would shout at us: "No holding back! If I see any of you holding back I won't play you!" We had grit and determination—and most importantly, we had an exceptional team bond. We were damn hard to break down. We were tactically solid.

The day was cold, a bit windy. The game started feistily, the ball moving quickly on the pitch. For the first half, we played the better football. In the twenty-fifth minute, the ball broke out wide, and it was Paul Ifill who created our scoring chance. Paul went on a wonderful mazy run, beating defenders, then lined up one of his cracking shots on target. The ball was saved by Sunderland keeper Mart Poom, but he could only parry it and it came popping back out.

I'd been tracking the play and, just outside the penalty box, I saw my chance. This was the culmination of everything my dad and Johnny Doyle used to tell me about being a box-to-box midfielder: to hold up my runs slightly, not arrive too early, be the trailing runner into the penalty area to take advantage of any opportunities.

When the ball popped loose I didn't have time for a first touch, so I went straight into the volley. Got my right leg up, made nice clean contact with the inside of my foot and struck the ball straight past two players, past the goalkeeper and into the roof of the net.

I peeled off, looking up into the stands, jersey off, swinging it over my head, and screaming. No one could catch me, though Neil Harris tried, as I sprinted the length of the Old Trafford pitch. I could see all our Millwall fans going berserk, drinks flying in the air, and then I spotted my mum and dad and my brother Sean. I knew they'd flown in for the match but I had no idea where they were in that sea of faces. It was crazy: in all that adrenaline-fuelled mayhem, how could I possibly have found them?

I ran up to my dad and my brother and threw my arms around them, shouting.

"What a goal, Tim!" they shouted.

I grabbed my mum and all I could hear was her screaming.

It was a big goal for Millwall, and the moment was made all the more memorable because my family was there to witness it.

When I came back into a huddle with my Millwall team-mates I was flying high. Dennis Wise was shouting that we had to get our heads back together—it wasn't even the half-hour mark. But we were such a well-organized and passionate team, we could sense we'd broken through, that that goal might be the winner.

"Focus!" Dennis kept shouting.

The challenges from both sides were intense. In fact, our captain, Kevin Muscat—the hard Australian who so perfectly fitted the Millwall badge—took a bad foul from Sunderland's George McCartney and had to come off the pitch in the first half. But we held our shape and kept defending furiously. It was only at the final whistle that it sank in: we were going to the FA Cup final!

That volley—especially because it came off a goal brilliantly set up by my mate Paul Ifill—still ranks among my favourite goals, even against better-known shots I would later score in World Cup matches, in Asian Cups, and in the Premiership.

That FA Cup semi-final goal was also a key moment in my career in ways I couldn't imagine at the time. It was because of that goal—seizing that moment—that selectors for the Australian national team began to take notice. In a way, that single moment paved the way for the rest of my career.

*

The FA Cup final was played in the Millennium Stadium, Cardiff, Wales, on 22 May 2004, against Manchester United.

If there had been low expectations for our performance against Sunderland, against Manchester United there were *zero* expectations for Millwall—none at all. For all our spirit and ability, we didn't expect to be the ones marching up the steps to the Royal Box, hoisting the cup overhead.

One of us even joked as we came up the tunnel: "If things go pear-shaped, lads, we might as well start a brawl. We'll win *that* for sure!"

That's one thing about that Millwall squad: we always backed ourselves as physical players. No one could intimidate us. Talent-wise, payroll-wise, Manchester United had it all. But what the hell: we were bloody *Millwall*. We were never going to get bullied on the park.

I remember walking onto the pitch, feeling almost star-struck. I'd had all the replica United kits as a kid, and even during my trial for Millwall I'd worn the official Manchester United Red Devils jersey. This was all I'd dreamed of from when I was a boy. I knew my family were in the crowd for that game, just as they'd been there for Sunderland, though at kick-off, again, I had no idea where they were sitting. I kept glancing around, hoping I could spot them.

That final is a blur of impressions: young Cristiano Ronaldo, wearing a pair of flashy golden boots—what a terror he was, dribbling, dazzling us with bursts of pace down the wing. No one could cover him. He was such a whippet-quick master of the step-over. Manchester United's whole line-up was star-studded: Ryan Giggs, Roy Keane, Paul Scholes, Gary and Phil Neville.

We came out hard, but they had Roy Keane bossing the midfield—one of the true hard men of the Premiership and at the peak of his powers. His ACL was clearly no impediment now, given some of the clattering he doled out on the pitch.

Still, we went at them completely without fear: hard challenges, real rough stuff, going after *every* loose ball. We were not backing down from them. We played to the limit of our physical abilities. It just wasn't enough.

Ruud van Nistelrooy scored twice for United, and Ronaldo nodded in a Gary Neville cross. The final score was 3–0, and it could easily have been 5–0 or 6–0. Though many news accounts called us "valiant"—and I guess we were—it's also true that we were simply outclassed. We were never really in the match.

As the final whistle blew, I remember thinking: *I want van Nistelrooy's jersey.* One of the top strikers in the world. I would have taken anyone's jersey, to be honest, but I really wanted Ruud's, since he'd scored that beautiful brace against us. I ran up and swapped jerseys with him and he signed his for me. Getting a player's autograph when you're on the losing side in an FA Cup final is not normal, but I didn't care. I was like a kid again.

*

That FA Cup run put me on the map, both domestically and internationally. It also taught me a lot about winning and losing. I never *accepted* losing. I was in every game, every moment, with a single objective in mind—to win.

But I was also in the game of football for the long haul. To do that, you've got to be mentally prepared for the ups and downs—successes, injuries, failures and inevitable losses.

You have to prepare yourself to maintain your mental strength over the duration, learning how to put the realities of the game in perspective. You'll win matches because of your team's efforts. Sometimes because of your own. You'll also lose matches—sometimes deservedly. Long-term mental toughness as a professional comes from making a deal with yourself. Be honest about what you did well and not so well and, most importantly, whether or not you played with all your heart.

No matter how hard you work, sometimes you're going to lose. That's football. What matters always is that you give every ounce of yourself to the effort.

I knew if I had the *desire* to win, gave my all on every play, in every match, I could live without the bitterness of regret. And I knew in that FA Cup run I'd done just that.

THE CALL-UP

WHILE I WAS OFF PLAYING for Millwall, Frank Farina was the Australian national team manager. Farina had been a striker in the NSL, playing for Canberra City, Sydney City, and Marconi Stallions before going off to a career in Europe with Club Brugge in the Belgian league. He'd been the manager of the Australian national team since 1999 and had reached out to Millwall, wondering if the Socceroos should be looking at calling me up. These things weren't secret within the club—I knew I was being observed as a potential international for Australia.

When I'd represented Samoa in that youth tournament in Fiji, no one—least of all me—could have anticipated I'd go on to do bigger and better things as a professional in the UK, or that those few minutes as a substitute in that Under-20 Samoan team would cause huge legal problems for me years later.

Farina selected me for the Australian team camp, only to find out that the Fédération Internationale de Football

Association (FIFA) would not grant me eligibility because I had been capped by Samoa in that Under-20 tournament. It seemed ludicrous. I explained that I'd really only gone to Samoa because my grandmother was sick. As the goalkeeper, Sean was the more valuable player to that Under-20 team and, truthfully, I never anticipated seeing match time. After all, it was a *men's* tournament and I was still only fourteen. But the facts were that I had come on as a substitute in a 3–0 loss against New Zealand, so in FIFA's eyes I had played for Samoa at an international youth tournament.

Behind the scenes, FIFA had to work out the legalities with the Oceania Football Confederation. There was little I could do—just keep battling, keep scoring goals for Millwall. But it was nerve-wracking. I was well aware that getting the honour or representing my country in international play lay in the lap of our legal appeal.

As for my eligibility, to me it had always been and always would be crystal clear: I was born in Australia, I grew up playing football in the parks and on the pitches of Sydney. I was an Australian; why on earth would I not be allowed to represent my home country as an adult?

The appeal dragged on and on. Frank Farina and a whole lot of other folks fought hard to get me cleared to play. In the end—thankfully—commonsense prevailed. By the start of 2004, FIFA had changed its eligibility rules to allow kids capped at junior levels to switch international allegiance as adults.

In fact, because of the strange rules of international football, Australia and Samoa weren't my only options for international honours. In 2002 Mick McCarthy, the former Millwall manager, who was coaching the Republic of Ireland, showed interest in me. Because my grandmother on my father's side was born in Ireland, I could have been called up for Ireland in the 2002 World Cup.

My international status may have sounded complicated, but to me it was simple and I told everyone as much at the time: "You can't represent a country if you don't even know the national anthem."

People would laugh: "What are you on about, Tim? Players do it all the time."

I didn't care what other players did. Different people, different motives. I could only speak for myself and my own beliefs. In my mind, you'd better know the national anthem of the country you're representing, better have passion for that jersey and that badge you're wearing, or else you shouldn't bother putting that shirt on.

Times have changed. It's now commonplace in international football for players to join teams based on the citizenship of their parents or grandparents, even though they've never spent a single day living in the country they're representing at the World Cup.

At the time, some of my Irish team-mates said I would have been better off picking the Republic of Ireland instead of Australia, for practical purposes.

"What are you thinking, Tim? Australia will never make it to a World Cup."

Australia had already played in a World Cup—but that was back in 1974, before I was born, and we hadn't won a single match or scored a single goal.

*

After all the complications of my eligibility and my case with FIFA were resolved, Frank Farina called me up to a camp right there in London. My first time representing Australia was in a friendly against South Africa. I didn't start, but what a huge honour it was to wear the green and gold among so many big-name players in that Australian national side, coming from some of the leading clubs of Europe and the UK.

These were the names that would become known as the Socceroos' "Golden Generation": Mark Schwarzer, Lucas Neill, Craig Moore, Tony Popovic, Stan Lazaridis, Josip Skoko, Mark Bresciano, Scott Chipperfield, Brett Emerton, Mile Sterjovski, Harry Kewell, David Zdrilic, Mark Viduka, John Aloisi.

Besides Lucas, my team-mate from Millwall, none of the other Socceroos knew much about me. I came into camp definitely sensing I was the young face who had to prove his worth.

I made my full debut for Australia on 30 March against South Africa at Loftus Road, in Shepherd's Bush, the home of Queens Park Rangers. Though I sat out most of the match, I was still a bundle of nervous energy. Mark Bresciano scored in the nineteenth minute and I came on as a substitute for him in the seventy-fifth minute. I don't know if my nerves showed in my playing for those last fifteen minutes, but after the final whistle everyone said I'd done well. We won 1–0.

For me, it wasn't about being a star in that team. My dreams were much more modest. I wanted to train hard, give my all and do well on the pitch. I wanted to do well primarily for Frank Farina, because he had fought hard to give me one of the most important opportunities—and honours—of my life. I'll always be indebted to Frank for that. It would have been all too easy for him to say: "Ah, the kid was cap-tied to Samoa, let's move on." But Frank didn't.

That debut was a proud moment and it certainly made for a great phone call home to my mum and dad in Sydney. Looking back, I realize it was yet another trial period, to see if I was actually good enough, to see if I was worth selecting again.

*

My first true test as an international came during the Oceania Football Confederation (OFC) Nations Cup and World Cup Qualifying Tournament. That's a long and unwieldy title for a tournament, so we always referred to it simply as "the Oceanias". In 2004, winning the Oceanias was a critical part of the two-step process of earning a berth in the upcoming World Cup.

I went into camp with the mind-set that I had to prove myself. That friendly at Loftus Road against the South Africans didn't count for much and the Oceanias tournament would be the first true test of my international career. I was given the

No. 10 jersey—quite an honour—showing that coach Farina had a lot of faith in me. The build-up to the tournament was brilliant. I became good mates with Jade North, who played for Perth Glory, and with Archie Thompson, who was with Lierse SK in Belgium. We had a lot of laughs in camp. That team was packed full of some really great, down-to-earth guys.

Back then, the Oceanias weren't seen as a difficult tournament—not by any means—but a potential banana skin if you didn't take it seriously. The Socceroos started off well: on 29 May 2004, we beat New Zealand 1–0, though I didn't play in the match. On 31 May, at Hindmarsh Stadium in Adelaide, I played my first full match as a Socceroo against Tahiti. I scored the opening goal in the fourteenth minute, then netted a second one. Just after the break, Mile Sterjovski came on as a substitute, scored a second-half hat-trick, and we went on to a 9–0 romp.

We won the tournament, beating Tahiti and Vanuatu, but suffered a bit of a shock with a 2–2 draw against the Solomon Islands. We prevailed in the two-leg qualification tie, winning 9–1 on aggregate.

The Oceanias was a milestone for me in that I'd scored six goals. I was the leading scorer of the tournament, but what I cared about—regardless of minutes played or goals scored—was whether I had made my mark. There were far bigger names than me in that squad—guys like Viduka and Kewell and Bresciano. It was important for me to go beyond scoring, to make myself a presence on the pitch in the minds of the other players.

*

I never took the honour and privilege of representing Australia for granted. When it comes to international play, you never know what will happen. Players are capped all the time, then dropped for a variety of reasons. Managers come and go and they tend to have their own sense of who's the best fit for their tactical system. Some brilliant young kid will pop up on the radar and be selected ahead of you. A team can only call up so many midfielders and strikers, and loads of amazing club players are never selected for their national squads.

I didn't fully understand how hard it was to be selected regularly for the national team until I got there. That's why I've got all my memorabilia from my earliest games to the present. I've saved them all, from the jersey I wore in my debut in the friendly against South Africa to tracksuits from the first Oceania tournament. I treasure all the mementos from the national team experience. Being selected to play for my country was one of the most difficult—and ultimately rewarding—accomplishments of my career.

We had great team camaraderie. Older players like Zeljko "Spider" Kalac, Tony Popovic and Kevin "Muskie" Muscat— the veterans who knew how to take care of you—they were the unquestioned leaders, focussed and disciplined.

Add into that mix men, like John Aloisi, who created the laughter. As a young player, you need those older and more experienced players to take an interest in looking out for you—on and off the park—much like Rhino had done for me at Millwall. We always went out together as a group, ate and drank together, bonded as mates.

No one was calling us the "Golden Generation" yet—far from it. Australia wasn't anyone's idea of a footballing powerhouse. At best, the Socceroos were seen as chronic underachievers—full of potential but short on delivery. But among that group of players, very early on, we had self-belief. We knew we were part of a potentially great national team.

PART
03

ONCE A BLUE, ALWAYS A BLUE

EVERTON

LEAVING MILLWALL WAS THE BIGGEST decision I'd yet faced. I'd done everything in my power to help this football team. I was nearing the end of my contract and had to decide whether or not I'd make a move to the Premier League. The previous season had been a cracker: I'd scored twelve goals—as a midfielder, not an outright striker—and finished as Millwall's top scorer for the season.

All told, I'd made 241 appearances for the Lions, scoring fifty-eight goals. My stock was high; moving up a division was more than just speculative talk. Offers were now official. My agent, Paul Martin, had four really good ones on the table. I knew it was time. I'd had some offers the year before, but I wasn't ready then. Now I was.

I had hoped Millwall would go further to reach the Premier League. I don't usually put much stock in speculation, but I had wondered, more than once, if with a little more investment, just a bit more quality, another striker thrown into the mix, it would have been possible.

The reality was that the owners didn't have that kind of money and we'd made the most of the cards we'd been dealt. We had achieved some great things together. We'd been promoted from Second to First Division, and in the 2001–02 season made it to the semi-final play-off for promotion to the Premiership, only to fall to eventual winners Birmingham City. We'd reached an FA Cup final and only lost to one of the great sides of European football.

It was clear that we'd gone as far as we could together. No one could have wrung another drop of effort and passion out of us. I was immensely proud to be a Millwall Lion. I also came to realize I needed to leave Millwall in order to advance in my career. I was twenty-four years old and knew that my next move should be to play in the Premiership as soon as possible.

*

I chose Everton because of its reputation as a stable club—one rich in history, loyalty and tradition. At the helm were David Moyes, the manager, and Bill Kenwright, the owner—two of the best footballing men in the UK.

But Everton was going through a miserable spell when they made me the offer. They had barely stayed in the Premier League, finishing seventeenth—fourth from the bottom— managing to avoid relegation to the First Division by the skin of their teeth. In the thirty-eight matches played, they'd only managed nine wins and twelve draws. It was not a club on an upward trend.

David Moyes knew he had to bring in new talent, make some tough changes and shake things up to keep the club competitive.

It was a multi-player deal: Everton bought me for £1.5 million and Marcus Bent for £400,000 and, shortly thereafter, they sold Wayne Rooney to Manchester United in a record deal worth £25.6 million.

When I signed with Everton, there were few expectations of me. Who was I? Some young Australian midfielder who'd done good things at Millwall? The Everton fans were already murmuring: why the hell did management decide to buy two unheralded young players—Cahill and Bent—at bargain prices, and sell a rising superstar like Wayne Rooney, albeit for a fortune?

Before signing I'd gone to Liverpool to speak to David Moyes face to face. It was a bit nerve-wracking going into that first meeting. I knew all about his background and what he'd achieved at a number of top clubs. He had a reputation for being a manager who could take on young players—teaching, nurturing and moulding them into more complete individuals. He also made them better team players, using their natural attributes to get the most out of them for the benefit of the club.

David Moyes is tall and blue-eyed, with a big presence when he enters a room. He's a serious footballing man. Intimidating, too. But in our meeting he turned out to be one of the kindest men I've ever met. When I greeted him, he smiled, shook my hand and started peppering me with questions about my personal life—nothing about football or business at all.

"How are you, Tim? Do you have kids? Do you like life in England? Do you miss Australia?"

As I sat across from him, nodding and answering his questions, any feelings of intimidation melted away. I'd dealt with gaffers like Dennis Wise and Rhino Stephens—imposing men until I got to know them on the pitch playing together. David Moyes was someone I'd only watched on TV. I saw him as one of the big-time bosses on the touchline whenever I'd watch *Match of the Day*. He dealt with star personalities like Duncan Ferguson, Kevin Campbell, Wayne Rooney. It takes a man like David Moyes—a no-nonsense and strong-minded Scotsman—to manage those oversized characters.

I assumed the first things we'd be talking about were my footballing position, my contract, the Everton club history, but here was this top Premiership gaffer asking me about all sorts of things that had nothing to do with football. For a good twenty minutes, we talked about our lives and families. He seemed mindful of the fact that I was shy and quiet, and straightaway made me feel welcome at Everton, asking what I wanted to do with my life, what my ambitions were for the future.

"Well, my dream was always to be a professional footballer," I told him. "Since I was a kid in Sydney, that's all I've worked for. And honestly, right now ... this is the biggest moment of my life. I know there's no guarantee that I'm going to play ..."

Everton had the likes of Lee Carsley, Leon Osman, Tommy Gravesen and Kevin Kilbane—quality midfielders—and I knew I'd have to work hard to make it into the starting eleven. That was my one major reservation about signing with the Blues, and I felt I could be frank with David Moyes about it.

"There's really only one thing I want to know," I said. "Will you really give me my opportunity? Will you give me a chance to show I can play?"

He stared at me hard before answering. "One thing I can promise you, lad, is that if you're good enough, you will play. If you're not good enough, I'll work you up to a standard where you can. If you're given the chance, though, you'd better take it."

"That's all I need to know," I said.

He looked at me a bit strangely, squinting.

Well, that's the only bloody reason I'm signing you, son. Of course you're going to get a chance! Why even ask?

It might have seemed an obvious question, but it's a huge issue in top-flight football. There are plenty of signings made simply for depth. I'd had offers from clubs in the Premiership where I knew I'd likely only be a squad player, coming on occasionally as a substitute. David Moyes could similarly have been signing me because he thought I'd be a solid squad player—someone to fill in for injured starters, a safeguard and backup—but not a regular starter.

I didn't want to make a move to the Premiership if it meant playing only with the reserves or going on for the final fifteen minutes in a few matches per season. That wasn't going to take me to the level I wanted to achieve. I felt I'd done my apprenticeship with Millwall and I was ready to play against the best now—all the big boys of the Premier League.

After our long conversation, I knew that Everton was definitely the club I wanted to play for. I knew David Moyes understood how to groom players of my calibre. And when I say "my calibre", I mean someone with potential who still needed the chance to develop. I was no superstar. I'd come from the Second Division, through the First Division, but I hadn't yet played a single minute in the Premier League. I was hardly some young phenomenon like Rooney. I'd worked my way up, and I needed a boss willing to take that chance to build on my potential. There were no promises.

*

After I'd agreed to the contract and was on the verge of signing, I had to tell David Moyes that I'd been called up for my nation and already agreed to play in the 2004 Olympic Games in Athens. I first rang my agent, Paul Martin, with the news.

"Look, Paul, I'll sign for Everton, but I'm going to miss the start of the season because of the Olympics, okay?"

Paul said, "Are you out of your mind?"

"Representing my country at the Olympics is huge to me," I said. "You go back and tell Everton that's my decision."

To my surprise, David Moyes agreed. I could miss the first three matches of the 2004 season. If he hadn't agreed, it likely would have jeopardized my contract. A lot of my mates thought I was mad, risking such a major contract like that, but representing Australia in the Olympic Games was worth it. Some opportunities come only once in your lifetime and you have to take them. I knew each Olympic squad was allowed only three over-age players and I was one of Australia's—the other two were John Aloisi and Craig Moore. It was likely my only opportunity to play for Australia in the Olympics.

The team arrived in the Olympic Village and we collected our accreditation. It was like nothing I'd ever seen before. People from all countries, travelling about in little buggies. Massive complexes flying national banners. We walked among the sprinters, swimmers, volleyball players and weightlifters. In our complex we had all the great Australian athletes— the Matildas soccer team, track-and-field stars, all housed in the same building. We mixed every day, shooting pool and playing table tennis with world-class athletes from every possible background. It was more than sport. It was a fantastic celebration of world culture.

We left Athens soon because most of our preliminary group games were played on the island of Crete, at Pankritio Stadium. We faced Argentina, Tunisia, and Serbia and Montenegro. We got off to a tentative start, a 1–1 draw against Tunisia, but soon enough we were flying. In our second match we beat Serbia and Montenegro 6–0 and I scored twice.

Then we faced an astounding Argentinian side that included two young players who would soon become greats—Carlos Tevez and Javier Mascherano. Argentina had just thrashed Serbia and Montenegro and were the firm favourites. We brought our do-or-die Australian mentality and maintained a solid formation, with me and Moorie as the older players in leadership roles doing a lot of the aggressive work. We actually held the ball for long stretches of the match, which is no mean feat against Argentina. We had our chances but just couldn't convert, and ended up losing 1–0.

At the final whistle, I remember swapping jerseys with Carlos Tevez—he was still playing in Argentina with Boca Juniors and wasn't yet a global superstar. But that day on the pitch I could already see the confidence, the swagger and the sense of self-belief. He was short, strong as a bull, with long black hair. I remember saying to Moorie: "This kid Tevez is bloody amazing. Watch him. Bet he's going to be a big star in a couple of years."

We advanced to the quarter-finals but had a mess on our hands in that both Moore and I were suspended for receiving two yellow cards in the group stage. In the quarters we drew Iraq and I remember Moorie and me jumping up and down from the bench, screaming ourselves hoarse, because Australia thoroughly controlled the game—bossed the midfield, hit the crossbar and the posts—but just couldn't score. We dominated every statistic of the match except goals: the Iraqis nicked one from us on a counterattack. At least it was a worthy goal, a brilliantly timed overhead scissor kick.

We knew we could have beaten Iraq on another day. We also knew we had enough talent in our squad that we should have gone further in the Olympic Games. We had held our own against the team that ultimately won the gold. Argentina trounced Italy 3–0 before beating Paraguay 1–0 in the gold-medal match. Still, our Olympic performance showed how far we'd come as a team, in terms of our confidence, that we dared to think that we had the quality to make it to the medal rounds.

Being knocked out of the Olympics so quickly was a mixed blessing. I was disappointed, but I didn't have an extra day to spare. The Premier League fixtures were well underway and Everton were waiting for me. I had to get back to England, get my family settled in Liverpool, and begin a new chapter of my playing career.

*

For me, leaving Millwall was quite emotional, saying goodbye to people like Debbie and Chris Grey, the Stanleys, the mates I'd made in south-east London—all had played such a big part in my life. Moving clubs was stressful, especially since I had my young son and partner with me, and we had to regroup quickly in a new home in the north. But that's professional football.

Your entire world can get turned upside-down in the blink of an eye.

As soon as Australia were knocked out of the Olympics, I flew to Liverpool and went into training with Everton. I could see at first glance that this was a family club—a tight-knit group of players who really cared about each other.

For all the big names in the squad, I could tell they played for the group, not for themselves. That's a signature of David Moyes. He always puts together teams that play *for* each other. I absolutely needed that balance and structure, needed to be part of a team playing as a collective, not a group of gifted and flamboyant individuals.

Before I played my first match for Everton, I went to Goodison Park to watch a match against West Bromwich Albion. Most people don't realize that the two storied clubs of Merseyside— Everton and Liverpool—play in stadiums less than a mile apart, separated by Stanley Park. Goodison nestles tight into the neighbourhood, houses flush against the stadium, local pub on the corner where the fans all gather. There's blue flying everywhere and the noise that comes out of the park is electrifying.

The West Brom fans were tucked away in one corner, the two ends full of loyal Toffees singing and chanting throughout the match, and I said to myself: "Bloody hell, this is the place, isn't it? Goodison! This is where I'm going to score some *serious* goals."

I was imagining doing special things for the club—building my life and career here. I'd signed a four-year deal, so I knew this was my long-term home.

The staff, the players, the fans—all were incredibly welcoming. When you join a club like Everton, it's not just about the players, it's also about the people who muck in, day after day—these sixty-year-old Scousers who've worked there for decades.

Danny Donachie, Everton's head of medicinal services, often reminds me that I was like a kid in a sweet shop. Everywhere I went, I was starry-eyed.

These old soldiers had seen the generations come and go. They knew all the history of the club. They were also the guys you shared laughs with, the guys you played football-tennis with—the guys who educated you.

I remember meeting the kit-man, Jimmy Martin; Mick Rathbone, the physio; Jimmy Comer, the masseur. All the groundsmen, the cooks, the dyed-in-the-wool Everton staff—all of them helped bring me into the fold.

That's what I mean when I say Everton is a *family* club—a rarity in today's Premier League. Everton is run by people who love the club. Being an Evertonian isn't a choice or a casual weekend pastime. It's generational. Their fathers and grandfathers were Blues. A lot of fans even have Everton tattoos, with the crest and founding date—1878—on their arms.

"Listen," Danny Donachie told me straightaway. "Pull your socks up, son, because this club can chew you up and spit you out *quickly*."

Every single day I learned something new about the club. I had one hell of a steep learning curve. It's hard to imagine now, but when I signed with Everton I didn't even know who Dixie

Dean was. The club's greatest-ever player, famous for scoring sixty league goals in the 1927–28 season, among other exploits. I never could have dreamed that I'd someday hold a club record with Dixie Dean: we're tied for most goals in the Liverpool–Everton derby.

Things like that don't happen overnight, of course. Over time I learned about the Everton Hall of Famers—Dixie Dean, Tommy Laughton, Alan Ball—mostly from the older guys in the club. Sometimes from retired Evertonians who would return and talk to us young lads. You heard stories, then you read up more about them—a slow process of learning what's meant by that expression: *Once a Blue, Always a Blue*.

I tried to take it all in. Day after day I spent time with the likes of Duncan Ferguson, Alan Stubbs, David Weir, Lee Carsley and Kevin Kilbane. Looking at Duncan Ferguson's tattoo of the Everton crest, I could see that these guys weren't playing for their own ego or for personal glory. They were playing for the badge.

True Blue. Literally. No one was allowed to wear anything red to training. In fact, you'd see nothing red in the entire complex. If I had a pair of red trainers or a tracksuit back at the house, you better believe I got rid of them quick.

*

Goodison Park was the mecca, but the day-to-day work was done at Bellefield, Everton's training ground. Built back in

1946, it had its own tremendous history and atmosphere. As you approach down Aysgarth Avenue, you come to a little lane that you can barely fit a van through; that opens up into a car park, then a couple of big buildings and two gorgeous training pitches. We'd play the small-sided games on the pitch on the right-hand side, then most of the full-squad games on the pitch immediately behind the Bellefield complex.

When official training was done, we'd go around the corner and play mini World Cups just for fun. Three v. three. One-touch, sometimes two-touch. Just to work on our technical abilities. And we'd play for *hours*. It didn't seem like work. It reminded me of being back in Sydney with my brothers Sean and Chris, with our mates like Anthony Panzarino. It was just footballing joy, with so much laughter.

We'd also play football-tennis on an indoor court with a proper net and two walls. We had players that could whip a ball like a helicopter around your head. Lee Carsley and Duncan Ferguson were beasts. But then we had the older guys like Jimmy Martin and Jimmy Comer who knew every spin and bounce off those old walls. They had so much experience and technique and know-how. Jimmy Comer had the best serve of any of us. My first few games, I was just spinning around, couldn't read the strange bounces off the walls.

We'd have big tournaments. And big arguments. This was football-tennis Everton style, by which I mean, guys could get hurt. Come to the net and get a size-eight shoe-print in your forehead.

"Unlucky! Well, don't put your head where it's gonna get kicked, lad!"

We'd finish our official training at 1 p.m. and I'd stay there until 5 p.m. playing football-tennis. Four hours of heated competition. The only days we wouldn't stay so late were on Thursdays and Fridays because we had matches on the weekend.

This was the Everton life, and I didn't want to miss a moment of it. We used to sit up in the dinner room and have darts tournaments—Fergie, Carsley, Stubbsy and me—or matches of head-tennis or golf outings. We'd all have a big meal and then head to the pub afterward. These nights weren't optional; they were compulsory. If you missed out, you'd be fined. We took what David Moyes had created with this strong group of players and built upon it. All this off-the-park time, the laughter and camaraderie, made for invaluable bonding sessions—and a much tighter, more connected team.

I was really lucky to have three great guides through the first weeks at the club—Nick Chadwick, Tony Hibbert and Leon Osman, who all became my close mates. They understood I was this young kid from Australia who felt enormous gratitude to be where he was. There was no hiding the fact. Sometimes they'd look at me with this expression that maybe I was too grateful, too nice, too wide-eyed, but I was simply appreciating that my life-long dream was actually happening. I was a professional footballer in the Premiership!

In one sense I'd made it to the Premier League, but in another I hadn't actually achieved anything except signing the contract.

Every day out on the training ground was a new test. Every training session, every touch I made, every bad pass, every shot on goal, I knew I was being watched. I was constantly being assessed and judged as to whether I had the right stuff to start for the next game.

The bar was set so high with these players. Believe me, shooting practice with Duncan Ferguson at Bellefield needed to be done *properly*. Ferguson was a machine: virtually everything he touched would hit the back of the net.

Fergie, who was 193 cm tall, was a top-class striker, born in Scotland. He'd played at Dundee United and at Glasgow Rangers but had been a fixture at Everton since 1994. We midfielders used to ping the ball out to his feet, he'd take one touch, stay within the arc at the top of the penalty box, and instantly hammer the ball in the back of the net. Other times he'd control our passes with his chest, swivel and volley into the top corner. Absolutely *effortless* technique. His finishing was pure class.

I was constantly getting guidance from Fergie and the other veterans. Sometimes on the pitch I'd drift out of position and David Weir, our captain, or Alan Stubbs, would shout from the back: "Left! Right! Where you going, lad?" And I'd hear Lee Carsley, with his thick Birmingham accent, shouting encouragement: "Go forward, Tim. Make the run! Fuck it! I'll look after here."

Also, in that midfield mix we had Tommy Gravesen, the brilliant Danish international, who could roam anywhere he liked. Tommy was such a creative, inventive player that Lee Carsley and I had to recalibrate constantly and readjust to wherever Tommy's position was on the park. If Tommy went out on the right, Lee would tuck in behind him and I'd shift forward on the left—that way, we allowed Gravesen to explore the pitch, but we still kept our shape. If Tommy tucked back and the ball broke out left to Kevin Kilbane, I'd make a third-man run with Tommy following in on my left. We started developing great chemistry, such instinctive and collective rhythm, in that squad.

Of course, we had Ferguson as the big target man up top, taking two or three defenders with him, which would then open up space for me as I'd follow him into the box.

The tone was set throughout the club by Ferguson, Stubbsy, Weir, Steve Watson and Lee Carsley. I love Duncan Ferguson to bits, but I could never say that he alone set the tone. Lee Carsley didn't say much, wasn't much of a talker, but he could drill a hole in your head with his eyes. As a young Blue, Lee was definitely one of the strongest influences on me. An international for the Republic of Ireland, he was the lynchpin, a holding midfielder, just in front of the back four and right behind me and our other midfielders.

If I'd upset him on the pitch by not doing my job properly, Lee would give me a withering stare. No shouting: the most you'd get from Lee Carsley was that look.

"You know what you did."

"Yes."

"*Fix* it."

On the other end of the leadership scale was Alan Stubbs. Man, did Stubbsy like to scream! He used to be on us 24/7. From the back, Stubbs used to shout at us midfielders until he'd practically shredded his vocal cords.

David Weir on the other hand—the skipper—didn't like to shout, but he was more verbal than Carsley. He'd pull you in to have a private chat, explain how you could improve your game. All these leadership styles are equally effective. Each one suited the man's particular personality.

*

My first big moment in the Everton jersey was our fifth match of the season—my second start for the club. It was Sunday, 12 September 2004, an away game at Manchester City. I was charged up, in fine form that whole match. When you're playing at the top flight, away from home, you've got to set the right precedent—straightaway—which means you need to let your marker know that you can't be bullied.

I learned that first-hand from Duncan Ferguson, David Weir and Alan Stubbs: *This is the Everton way. Don't let them think you're soft. Stand your ground, son.*

I started to have issues with Manchester City's Joey Barton almost immediately after kick-off. Barton was a strong character. He wasn't singling me out. I could see he was just trying to mess with everyone in our line-up.

Barton was known for being one of the more thorny players in the league and we were at each other the whole first half. Then, nearing half-time, Joey and I had some words that turned into a minor scuffle.

I wasn't about to back down from Barton. I didn't care what his reputation was. I got into it with him for the purpose of helping my team, not some personal agenda, not wanting to be seen as tough. The referee gave me a yellow card and we went into half-time.

After the interval, we came out flying. On the hour mark, I saw my first big chance. The ball was played wide, Tony Hibbert made an overlapping run, put over this beautiful cross, the ball hung there for what seemed a lifetime, curled back over, and I angled my run into the penalty box and jumped early. The goalkeeper's eyes were fixed on the path of the ball. The City defenders lost sight of me—I'd run off the shoulder, angling inside. My jump was well timed and I knew if I could get good contact I was in the 70–80 per cent range for scoring.

As the cross curled in, I knew instantly that my contact was great. I whipped it back across the goalmouth, could see the ball travelling through the air like a bullet, hitting the back of the net.

A massive goal. Fifth match of the season and I'd scored for my new club!

I wheeled away at full sprint, arced my run to the left side of the pitch, hugging the boys. And, in one motion, I grabbed my shirt and briefly lifted it over my head. Then I broke through the pack and ran straight to the manager. I hugged David Moyes, saying, "Thank you!"

Among professionals, with years of experience playing in the top leagues, running to the manager, hugging and thanking him? Unheard of.

Even as I did it I could hear the boys laughing; I could see their sarcastic expressions. Hugging the gaffer? What's this kid Cahill thinking?

I knew I was probably going to get stick for that, but I didn't care. I've always worn my heart on my sleeve. I felt like hugging David Moyes in the heat of that moment, so I did.

As I walked back to the centre of the pitch, the referee pulled out a second yellow card. I didn't understand at first. But he was booking me for the shirt-off celebration. *What?* I'd lifted my jersey over my head and put it down quickly. I had no idea that the Premiership was starting to crack down on guys removing their shirts that season.

Twice in the book.

Now the referee was flashing a red card.

My jaw dropped to my knees. So much was swirling around my brain as I walked off to the touchline. That could have been the best and the worst day of my Everton career. What if we lost the match because of me, because we went down to ten men?

I'd scored in the sixtieth minute and there were still thirty minutes to play.

I didn't know whether to laugh or cry. I sat on the bench for the longest half-hour of my life.

It was a good thing the lads held their shape. All those experienced veterans like Stubbsy and Weir and Carsley could cushion mistakes and deal with any contingency—even a sending-off with only an hour played.

I don't know if there's another case of such a strange scoring debut in the Premiership, a player both scoring his first goal in the league and being ejected from the match.

When the final whistle blew, giving us the win, that image of the red card left my head instantly.

I'd scored my first Premier League goal and it was the winner against Manchester City. I was on top of the world. Nobody would ever take that feeling away from me.

But back in the changing room, I got hammered. Stubbsy, Carlsey, Weir, Fergie—all the boys started in.

"What the hell were you hugging the gaffer for?"

"Oh, Christ, Cahill—what are you? The gaffer's pet?"

"Gaffer's pet!"

"Bloody hell, Cahill! You're *Son-of* ..."

Son-of. I forget who came up with that one, but it became my Everton nickname for a long time. It was short for *Son-of-the-Gaffer*.

I laughed it off. "Say whatever you want. This is me. This is *me*, mate!"

I've always been that way. I do things because I want to do them, not because it's supposed to be cool.

I got smashed by the boys the whole time we were in the dressing room. The boss walked in and he was laughing, too. But David Moyes understood why I did it.

I didn't hug the gaffer because of that debut goal. I was showing my gratitude for David Moyes having signed me from Millwall, for scouting me and giving me my chance in the first team instead of just leaving me as a squad player.

After a bit, they all understood. I was that loyal kid, always appreciative. But they never did let up with that business about me being *Son-of-the-Gaffer*. And sometimes my team-mates would refer to David Moyes as *Timmy's dad*.

"I dunno, Watto," Stubbsy would say. "Why don't you go see Timmy's dad?"

That line always had everyone in the changing room laughing.

*

That 2004–05 season ran on a razor's edge for Everton. There was such a fine balance in our squad, that mix of young and old, talent and scrappiness. To be at our best, we *knew* we needed nine players playing at 95 per cent to win.

If we had three players at less than their top form, well, that might just be enough to get a result. But if we had four players under-par, we knew we couldn't win the match. We always felt—and this came from the top down—that Everton needed to do more than any other club. We had to defend harder, stay mentally sharper, always fire on all cylinders.

That was David Moyes. He knew where our strengths and weaknesses lay. He knew how we compared to our opponents. He knew, playing away, that we had to hold our shape and hit teams on the counterattack. The discipline in our defending was unbelievable. Midfielders, centre-backs and full-backs used to throw their bodies on the line. Blocking every shot. There was such fire and work ethic in our entire line-up.

Tactically, most of that first season, we were top-class. We were as sharp as any club in the Premier League. We had enough players in that team who knew how to hold the fort, and had enough quality up front, that even if we'd been under pressure the majority of the match, we could always steal a goal. We won a bunch of matches in my first season 1–0 away from home. Up front we had that pace of Benty, that strength of Ferguson and Campbell. Then I would come in as a third-man runner, sprinting from midfield deep into the box, always a risk to score.

One thing David Moyes understood was player psychology. Players' mentality changes throughout a season. A good manager knows this and will recalibrate expectations. One year you score eight goals. How do you motivate yourself to get out there in front of 40,000 fans to score ten goals the next season?

Fans aren't stupid. Many fans know more about the game, overall, than the average footballer. Especially Evertonians. They see right through the players. You step out at Goodison and the hard-core fans can see if you're True Blue, if you want to play with intensity and passion for the club, or if you're just an individualist out for personal achievement and the pay cheque.

If I had an off-day on the park, David Moyes would say to me after a match, "That was *not* Tim Cahill out there on the park today. That was not your game, son. If you don't fight, work, hustle for the *entire* match, if you don't go above and beyond, you'll lose your identity. Keep that, Tim. That's what makes you who you are."

By the autumn of 2004, I was putting together a good string of matches and started scoring fairly consistently. The boss was pleased. David Moyes only ever offered muted praise—much like my father had when I first started playing football as a boy.

David never said: "Tim had a cracking match." He'd say things like, "Tim worked hard today", and I knew that was his highest praise. On the other hand, I knew when he laid into me with some tough criticism—which was often—that he did it out of true concern and affection. He wanted me to improve my game all the time.

As the weeks turned into months, I became a regular starter and learned the strengths and weaknesses of my team-mates. As a midfielder, my most important job was to link up well with our forwards, to make sure they got the best possible service.

Duncan Ferguson was strong enough to play with his back to the goal, and be relied upon to bring the ball down and beat his markers. He was our star man, but more multi-dimensional than the typical big powerful centre-forward. Marcus Bent was a great striker, too, but his gift was speed. We called him a "one-in-three man". If I put a ball in front of Benty, he'd score in one out of three opportunities. But you had to lead him with a well-weighted through-pass. Get the ball perfectly in front of his feet. He wasn't the big target man that Ferguson was, but if you put the ball in front of Bent where he could use that burst of pace, there was no touching him.

There were moments, that first year, where I could do little more than marvel at the quality of the guys I was lucky enough to be playing with.

GLADIATORS

THE SOCCEROOS FACED A FIERCE, uphill battle on the road to the 2006 World Cup. FIFA had allotted the last spot in the 2006 Cup to the winner of a special CONMEBOL (South American Football Confederation)–OFC qualification play-off designed to break a two-legged tie between Australia, the winners of the Oceania qualifying tournament, and Uruguay, the fifth-place team from the South American qualifying tournament.

It was a home-and-away set-up, with the games scheduled for 12 and 16 November 2005, in Montevideo and Sydney. I was called away from my duties with Everton for that November play-off. By now, Frank Farina was gone. Our failure to perform well at the 2005 Confederations Cup had spelled the end of his run with the Socceroos.

Guus Hiddink was now our national team manager.

We travelled the long haul to Montevideo for the first leg. We all knew we were entering a place of football lore. Along with Brazil and Argentina, Uruguay is one of the traditional Big Three teams of South American football. For a nation of fewer than three-and-a-half million people, Uruguay is a hotbed of the sport. They were the winners of two of the first four World Cups, including the 1930 inaugural tournament in which they were the hosts. They also pulled off one of the great upsets in football history by beating Brazil in the Maracana in 1950.

National team life was still new to me—travelling business-class with the very best Australian players, seeing all these beautiful countries, where football is woven so deeply into the fabric of society.

In Montevideo, it was madness from the moment we landed. Even at the airport we felt the fans' hostility. We knew we were going into what was sure to be both a psychological and a tactical battle, led by a new coach. I felt we were in good hands. Guus Hiddink had a reputation as a master of chess on the international level. He'd also been the manager of some top continental clubs—Valencia, Real Madrid, Real Betis, PSV Eindhoven. And he'd managed the Dutch national team from 1994 to 1998.

Still, we were under no illusions. The Uruguayans were formidable, a side gifted with all the Latin technique and flair but also known for being rough. For that first away game in Montevideo, we knew we had a chance, but the odds were stacked against us.

Guus Hiddink was still a brand-new manager for me. I couldn't read him at all. He kept his distance from the players and was direct and forceful in all his communications. I think he intentionally erected a barrier between himself and the players so that he could maintain respect 24/7. Different managers have different styles. Some don't mind messing about with the lads. Not Hiddink. He was always on a different level. There was no banter, socializing, or joking with us. Strict discipline and respect at all times.

Johan Neeskens, the legendary star from Ajax and Barcelona, came with him as assistant coach, but there was never any question about who was the boss. I remember an incident in camp just before the match. Hiddink had asked me to do something on the pitch, and due to his heavy Dutch accent I didn't understand. I asked a question, trying to clarify what he wanted, and he shot me an angry look.

"Get on with it."

I knew then that Hiddink and I had gotten off on the wrong foot. He gave that same look to any player who questioned him or made what he considered to be a comment undermining his authority. The only way you could play for Hiddink was to buy into his method and ask no questions.

As we pulled into the old concrete stadium, it seemed as if tens of thousands of people were already there, hours before kick-off, making an ungodly noise. Fans booing, throwing things, banging on the sides of the bus. Estadio Centenario, built when Uruguay was hosting the 1930 World Cup, is one of the sport's classic venues—in a class with the Maracana, Wembley Stadium, San Siro and the Bernabeu.

From the windows of the coach, it looked like an imposing fortress. We entered the halls of that old, damp stadium, into a changing room that had not been upgraded since 1930. On those bare concrete walls, on the old wooden benches, you could smell the decades of tradition—you could almost hear the echoes of players' voices down the years ...

Being in the bowels of the Centenario almost felt like you were a gladiator. As we were getting ready, we could hear the fans thundering in Spanish, jumping and pounding their feet over our heads. The walls and roof visibly shook—actual tremors like in an earthquake. THUD-THUD-THUD. The concrete shuddered, and I remember we glanced nervously at each other, as if the walls of the changing room might cave in.

I'd played in the Den and in front of plenty of rabid English fans. I'd seen some drunk tattooed skinheads in my time, but I'd seen nothing like this. When we jogged out onto the pitch for warm-ups, the animosity grew even more intense. The fans were hurling abuse at us, non-stop, through the fence.

I don't believe Uruguayans hate Australians, of course, but I'd never seen anything approaching their level of intimidation. Such anger in their eyes. Anger that anyone would dare come to their stadium and try to deny their national team entry to the World Cup.

*

I started the match on the bench, knowing it was possible I might come on as a substitute for Bresciano or Viduka at some point, but Guus Hiddink was impossible to read that way. My role in the Socceroos had always been clear to me before, but I didn't know if Hiddink thought I could be useful.

I never assumed I deserved a spot in the starting line-up. My attitude was that if my role was to be a substitute, then I'd come on and do everything in my power to score. That was always my mentality throughout my international career.

It was an incredibly difficult match and, unfortunately, I didn't get the opportunity to go on. Our boys had a few chances and for the first half-hour we were with the Uruguayans stride for stride. They had incredibly gifted technical players in their sky-blue shirts, swinging pinpoint passes all over the park: Diego Forlan, Alvaro Recoba, Marcello Zalayeta. Though still young, playing with Villareal in Spain, Forlan was someone you just marvelled at. He was a brilliant, creative No. 10 who would go on to win the Golden Ball as the highest scorer in the World Cup in 2010. He wasn't fully fit, though, and hobbled off the pitch after seventeen minutes, which was a bit of a break for us. Recoba, the Inter Milan attacking-midfielder, then began bossing the game, a wizard with long precise passes and set plays.

It was Recoba who did us in. In the thirty-fifth minute, we conceded a free kick on the right, just outside the penalty box. Recoba swung in a perfect curling ball to their fullback, Dario Rodriguez, left unmarked at the far post. Rodriguez dived and headed the ball low and hard into the goal past Schwarzer. After that, the crowd became even more deafening.

We tried our best, but we couldn't get back into the game. The final score was 1–0. Back in the changing room, we knew we still had a fighting chance. If we could beat them at home, in four days' time, by a larger margin, we'd still go to the World Cup. I remember Mark Viduka, our captain, talking to some reporters.

"In Sydney," Dukes said, "we'll have 85,000 Aussies screaming for us to go to the World Cup. It's going to be like a twelfth man, isn't it?"

To a man, we shared the captain's belief.

*

My experience in the 2004 Oceanias proved I could play and score goals at the international level. Since I didn't start in the away leg, as we were flying back home to Australia, I kept wondering if I'd possibly get a shot in the starting eleven for Sydney.

Hiddink played his cards very close to his chest. Even when we set up camp in Sydney, he gave nothing away about his potential formation. He gave nothing away to us at training. He gave nothing away to the media—all of whom were curious, of course, to see if Guus was going to change the line-up.

Come game day, I was named on the starting team. With the 1–0 loss against Uruguay, and needing a big performance, Hiddink had decided on an aggressive attacking formation. When I saw the sheet of paper with the starting eleven, I smiled.

"About time. We can get a result with this line-up."

Our team was fierce, fast, hard. We had our most skilled players as well as some battlers. Since Montevideo, I'd barely spoken to the coach beyond hello or goodbye. In fact, when he picked me for that starting eleven I was a bit shocked. But I've always said you don't have to be mates with your boss to play well for him. It's professionalism. My relationship with Guus Hiddink was not like the relationship I had with David Moyes, but that didn't mean I couldn't perform at my highest level with him at the helm.

The sixteenth of November felt like potentially the biggest moment in Australian football history to date. We knew the stakes. A 0–0 draw would do us no good, and a 1–1 draw would be just as useless. We needed to score two goals and hold Uruguay goalless in order to advance to the World Cup. We felt like we had the whole nation on our shoulders.

Stadium Australia was jammed with more than 80,000 in attendance. I'll never forget coming out of the tunnel in our green and gold, to that thunderous roar, knowing my family was out there in that crowd, that all our mates were watching on TV. It was an incredible feeling, walking into that stadium, thinking I could be part of changing our country's footballing history.

The national anthem started and we belted out every single word. When the Uruguayan anthem played, our fans were booing, trying to put the South Americans off their game—a bit of a payback for the intimidation we'd faced in Montevideo. I could feel the adrenaline flooding my muscles, ready for the opening whistle.

I tucked in my shirt, checked my socks and shin guards, even my boot laces.

We knew how many millions were watching this moment on TV at home and around the world and we wanted to represent near-perfection—as footballers and as Australians.

All the players were saying the same words to each other.

"Let's give it everything, boys ..."

The opening whistle sounded and a roar rose up from those fans. Balloons everywhere, giant Australian flags, billowing yellow banners.

Uruguay dominated the opening exchanges and peppered our goal with several dangerous kicks into the box. A corner from the boot of Recoba in the eleventh minute almost gave them the lead, but the header went wide. Our first clear-cut chance came in the sixteenth minute: Scott Chipperfield was fouled just outside the penalty area. My midfield partner, Bresciano, stepped up but his kick sailed over the bar. A minute later we dodged a bullet when a goal kick was headed forward and Recoba burst through our back line to latch on to the through-ball. He only had Schwarzer to beat, but his left-footed shot went wide.

Recoba continued to cause us trouble, and on the half-hour mark he took an elbow to the face from Popovic. The referee produced a yellow card and Tony was replaced by Harry Kewell. Immediately Kewell gave us some danger on the left, working well in our formation, and then came some lovely interplay between Harry, Dukes, Bresh and me.

*

It's the thirty-fifth minute of play: there's a throw-in from the left side of the pitch, Kewell brings it down and makes a clever backheel pass to Chipperfield, who plays the ball in square to me. I beat my man and send a crisp pass to the top of the box which Viduka flicks—another lovely backheel—into the path of Kewell. Harry takes a touch, then swings at the ball and miskicks—the ball scuffs across the box and straight to Bresciano.

Bresh lashes it—first time—a hard shot pinging past Carini ...

Roof of the net!

And then Bresh stands there in his Cantona-like celebration. He looked fierce, with his shaved head, briefly savouring the moment.

The rest of us just went mad. We jumped on Bresh, knowing we'd kept ourselves in the game, dug deep to score the equalizer, but that we'd by no means finished the job.

Back in play, we kept pressing. Bresh and I were combining well and I thought I could head in the winner, a good cross in from Kewell, but Carini jumped and intercepted the ball. In the seventy-seventh minute I had another chance, this time Bresciano delivering the cross. I was unmarked, but my header went wide. Three minutes later Kewell found himself in open space with a chance, but Carini's outstretched hands denied his right-foot strike.

We were playing without fear, dominant in those final minutes, but we just couldn't knock the Uruguayans out, and they held on for thirty more minutes of play.

In extra time, we had our chances, they had theirs, but it ended in stalemate.

Penalties.

There was no question in my mind that the right group of guys stepped up to take the spot-kicks. Our most experienced five players. We were all at the halfway line, linked arm in arm.

Harry Kewell went first. He ran up, fooled Fabian Carini by looking to his right, the keeper dived to the right and Harry banged in a perfect, powerful penalty to the left.

Then we all waited on Schwarzer. Defender Dario Rodriguez, who'd scored that winner against us in Montevideo, was up first for the Uruguayans.

Rodriguez stuttered his run, trying to psyche out Schwarzer, but Schwarzie leapt perfectly across to the right post, stood his ground and made a massive save.

Then up stepped my mate Lucas Neill. Pressure? *What?* He shot a textbook side-footed penalty inside the post. 2–0 Australia.

Tony Vidmar scored handily to make it 3–1, another calmly taken side-footed beauty. Fabian Estoyanoff stepped up for Uruguay and tucked it away perfectly, with power, mid-height to the right corner. Now it was all up to Viduka, our captain ... the run up ... a *miss*!

Dukes slid it just wide of the post. I knew that some of the greats like Roberto Baggio, Michel Platini and Zico had all failed to convert important penalties in World Cup games. Penalty shoot-outs are all about mental focus, a battle of nerves, and no one on the Socceroos faulted Dukes for that miss.

Now things were tense and everything rested on Schwarzer.

Could he possibly save again?

Zayaleta's kick was hard and well directed, but Schwarzie leapt brilliantly, making a one-handed block. It was just a phenomenal save. To this day, I consider it one of the most extraordinary reaction saves I've ever seen.

His body diving to the left, parallel to the ground, shoulder going down, and he reaches up with his right hand and fully blocks the hard shot. If he'd dived half a second earlier, or if Zayaleta had shot even a few inches higher, the pace of the ball would have made a save virtually impossible, but Schwarzie had timed it perfectly.

At the halfway line we leapt up and down in disbelief. As John Aloisi prepared for his spot kick, the stadium went from a roar to near silence.

Johnny lined up and then confidently blasted the ball past Carini, wheeling away, screaming, ripping off his gold shirt and waving it over his head.

All the boys started running like mad, chasing Aloisi down the touchline, but I broke off running after Schwarzer to jump on his giant shoulders. I landed on our keeper, piggyback-style, screaming.

"Schwarzie!"

It was just madness. By now it was past 11 p.m.—we'd just played a hard ninety-minute match, plus thirty minutes of extra time but, fuelled by adrenaline, we were running the length of the pitch to celebrate.

It didn't feel real at the time—sometimes, even now, it still doesn't. The first thing I could think of was my parents, my brothers, my sister, Bek and my kids.

Had we honestly done this, beaten the great Uruguayan national team to advance to the World Cup?

One thought kept flashing through my brain.

I wasn't supposed to be here, was I?

For years, as a kid, I was told I was never going to make it as a footballer.

Too small, not strong enough, not fast enough.

But here I was: a member of a team full of self-belief and vigour and pride. We'd beaten two-time World Cup winner Uruguay and qualified for the 2006 World Cup in Germany.

Thirty-two years after our last World Cup appearance, we had just delivered the biggest day yet in Australian football history. What an unlikely crew! Half of us hadn't even come up through the Australian football system. We'd defied all the odds. Many of our players had stories just like mine, with my cobbled-together journey to London, my trial at Millwall with hopes of becoming a professional. Loads of us had gone overseas, risking everything to follow our dreams. And now here we were, back at home in our national stadium, taking Australia to the greatest tournament in all of sport.

ONE CITY, TWO COLOURS

IN LIVERPOOL, IT'S OFTEN SAID, you're born either Red or Blue. Team allegiance is passed on through the family bloodline. If your dad's Blue, you're Blue. If your dad's Red, you're Red. And to the fans of Liverpool and Everton, the derby is the most important game of the season. For some fans, ending the year on top of the rival team is actually more important than winning the league.

What's unique about the Liverpool derby is that, be it at Goodison or Anfield, the fans often go to the match with their friends, even if they're wearing opposing colours. Unlike other famous UK derbies—Celtic–Rangers in Glasgow, for example— the match is not so tribal or religious. It's not Catholic versus Protestant. It's rarely violent. On Merseyside, it's about pride and bragging rights. That's all. Just football.

The 2004–05 season was turning into a great one for Everton and we entered the derby as the third-placed team in the Premiership, nine points clear of Liverpool, who sat in seventh place.

I always felt a huge responsibility playing for those Goodison fans. I knew football was a way of life for them, not just another game. They went to work from Monday to Friday to earn their money to go to the pub with their mates on Saturday, then to the match to enjoy ninety minutes of passion and craziness for the game they loved. The outcome of the derby would carry them for the next week, the next month, all the way to the next derby. Victory was a matter of honour on Merseyside.

As a player living in Liverpool, if you didn't win the derby, it was best you didn't leave your house. If you *did* win the derby, it was *definitely* best you didn't leave your house. The Everton fans would mob you. They were out in the pubs and in the streets celebrating for days.

Liverpool is an enormous global brand. It's also a football club for which I've developed a deep respect. I've watched their games over the years, seen their evolution, the managerial and ownership problems they've survived. What I've witnessed recently is a club brave enough to give one of their greatest icons, Steven Gerrard, the chance to leave the club to end his career in the United States. That was an act of generosity as much as of respect.

I look up to Steven Gerrard a lot. I played many tough derby matches against him. I've watched his growth from being a young, hard-tackling midfielder who could also score goals, to a mature man and player, one of the top men of the

Premiership, also wearing the captain's armband for England. In every sense, Gerrard is a complete footballer. People can nit-pick about his abilities. True, his left foot isn't as great as his right, but you can never put a price on the passion and love he has for his club and the dignity he brings to each match.

You want to talk about club loyalty—those Merseyside derbies breed it into your bones. No amount of money in the world would ever entice me to play for Liverpool. People may laugh at that, but I say it with the utmost respect, because I know what it means to be a Blue. I know what it means to play for a badge—and if a person ever left a team like Everton to go to play for their fiercest rivals, how could they give themselves to it with the same love and passion?

For me, it'd be impossible. I'm sure Steven Gerrard would say the same thing. Nothing could entice him to play for Everton. He loves and respects the Liverpool badge too much. It'd be like betraying your family.

When you play in the derby for the first time, no matter how much you think you're ready, no matter how much reading you've done before the match, or how many stories you've heard from the old guard, *nothing* prepares you for the intensity. The media bubble in a derby goes beyond Liverpool. There are fans glued to their screens throughout England—and worldwide. The press covers the build-up, bombarding players with questions.

Personally, I never like to talk up a game. I talk up the *occasion*—how much the match means, how thorough our preparation has been—but I never predict how good we'll be on the park.

On match day, you get to the park early. You walk onto the grass of Goodison to the Everton theme song, "Z Cars"—the title music of a 1970s TV cop show set in Liverpool. The Red side belts out "You'll Never Walk Alone".

Standing in the line-ups, I would look to where my family would be. Usually Bek was there with my two young sons, Kyah and Shae. If I ever felt in trouble in a derby, I'd turn around and look at Lee Carsley and he'd just give me the nod. Or I'd look at Duncan Ferguson, see him clenching his fist, and I'd mentally click into another gear. Just like in my early days with Millwall, it was so important to have that sense of security, that feeling that your team-mates are in there fighting with you. You need to know when you're coming into a challenge, even if you've lost it, that one of your mates is coming in straight behind you. I wanted that in my team-mates—and *got* it. I always wanted to be that player to them. I think I was. If there was a scrap to be had, I made it a point to be in it.

Whenever we played Liverpool, home or away, I had one goal: stop Steven Gerrard. Gerrard was the heartbeat of the team. When anything went pear-shaped for the Reds, they always turned to Gerrard. Leaders always lead with actions. Gerrard, with a pivotal goal or his hard tackling, could always change the game.

Throughout my time with Everton, I learned that the derby is almost always won with that very first tackle. Who's going to put in the first heavy-hitting challenge? Who's going to kick someone into the air to get our crowd fired up and passions soaring? And, yes, put some fear into the heart of the Reds.

I saw Gerrard do it to us all the time. Even before I played in a derby, I watched clips where he'd go out, right after the opening whistle, and munch everyone he could get near wearing an Everton shirt.

When you're on the pitch, living in the heat of those moments, you don't realize how intense it looks. You go flying into challenges, fearless—borderline red-card stuff—but if you get your boot to the ball and not the other man's leg, it's clean, and the crowd will go wild for it. To me it often felt like the Goodison crowd was right down there with us, fighting with us in spirit.

*

The 200th Merseyside derby—11 December 2004.

My first as a Blue.

You could feel the pent-up energy in both teams, ready to be unleashed. Liverpool arguably had a bit more quality on the pitch than we did, but our desire and discipline always made Everton dangerous. If we were going to win the derby, I knew it would not be through technique but through grit.

For the entire first half, the two teams battled to break through. Then midway through the second, from twenty metres,

Lee Carsley launched a rocket into the net. That beautiful strike left Liverpool goalkeeper Chris Kirkland motionless.

After Carsley scored, we killed him. Absolutely buried him. I'm amazed he came out of that pile still breathing.

On the heels of that amazing goal came an image that went worldwide. It would become one of the most iconic pictures ever taken of Everton. A massive pile-up of players with this young Aussie lad on top of the mountain, knees in the backs of the boys. My left arm thrust up in the air, shouting to the Everton faithful.

To this day, if you visit the homes of Everton fans, you'll see that picture on the walls or on their laptops as a screensaver, or as the wallpaper on their iPhones. That photo—that snapshot of us celebrating, piling on each other—just embodies the spirit of Everton.

We won that match 1–0, and it was Everton's first win over Liverpool in five years. It also put us twelve points clear of the Reds, in second place in the Premiership.

David Moyes hadn't won a derby until that day, and I'm proud to say I'd played my part in helping win it. It was a small way to repay the gaffer for signing me.

It's very tough to get David Moyes to smile. He wears that stern expression most of the time. But when he came into the changing room after that derby win, man, he was smiling like a ten-year-old boy.

*

Our battle against Liverpool continued hot and heavy into that spring. Every week was a battle to see who'd finish higher in the Premiership table. By the time we hosted Newcastle at Goodison Park on 7 May 2005, we knew the result would have far-reaching repercussions.

If we won this game and Liverpool lost the next day to Arsenal, playing away at Highbury, we'd finish fourth in the table and could qualify for the European Champions League for the first time in years.

It was tight against Newcastle until just before half-time. The Magpies had their chances but kept failing to convert. Then, in the forty-third minute, we won a free kick and Mikel Arteta, the brilliant Spanish midfielder who'd come to us on loan from Real Sociedad, sent a perfect ball in for David Weir to head home. After the interval, in the fifty-ninth minute, Arteta shaped up again, this time to shoot with his left.

I made a run on his right shoulder, just in front of the back four. Mikel scuffed the ball with his left foot and I stayed in my run as the ball came straight to me. I took a good first touch, adjusted, set the ball. The goalkeeper, Shay Given, stood tall as I reached the penalty spot. I moved to put the ball into the right-hand corner, forcing Given to lean left, but I'd given him the eyes and whipped it across his body.

Giving the keeper the eyes is a perfect way to feint mentally—look one way and shoot the other—sending him in the wrong direction. The ball lashed high into the back of the net.

I remember glancing up into the stands to see fans shooting up like dominoes in reverse: all these people leaping in waves to their feet and a roar from our home supporters.

Mayhem. Back-slapping, laughing, cheering, drinks and food flying everywhere. I curved my run, screaming down the touchline to where our dugout was.

I knew then—as did all the fans at Goodison—that we'd done something special for Everton. We had to win to finish fourth and we'd done it, putting Liverpool in the position of having to win away against Arsenal. They didn't. The Reds lost 3–1. We secured our place and qualified for a play-off in the Champions League.

Everything that Everton had been through the season before—the controversial selling of Wayne Rooney, the purchase of Marcus Bent and me—that was now left behind.

Every week of that first season you'd been hearing it in the news or reading it online: "When is Everton's bubble going to burst?" Among the players, we never felt the bubble was in danger of bursting. We weren't looking at the big picture, the overall span of the season. We just took it one game at a time. "Come on, lads, we just need one point." Or: "Come on, boys, these three points are ours."

All season long, day after day, we continued to grind out wins. We never let up, not a single match. Injured players strapped themselves up and hit the park like they were perfectly fit. If you said you had a back problem, rather than sit out, you'd strap it up and hit the pitch running. If Lee Carsley had a cut on his leg, he'd say, "Fuck it", slap a bandage on it and get back out on the park. That's the spirit we all had. Even if you were banged up, you didn't want to miss a game.

I think it was all the result of a special blend of leadership and personality, experience and youth, and it came together in that 2004–05 Everton side. We sensed we were a part of a magical season. It didn't matter if it was Sunderland away in the freezing cold, every player wanted to be on the pitch for the full ninety minutes. And now that I've played a lot longer—now that I'm thirty-five—I know how unique it is to find that attitude within a football team.

The year before, Everton had finished seventeenth—only one up from relegation. Now we'd finished in the top four—but most importantly for the Merseyside faithful, we'd finished ahead of Liverpool. To True Blue folks, the real Evertonians, that's their real championship: finishing on top of the Reds in the table.

Personal records never mattered much to me as long as the team was winning, but it was great to be told that I'd finished as the club's top goal-scorer and was voted the Everton fans' Player of the Season.

My first year in the Premiership was off to a pretty good start.

THE BOYS IN BLUE

AT EVERTON, MORE THAN AT any other club I've played with, you had to be one of the boys. You had to do *everything* the lads did. As I've said, those off-the-park activities and nights out were compulsory.

"We win together, we lose together."

For us that was more than a motto—we really lived it, day in and day out.

During my first off-season, we got news of a major new signing for the Blues, one that might possibly disturb our team chemistry. On 4 August 2005, Phil Neville came over from Manchester United, joining Everton on a five-year contract for a fee in excess of £3.5 million. We all knew Phil Neville's exceptional leadership, attitude and work rate. We'd played against the Neville brothers in some heated and intense matches. It was great for us, of course. A world-class player with tons of trophies to his name. But everyone was asking the same question. Would he fit in with the lads?

When Neville first came to Everton, he was a bit of a loner. Because he'd come from Manchester United and played for the English national side, I guess there was a bit of a distance. There were times he was seen more like staff than a team-mate. He'd give out instructions and a few of the lads would say, "Okay, Nev", and then, under their breath, "Whatever—piss off." Phil noticed, and finally he came to me and said, "Come on, Tim, can you talk to the lads for me?"

I had been there longer, was seen as part of the group and, while everyone respected Phil, he hadn't crossed over to being one of the lads yet. So, in effect, I became his lieutenant. Whatever he wanted done, I'd be the guy to make sure the boys went along with the program.

As we closed the distance, I came to realize that Phil Neville, strictly from a professional standpoint, was one of the best I'd ever seen. His commitment to the sport was total. He got up at 5 a.m. and went to bed most nights around 7 p.m. He treated football as a job, a life commitment, not just a game. Some footballers are on a completely different level when it comes to professionalism. Neville was the peak. I can't give any higher praise than that.

On and off the park, Phil taught me how to be better with my family, my training and my business decisions. He gave me advice about balancing international commitments with club duties. As a leader in the team myself now, I would sit with Phil and talk about how to make the Blues better, how to make sure we won the fans over early in the match and got that crowd energy behind us to help us win the game.

Despite the fact that the lads, at least in the beginning, would shrug off his comments, he developed over time into the perfect Everton captain.

For anyone outside professional football, it's tough to understand how much a player's external life affects his on-the-park performance. If the elements are not right at home—with your mum and dad, your kids, your girlfriend or wife, if you have some financial foul-up or tax problem or trouble with the mortgage that month—it weighs on you and affects your play immensely.

As team-mates we see that. Even if it's not openly discussed, we sense it. There were a few nights at Everton, I'd be sitting with Neville—by then we'd grown close enough for me to call him "Fizzer"—and mention that one of the boys was not himself on the pitch.

"You noticed? He's not up for it. Fizzer, we need to talk to him."

"Is everything all right at home?" Phil would ask.

If you're going to have a serious talk to one of your team-mates, you've got to decide your strategy. With some players, you can speak to them directly about their lack of focus. With others, you have to back off and work strictly through football.

Fizzer hadn't been there long enough to know all the personalities in our team, so he'd consult me. We'd toss it about and decide our approach.

"Nah, let's just give him a bit of confidence," I'd say. "Get him loads of touches on the ball. If we get him playing, I reckon he'll sort himself out."

There's no one-size-fits-all solution. Some players can handle a dose of screaming from the gaffer or the captain. Others just need to be brought gently into the mix, need their confidence lifted, and that, over time, fixes the mental issues. When you've played with someone long enough, you learn what switches them on. Some guys need a kick in the arse, others need their egos massaged.

It didn't take Fizzer long to figure what makes me tick. He would say: "Cahill always needs to be tested." Completely true. Some of my best moments as a player—at Millwall, at Everton and with the Socceroos—came when I was tested, both as a player and as a person.

It's the hard times that make you: the moments when you've got to show what you're made of.

I often say: when it's good, *everyone's* good. Everyone wants the ball. You're riding high, feeding off that energy from your team-mates, your own talent and fitness, the fans singing in the stands. When things are bad, though, you're alone—dealing with fear, doubt, injuries. In bad times, the obstacles you face can't be sorted by anyone but you. Some people can rise to it, others can't, but whatever the situation, it helps to have good leaders like Phil Neville guiding you through.

Over those first few months, Fizzer and I developed a really warm connection. I loved to give him stick about his monotone voice. If I could pick one person to sit next to on a long overseas flight, it would be Phil Neville. He's the only guy that could put me to sleep in seconds talking about football!

But that's just one side of Fizzer. He's also one of the funniest guys in football I've ever met. One off-season we were in Barbados, at Sandy Lane, together. I was with Rebecca and our kids, and Phil had his family there, too. We didn't know it to begin with, but Wayne Rooney was there in the same resort and he swam over to say hello. As soon as he saw his ex-team-mate from Manchester United, Phil stood up and said, "Excuse me, mate. No autographs".

"What?" Rooney said.

"I said piss off, mate, no autographs. We're trying to chill with our families."

Fizzer said it straight-faced too. And finally Rooney let out a huge laugh.

On that trip, Wayne Rooney was already a superstar and, thanks to that introduction from Phil Neville, he came out of the water and played football on the beach with my young sons.

I'd never met anybody at his level of fame who was still as down-to-earth and sociable. He was great with my kids. Just a simple sand kickabout. Priceless! To this day, my boys still talk about it. Whenever we go to the beach back home in Sydney, they'll say, "Dad, remember that time Wayne Rooney had a kickabout with us?"

*

If Phil Neville was usually in bed just after dinnertime, Mikel Arteta was just the opposite. The classic Spanish night owl. When Mickey and I hung out, we wouldn't start cooking our steaks until nine or ten at night. That's the Spanish way. Late nights, eating, talking, singing.

Fizzer and I took some time to develop our friendship. With Mikel Arteta it was instant—from the minute we met, Mikel was like my brother. We laughed together, competed together, argued like brothers.

David Moyes bought him for next to nothing—a bit like myself. But in Mikel, David saw a talented player and figured he could resurrect Arteta's career. He saw that Mikel was a great footballer—amazing technique, wonderful passing ability and a hard shot. Simply class at free kicks and other set plays. Arteta would also add a different dimension to Everton, give us a bit of flair.

Mikel and I grew close very quickly. I was always close to the foreign-born players. That's just my personality—at every club. Any new player who comes—like Fizzer—I'd be the first to welcome him into the fold. I didn't care if he was playing the same position as me, or that he might be a threat to my starting spot.

Mickey had great footballing ability. To have a talented European player like him was like finding the missing element in the Blues. He had the rare vision and touch that unlocked defences.

We started hanging out off the park. Soon we were in each other's pockets. We'd talk about football but also do a lot together with our families. Mostly I remember us cooking together. He'd cook at his house, I'd cook at mine. It was actually comical how domesticated we were. We'd do a big shopping together, wheeling trolleys around the supermarket, loading up mountains of food, then go back to one or the other of our houses and start cooking steaks and pasta, chopping up salads.

If I had a drink, I'd share it. If he had sweets, he'd share them. At the dinner table, we'd serve each other. It's the Spanish and the Samoan way. And, we always had each other laughing.

We'd go out for tapas and Mikel would order this expensive, thinly sliced ham—a real delicacy. He'd turn his back for a moment and I'd gather all fifteen slices on a piece of bread and wolf it down.

He'd turn around and slap my hand.

"Tim, slow down! *Tranquilo!*"

"Come on, I'm *Samoan,* man. I see food, I eat it!"

"*Tranquilo … tranquilo …*"

Relax—that was his favourite expression with me. *Just chill, Tim.*

Mikel was born in San Sebastian, in the Basque country, but he'd been a youth player with FC Barcelona at the age of fifteen, so he brought the techniques he'd learned in Spain to our club in Everton. His prehab-rehab was on another level. All the strengthening, stretching, massage. He had his own physio, too. Today, I still follow pretty much the same prehab-rehab regimen I picked up from Mikel.

At Everton, whenever we had an away game, we'd share a room. Mikel and I are exactly the same size—same height, same weight—and before I knew it he'd have my suitcase open and be putting on all my clothes. I used to bring two sets of clothes to any away game, because I knew Mickey would snatch my best shirt, my new jacket, my favourite jeans.

We were in each other's pockets all right, but in training there was always a contest and sometimes serious arguments. It reached the point where David Moyes and Steve Round, Everton's assistant manager, would never put Mikel and me against each other in practice. If Mikel played in one team and I played in the other, we'd be all over each other. If I saw Mikel with the ball, I went after him, and vice-versa. If he beat me with the ball, I'd foul him and he'd roll around or wave his arms in complaint. Very rarely did he foul me—he's not that type of player. But we could argue for hours. We'd argue over offside or whether a ball had gone into touch—until finally the boss decided we'd never clash with each other again.

"Nah, not putting you on separate teams no more."

All that off-the-park time we spent together led to some great moments on the pitch. He played in the midfield with me, sometimes on the left, sometimes on the right. He was versatile enough to move to a lot of places. When I look back at our time together at Everton, when I count up the number of goals Mikel put perfectly on my head—the big game-changers—I'd have to say a lot of those were the result of the close friendship we'd formed.

There were moments for Everton when the understanding we had of one another was almost uncanny. A few combinations I remember particularly well. Sunderland at home, for example. Mikel looked to the left, winked, I dropped the shoulder, ran the arc round to the back post. Mickey put the ball in the air at the back post. I headed it right into the net. A perfect link-up.

Another great combination play came against Newcastle away. We're at St James's Park, Mikel's on the wide right, he can see me on the back post, sends a long, whipped-over cross. I leap for the header—another goal.

Liverpool away. I'm standing near the keeper, Pepe Reina. Mikel's running with the ball, close to the touchline where our Everton supporters are. We make quick eye contact, I point down the pitch. *Whip it down there, Mickey—near post.* I slide over, stand inside the goal area, then out, two steps left; Mickey whips it in, I just touch it: goal.

Off the park, that competitiveness never went away. One break in our season, I took my family to his house in Spain. Our wives were preparing pastas and salads, while Mickey and I were outside on his Spanish barbecue cooking huge chunks of meat.

We relaxed after eating, had a few good glasses of Spanish wine. He's got a beautiful volleyball court with sand, where you can play paddle tennis. It was nearing midnight. Our wives were sitting up in a small alcove. Mikel and I took off our shirts and challenged each other to paddle tennis. We started playing for fun. It was a clear night, you could see the stars and moon, and suddenly we're playing seriously. One set to him, one set to me. The competition's on. We're down to match point and we get into this huge dispute.

"On the line!" Mikel shouts.

"You blind? It was out!" I shout back.

It's two in the morning and we're standing there screaming, getting more and more heated. From the alcove above, our wives shush us.

"You'll wake up the kids!"

We're swearing at each other, drenched in sweat. I throw the paddle at him, he whips the ball at me.

"If you're going to lie, Tim, I'm not playing!"

"Fuck off, if you're going to cheat, I'm not playing."

Screaming, sweating, chucking bats and balls at each other. We both had to shower off before we could join our wives and have some wine.

But it wasn't always fooling around with us. Mikel and I shared some life-changing moments. In 2010, when I finally married the love of my life, Rebecca, Mikel flew out to Las Vegas to join us. And when Mikel got married in Spain, I was there in the wedding party. The best men were Pepe Reina, Xabi Alonso, and me. It was an amazing wedding, held at a private castle in the middle of the Basque country.

As I write this, Mikel is now the captain of Arsenal, and we still text each other all the time about all our major life decisions. I never could have predicted this when Mikel came on loan to us from Real Sociedad, but the time we spent together blossomed into a remarkable, long-lasting friendship.

Fizzer and Mikel—both phenomenal players with such differing styles and temperaments. But to this day they remain two of the most valuable relationships I made in my days as a Blue.

MAKING HISTORY

THE NATIONAL TEAM TRAINING CAMP leading up to World Cup 2006 was one of the hardest I've ever experienced. It was run with strict military discipline, once again, by Guus Hiddink and Johan Neeskens. Guus also brought in former Australian international striker Graham Arnold as his second assistant.

Guus Hiddink knows about performing in big tournaments. He knew Australia's talent base, if drilled right, could be a force. He also knew that actually *delivering* in a tournament as highly pressurized as the World Cup—well, that was a much trickier proposition.

Hiddink maximized our potential. Look at our running statistics and other data from the tournament: Hiddink wrung every last drop out of every single Australian player.

He prepared us scientifically, tactically, strategically, mentally. He made it clear to us that *nothing* was guaranteed—certainly not a starting position, much less a spot in the team.

Australia came into the 2006 World Cup ranked second lowest of all qualified nations. We would have to face Japan, Croatia and Brazil in the group stages. From the beginning we were written off as the whipping boys of Group F.

Our attitude was still optimistic. We weren't going down without a fight. For me, being in that World Cup wasn't just the fulfilment of a lifelong dream. It was really a test of character.

Come the final week of camp, the nervous tension hit its peak.

"In this team," Hiddink told us, "there are no egos. If I see any egos, I'll get rid of them."

He wasn't messing about. Even in training games, if you gave the ball away sloppily, did the slightest thing wrong, any one of us—Bresciano, Viduka, Kewell, me—could be told by Hiddink or Neeskens: "Give the bib away—swap sides!"

The sense of uncertainty never let up. The night before our opening match against Japan, I was in the starting eleven. I asked Ron Smith, the Socceroos' technical manager, to come up to the room I was sharing with Luke Wilkshire and show me video footage and statistics on Japan.

I wanted to understand more about their defenders: how tall they were, how they moved. How big were their centre-backs? What statistics and information did we have about the left-back, right-back and defensive-midfielders? I wanted to know if I could out-leap them if a cross came my way. I wanted to do all my homework—anything that was going to give me an edge, whether it be from a free kick or a corner kick, or during open

Top: Not looking at the camera, in my third-grade class photo, 1988

Above: Me in 1988, aged eight

Right: Me, mum and Chris celebrating Chris's fifth birthday, 1989

UNDERCLIFFE
PUBLIC SCHOOL
1988

CLASS 3/4

Top: The mighty Banshee Knights. My dad is in the back row, at the far right.

Left: With the Samoan soccer team. My trip to Samoa allowed me to learn so much about my heritage and culture.

Above: In the line-up for the mighty Sydney Olympic as a 16-year-old

Below: With William Cook at my digs in London, 1999

Right: Training at Millwall

Top: Celebrating my goal for Millwall against Sunderland in the FA Cup semi-final on 4 April 2004 at Old Trafford — no one could catch me as I sprinted the length of the Old Trafford pitch! That volley still ranks among my favourite goals. *(Laurence Griffiths/Getty Images)*

Left: "What a goal, Tim!" It was fantastic to find my father and brother in the crowd and share the moment with them. *(Matthew Peters/Manchester United via Getty Images)*

Going into a challenge with Roy Keane. Playing in the FA Cup Final against Manchester United, on 22 May 2004, was a dream come true for me. *(John Peters/Getty Images)*

One of the most iconic pictures ever taken of Everton. Arm aloft in celebration I sit atop a massive pile-up of team-mates. Somewhere at the bottom is Lee Carsley, who had just scored the winning goal against Liverpool at Goodison Park, on 11 December 2004. *(Ross Kinnaird/Getty Images)*

Above: Being congratulated by Joseph Yobo and Tony Hibbert after scoring the second goal against Newcastle at Goodison Park on 7 May 2005, which gave us a fourth-place finish in the league *(Michael Steele/Getty Images)*

Right: In a bear hug with Mark Viduka after Mark Schwarzer saved a penalty to give us victory in the second play-off against Uruguay at Telstra Stadium, Sydney, 16 November 2005 *(Cameron Spencer/ Getty Images)*

Sliding in on Thierry ... We would discuss this tackle in person when we later became team-mates at the New York Red Bulls.
(Shaun Botterill/Getty Images)

It's 1–0 against Japan at Kaiserslautern, Germany, on 12 June 2006. All I can remember next was the screaming. I'd scored the first-ever goal for Australia in a World Cup. *(Sandra Behne/Bongarts/Getty Images)*

When I got to the corner flag, my emotions were running so high I forgot to do the final hook in my usual routine! *(Torsten Blackwood/AFP/Getty Images)*

Tackling Ronaldinho in the World Cup Group F match against Brazil, Munich, 18 June 2006 *(Roberto Schmidt/AFP/Getty Images)*

Sharing the moment with manager David Moyes, after scoring a goal against Portsmouth at Goodison Park, 2 March 2008
(Alex Livesey/Getty Images)

Disappointment following a miss during the penalty shoot-out win over Manchester United in the FA Cup semi-final at Wembley Stadium, London, 19 April 2009 *(Carl de Souza/AFP/Getty Images)*

Above: One of my favourite photos: on holiday in Samoa in 2008 with my extended family

Right: Having my tattoo done in Samoa, 2008

Below: With Rebecca and Giorgio Armani *(Billy Farrell/BFA.com)*

Tussling for the ball with Steven Gerrard, at Anfield, 6 February 2010 *(Paul Ellis/AFP/Getty Images)*

Scoring against Liverpool at Goodison Park, 17 October 2010 *(Paul Ellis/AFP/Getty Images)*

Our wedding in Red Rock, Las Vegas, in 2010

Wedding party: Chris, Rebecca, Fea (my cousin), me, mum, Sean and Opa

At the wedding with, from left to right, my mum, my wife Rebecca and my dad

With Rebecca and the kids at the wedding

Getting a red card from referee Marco Rodriguez after my tackle on Bastian Schweinsteiger during the 2010 World Cup Group D match against Germany, in Durban, South Africa, on 13 June *(Jamie McDonald/Getty Images)*

Scoring against Serbia in the 2010 World Cup Group D match on 23 June at Mbombela Stadium in Nelspruit, South Africa *(Christophe Simon/AFP/Getty Images)*

Saluting the fans after our elimination from the 2010 World Cup following the match against Serbia on 23 June in Nelspruit, South Africa *(Ezra Shaw/Getty Images)*

Enjoying a light-hearted moment in training with Phil Neville at Finch Farm, as David Moyes looks on, 21 October 2011 *(Clive Brunskill/Getty Images)*

Even though Mikel Arteta (right) is one of my closest friends, it's always fun to compete and we don't give an inch. *(Glyn Kirk/AFP/Getty Images)*

Meeting the Queen at Buckingham Palace during a reception for prominent members of the Australian community in Britain, 13 October 2011 *(John Stillwell/ AFP/Getty Images)*

Kiah singing the US national anthem at a New York Red Bulls game in 2014 with his very proud dad in the background

With Thierry Henry at a Giorgio Armani fashion show in New York, 2013 *(Emmanuel Dunand/Getty Images)*

Flying high. Scoring a match-winning header against Toronto FC in Toronto, April 2013 *(Lucas Oleniuk/Toronto Star via Getty Images)*

Heading past Chilean keeper Claudio Bravo in the World Cup match at the Pantanal Arena in Cuiaba, Brazil, on 13 June 2014 *(Juan Barreto/AFP/ Getty Images)*

With Ange Postecoglou at the 2014 World Cup *(Cameron Spencer/Getty Images)*

The greatest goal I'll ever score? The first strike against the Netherlands in the Group B match in Porto Alegre, Brazil, 18 June 2014 (*Dean Mouhtaropoulos/Getty Images*)

My scissor-kick goal in the Asian Cup quarter-final against China, 23 January 2015 *(AAP Image / AP Photo / Tertius Pickard)*

With my kids after winning the Asian Cup, Sydney, on 31 January 2015 *(Robert Cianflone/Getty Images)*

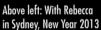

Above left: With Rebecca in Sydney, New Year 2013

Above right: Bek's birthday, 2014, at Saddle River, New Jersey

Right: All of my children, nieces and nephews together. Getting together with all of my family is always an amazing time.

Left: With my close friend and mentor, Chris Elder, 2015

Below left: My boys covered in "tattoos" to look like dad, Florida 2012

Below right: With Sean and Chris, Christmas 2014

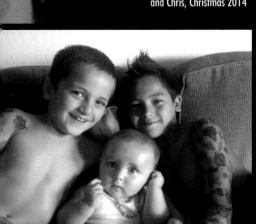

play. This was my first World Cup, the most important game of my life and I wasn't going to let my team or myself down because of lack of preparation.

By the time Ron Smith left the room, I knew I'd done everything possible to prepare myself.

Early the next morning the phone rang. It was Graham Arnold, saying I should meet him downstairs. Guus Hiddink and Arnie sat at a table over cups of coffee. I joined them and Guus told me, in his blunt manner: "I'm not starting you against Japan."

He started to explain his tactical reasoning, why it was better to line up a certain way against the Japanese. I didn't say a word. I knew it was pointless to debate him. I could see he'd made up his mind.

But I was confused. How could I go from starting to not starting? What had I done wrong in the space of eight hours?

Hiddink offered some more explanations and I stared back at him.

"That's your final decision?"

"Yes."

"I respect that."

I got up from the table and went back to my room. I was crushed. Gutted. It wasn't self-pity. I was just in disbelief. I'd been in the starting eleven the night before, and now I was being told, hours before the match, that I wouldn't be on the pitch when we sang the national anthem—when the whistle blew for kick-off?

The only positive I could find was to remind myself this was Australia's big moment, not mine. We were there as a nation, a collective, not as individual players. I was part of a squad about to play its first World Cup in thirty-two years. It was not about me.

I tried to adjust my perspective, reminding myself I could be sitting on the bench here in Germany, waiting for the boss to play me, or I could be at home watching with millions of others—including the dozens of other good players who hadn't made the final squad.

As always, I had no idea what Guus had in mind, but at least the possibility existed that I might still come on as a substitute.

*

A few hours before game time we drove to the stadium in the team coach. I just kept trying to put all the disappointment out of my mind. One of the ways I prepare—a lot of the boys do as well—is through music.

The whole drive in the coach, I had my headphones on, blasting songs that had personal meaning for me: "All My Life" by K-Ci and JoJo—Bek and I both loved that song when we were in high school. I listened to some Boyz II Men, which was the first ever concert I'd gone to in Sydney with my brother Sean. I listened to UB40. Growing up, that was the soundtrack to all my Samoan family gatherings—dozens of us around a barbeque, blasting that British reggae until 2 a.m.

But the big song during that coach ride to the stadium was Bernard Fanning's "Wish You Well". I had that on repeat and must have played it a dozen times straight. It wasn't specifically a Socceroos' World Cup song, but a lot of us loved it because it felt like it came straight from the heart of our Australian fans, wishing us well in the tournament.

I kept the volume on those songs up loud. Then, halfway to the stadium, I decided I should text my parents to tell them I wasn't in the starting eleven.

They were disappointed, too, but I texted straight back: "Don't worry about it. Everything will be okay. It always is."

I had forced myself into the right mental zone: I wanted my team to do well. That was my only concern.

*

As we neared the Fritz-Walter-Stadion in Kaiserslautern we began to see green and gold everywhere—our fans were out in force. Then we saw the Japanese fans were there in big numbers as well—they had a heavy presence in Germany. Security and police cars drew in around our coach, escorting us into the stadium proper, and that was when it hit us. The whole of Australia would be up in the early hours of the morning watching us out there on that pitch.

It was bloody hot on the park. You could barely breathe. They say it was 38 degrees, but it felt a lot hotter.

Guus Hiddink wore a white button-up shirt and black trousers. He was drenched even before kick-off. Getting up, sitting down. He was a bundle of nerves, glancing down the touchline to his opposite number. Japan were coached by Zico, the former Brazilian midfielder I remember watching in the World Cup as a kid.

As the match started, I was on the far end of the bench, away from the staff, sitting with Spider Kalac and some of the other substitutes. Back and forth the ball went. A tense beginning. Few chances either way, then two bullets from Viduka, one after the other right near the Japanese goalpost. The keeper, Kawaguchi, knocked the first back and sent the second one over the top and out.

Then in the twenty-sixth minute, Japan sent a long, sailing kick from the left. Schwarzer came out to grab it, and the Japanese and our players bunched. Schwarzer jumped but was impeded. The ball nicked Schwarzie's outstretched fingers, bounced high and went into the net.

On the bench we were all shouting—at the linesmen, at the referee—because we knew Schwarzie would have grabbed the ball had he not been blocked.

But the goal stood.

Not even a half-hour gone and we were down 1–0.

We watched the minutes tick away. After half-time, I got the call from down the bench to get ready to go on. Minute 50: I found out I was to replace Bresciano. I put on my shin pads, pulled up my socks and tucked my jersey in. The heat seemed even more brutal. I was drenched before even getting on the pitch.

Minute 52: on the touchline, I was stretching, limbering up. Guus Hiddink called me over and was giving me instructions.

To this day, I can't tell you what he said because I wasn't listening.

It didn't matter what Hiddink or Neeskens or Arnie or anyone else said to me in that moment. I knew exactly what my job was.

I had to come in and change the game.

I ran on for Bresh. Immediately got into the mix. We were chasing the game furiously. Minute 60 … minute 68 … minute 70 … Zico had his Japanese team playing very smart tactically.

*

John Aloisi comes on in the seventy-fifth minute—some fresh legs—replacing Luke Wilkshire. We're storming forward, taking it to the Japanese again and again.

We have nothing to lose. We aren't trying to hold a lead. I demand the ball. I'm tracking back. Challenging hard. Pressing high up the pitch.

Minute 80: the ball goes into touch on the left. Lucas Neill executes a perfect long throw-in, as good as a corner. Kawaguchi makes a muffed attempt to punch it out.

Harry Kewell takes a shot—blocked—and the ball squibs loose in front of me.

Half a chance. Here it is.

I strike. Pure reaction. Like in the playground: a maze of legs in front of you—*Just kick the ball!* Low and hard—I watch the ball as it whips past Aloisi, left of a defender, right of the keeper, and rips into the back of the net.

*

All I can remember next was the screaming. I was screaming—we were all screaming. I'd scored the first-ever goal for Australia in a World Cup. But that's the last thing that goes through your mind on the pitch. You don't have time to think about it. You're in the heat of the match.

After I scored, I sprinted off to the corner flag to do my boxing celebration: left jab, right cross, left hook, duck under, then a second left hook—but the emotions were running so high, as I punched the corner flag, I even forgot to come up and do the final hook.

I was swarmed and smothered by team-mates—Archie Thompson, Lucas Neill, Luke Wilkshire.

Foremost in my mind was the thought to press on. We could win this.

We had the edge in possession. All credit to Guus—his intense fitness preparation was about to pay off. We were running like dogs in 38 degrees of heat. We were on the scent of the win. No way were we playing for the draw.

*

Minute 88: Aloisi lays the ball off, I control it with my right foot. The defender holds back, fails to close the space. In that split second I roll the ball forward with my studs. A gap opens on the right side—a second defender runs into the centre, blocking the keeper's sight line. Another gap opens on the left. I shape to go right, give the keeper the eye, misdirecting him, then at the top of the penalty arc I launch the shot, twenty metres out, curling left.

Not a ton of power, just curl it with the inside of my foot.

If my first goal was poaching instinct, this second goal is all technique. As it leaves my boot I say to myself: "Keeper's got no chance."

It hits the top left of the post, then bounces right across the length of the goal and settles into the back of the net—one of the sweetest strikes I've ever made.

Barely two minutes left in regulation time, I'd gone and nicked it. Like my brother Sean used to say when we'd tussle in the back garden: *Take your shot at the title, mate.* I'd had two shots at the title—two scoring opportunities. I'd hit both.

I was smothered by my team-mates, even the substitutes and staff. Then I took off running down the touchline. Guus Hiddink went to high-five me, but I ducked his outstretched hand and ran past.

Back in position: play started up and less than two minutes later we iced it. In the ninetieth minute, Aloisi burst through the middle of the Japanese defence, finishing coolly.

Final whistle: 3–1 for Australia.

I could hardly believe it: in the space of mere minutes, I had changed the game and Aloisi had shut the door. We'd made history.

*

I was named FIFA's Man of the Match, the first Australian to get that honour. During the press conference, I kept hearing it was a landmark day and people kept asking me how I felt. The truth was, as I'd texted my parents, I'd never lost faith.

Afterward, in the changing room, Guus Hiddink was talking to me and I still couldn't hear a word he said. I was in a daze. I'd been crushed not to start and now I was ecstatic.

Our boss looked like a tactical genius for having brought on both Johnny Aloisi and me to score all three goals in the final six minutes of the match.

Did I score as the result of Guus's tactics? Holding me in reserve and bringing me on as fresh legs, with all my pent-up energy and desire? Maybe even deliberately frustrating me by using me as a substitute rather than as a starter, just to inspire me?

Sure, it sounds like a master psychological chess move: know your players' strengths and psychology. If that's what he did—and only Hiddink knows the answer—then I've got to raise my hat to him. Tactically brilliant!

As a player, though, I just don't see football that way. For me, football is about feelings, action—*heart*—not abstract tactical thinking. I'll leave that to the coaches. My job is to score and battle hard. To serve my team as best I can.

Emotionally, that match against Japan was the biggest roller-coaster of my footballing life. In a matter of minutes, I went from personal disappointment to being at the centre of a moment of football glory for Australia.

ALL GOOD THINGS

WHEN YOU'RE AT A WORLD Cup, thousands of miles from home, you have no sense of how the public back home in Australia is reacting. We found out later that fans flooded the pubs and the commentators were in rapture.

We didn't see any of it at the time, of course—though now on YouTube I've seen the clips—as have my kids.

Simon Hill was screaming: "Tim Cahill has done it again! 2–1 for Australia. Oh it's a wonderful moment in Kaiserslautern. Tim Cahill has come off the bench and maybe won the match for the Socceroos. Magical stuff! It's a wonder-strike by the wonder-boy of Australian football!"

It does make you smile.

*

Before I knew it, I was back in the hotel—complete isolation, ice bath, rehydrating and post-match recovery. Just thinking about our next game in Munich against the most dominant team in World Cup history—Brazil.

Did I experience a high from the Japan game? Not really. It fizzed past, and I was immediately doing my rehabilitation routine and focussing on the next match. There was no time for emotion. I learned that very early in my career. This is what top-level football's about. No resting on laurels. That's what keeps you mentally strong.

In a World Cup group stage, the pressure is far more intense than in routine club play. That first win against Japan had bought us breathing space, but it guaranteed nothing. We could be knocked out in our next two matches and it'd be over. Each win bought our survival for the next game, so the struggle didn't let up, even after the final whistle.

For me, preparing for Brazil was like reading a list of legends. They had Ronaldinho, Rivaldo, Roberto Carlos, Cafu, Kaká, Ronaldo—an amazing starting eleven. But by no means were Brazil taking us as a pushover.

We were honest about our expectations.

"We're Australia—no one rates us. What have we got to lose?"

Our attitude before the match was simple. Try not to fear the name, because just seeing Brazil's crest with its five World Cup championship stars could mentally unwind you before you'd even started.

*

When the Brazil game kicked off, I remember we were all stunned by the level of their technique. If you ask me who is the most skilful player I've played against, without question the answer is Ronaldinho. Things were happening on the pitch that made me do double takes. He had skills straight out of a video game. Step-overs. *Elasticos*. Feints that had us flailing at thin air.

At one point I tackled Ronaldinho and someone captured the image with a perfect photo. I didn't get a yellow card, but I probably should have. I'm coming in on a sliding tackle, he's going over the top, and I'm nowhere near the ball. I didn't set out to foul him, he was just a magician with his close control. Against Ronaldinho, the minute you think you have a chance to get the ball, he goes into his bag of flicks and tricks and leaves you looking foolish.

No one watching that game could ever say Australia versus Brazil was a mismatch. We fought them all the way. We kept it scoreless until half-time, then at forty-nine minutes Ronaldo squared Adriano a beautiful pass and he slotted it in from fifteen metres.

We had our chances. I had a few, Viduka as well. Dukes had a lob that looked as if it was going in but landed on top of the net.

Our best chance was when their keeper, Dida, dropped a cross and Harry Kewell, who'd come on for me as a substitute at fifty-six minutes, blazed a rocket over the unguarded goal. Then Kewell almost embarrassed Dida, dipping a forty-metre shot centimetres over the bar after spotting that the keeper was off his line. We kept chasing the game, trying to equalize, but Brazil's striker, Fred, tapped in a rebound off the post at the ninetieth minute to seal the win.

We'd given our all and made them earn the win. In the end, our efforts just weren't enough. We lost 2–0, which was probably a fair reflection of the gulf between the two sides.

A personal highlight from that game came at the final whistle. I walked straight toward Ronaldo—whom English-speaking footballers often call "the original Ronaldo" and Brazilians call *Ronaldo Il Fenomeno*. I asked the original Ronaldo to swap jerseys with me. He happily agreed. It's one of my prize mementos of the many top players I've played against—the No. 9 shirt of Ronaldo from our World Cup 2006 match.

*

Now we had to prepare for our defining group match against Croatia in Stuttgart. A win, or possibly even a draw, would be enough to secure us a place in the Round of 16. We were sitting on three points, but if we could claw our way past Croatia, it would be a huge moment for the Socceroos.

Croatia and Australia have strong cultural ties. Big enclaves of immigrants from Croatia live in Australia and two of the leading clubs of the old NSL were Sydney Croatia and Melbourne Croatia, where Mark Viduka started his professional career. In our squad alone we had four or five players of Croatian descent—Viduka, Popovic, Kalac and even Bresciano, whose father was Italian but whose mother was Croatian. And the Croatian side fielded a few players with Australian family ties—some born in Australia, actually.

Guus Hiddink made a major decision in that game to drop our starting keeper Schwarzer and play Zeljko Kalac. To this day, I don't know why that decision was made. I doubt Schwarzie or Spider has a clue either. Again, it could have been a matter of tactics, Guus assuming that Spider would "show up" against the country of his descent. Or maybe he thought Schwarzie needed a break. Whatever the reason, it was a shock to everyone.

That was always Guus Hiddink. A mystery.

But having led us this far in the World Cup, Guus was a popular figure back home and in the German stadiums. People were even calling him "Aussie Guus". The Socceroo fans chanted "*Guuuussssssss!*" during our matches and you'd see T-shirts and banners saying "No Guus, No Glory".

We had no doubts about Spider Kalac as our net-minder. He was a dominating physical player, at least 203 cm tall, and at that time a top keeper for AC Milan. It was just one of those matters of chemistry and camaraderie—if Schwarzie was playing so well in our first two matches, why drop him in favour of Spider?

Within two minutes of the match kicking off, we were up against it. Darijo Srna lined up to take a free-kick from thirty metres out. Right footed, Srna struck a beauty, curling the ball over the wall and past the outstretched right hand of Kalac into the top left-hand corner of the net.

We'd barely settled into a rhythm and already we were chasing the match. Then Mark Viduka was nearly rugby-tackled in the penalty area, but the referee didn't give us the spot kick. A cross came in to me at twenty-nine minutes, I rose to meet it in the goal area, but their keeper made a great save. I ran my hands through my hair, wishing I'd been able to direct it better into the far corner.

Back and forth it went the whole match, like two heavyweights trading punches. The entire match was so physical. You just knew guys were going to get sent off. Brutal challenges and yellow cards.

In the thirty-ninth minute, a great cross came in for me and one of their defenders, Stjepan Tomas, handled it. Whistle: the referee pointing to the penalty spot.

We had some top attacking talent out there: Viduka, Kewell, Bresciano, me—proven scorers—but it was our central defender, Craig Moore, who took the penalty.

With the Socceroos, it was always Moorie or Muskie stepping up for spot-kicks. We all felt they were the strongest mentally in that entire squad. Penalty kicks in a World Cup match require players with great mental discipline, and if you're looking for mental toughness, I'd pick Moorie or Muskie any day.

Moore stepped up and calmly smashed home a perfect penalty. It was unstoppable; into the roof of the net. We were level.

Then, unfortunately, Spider Kalac misjudged a long-range shot from Niko Kovac and conceded what he later described as a "shit goal". It was a howler. Spider dived and seemed to have stopped the shot easily, but the ball popped over his body and into the net.

That was demoralizing, because we'd worked so hard to level the score. We couldn't help questioning Hiddink's decision to bench Schwarzie, who'd been in fantastic form, in favour of Spider.

At 2–1 we had an uphill battle, but we were all getting chances—Dukes, Harry, me. In the seventieth minute, Kewell shot from ten metres, but their keeper made a brilliant reflex save. Then there was a crazy moment—unique in World Cup history, I believe—involving their defender Josip Simunic. He was actually born in Canberra, had trained in Australia and had started his professional career with the Melbourne Knights. He was eligible for the Socceroos but chose to play for Croatia. Simunic got his second yellow card after blatantly dragging down Josh Kennedy in the midfield, but—bizarrely— the referee didn't send him off. We were mystified.

In the seventy-ninth minute, we got one back. The ball came through, Kewell took a sweet touch with his left, put it onto his right and fired home. Great goal and I ran immediately to hug Harry, but at 2–2 we weren't sure if we'd done enough to advance.

We were frantically clearing our lines and then, at the death of the game, we got a throw-in and Dukes scored what looked to all of us like the winning goal in injury time. But the referee ruled it out. Supposedly, the final whistle had been blown, but we hadn't heard it. In the confusion the referee now showed Simunic a third yellow card, sending him off finally with the red as the game came to an end.

That's the type of physical match it was. In the final ten minutes, three men had been sent off: Dario Simic, Brett Emerton and Simunic. The full-time whistle sounded and our entire bench emptied onto the pitch. We didn't need the win, as it turned out, given the other result in our group. A draw would have been enough to put us through. The Croatians knew it, too, and slumped to the pitch, gutted, as we celebrated.

For all the bizarre decisions, Spider's soft goal, our denied winner, all those hard challenges and bookings, that match was thrilling. Many at the time called it the most entertaining of all the group-stage matches in the 2006 World Cup. And we'd exceeded all expectations to make it through to the knockout round. The Socceroos had an aura of confidence now.

*

For our second-round clash we faced the Group E winners, Italy. As with Brazil, we tried not to be overawed by the Italians' three World Cup trophies. But because I always do loads of pre-match research into the defenders I'll be facing, I was giving those Italians a lot of respect.

Fabio Cannavaro, for example. Not a tall player, but strong and solid, and very tactically aware of position. Brilliant defender. You think you can beat him in the air, he'll have you covered; you think you can beat him on the ground, he'll position himself to shut down your run.

Alessandro Del Piero, Francesco Totti, Andrea Pirlo, Gennaro Gattuso, Luca Toni—so many class players in that *Azzurri* roster. Not only did they defend well, they were technically gifted players too.

Italy were mentally tough. A team built for tournaments. Their discipline was immense. They held their shape. They didn't rush the ball. It was measured, calculated, always intelligent.

The thing I remember most about that match was the battle I had with Marco Materazzi. Throughout the game, we were on each other's shoulders, pushing and tugging, battling in the air.

Materazzi is a master of winding you up. He and I were clattering into each other throughout the match and he was yapping non-stop. Materazzi is about 193 cm, tall but lanky— and one of those guys who acts tougher than he is. After one really physical exchange, I told him, "You need to get on the weights, mate, you're a bit frail."

He acts like a hard man, but he was nowhere near as tough as some of their other guys, like Cannavaro or Gattuso, for instance. Now Gattuso—that's a pit bull of a player. If you went into a challenge with him, he'd rattle you.

Right from the kick-off, the match was fast. We were giving no quarter. Again, there were so many hard tackles and yellow cards. On their side, Grosso, Gattuso and Zambrotta were all booked. On our side, Grella, Wilkshire and me.

We were holding our own, certainly not being played off the park, and then Materazzi got a red card. Six minutes after half-time he came in on a hard challenge on Bresh and was rightly, in my view, shown a straight red.

With an extra man we should have been able to press our advantage, but no team is better at playing with only ten men than the Italian national side. If there's one thing they know how to do, it's shut up shop and concede nothing.

Throughout the game we had our chances but failed to convert. And if you don't bury your chances against the Italians, they'll bury you.

Well into injury time—the ninety-third minute—we were already mentally prepared to play the extra thirty minutes, but then Grosso, Italy's left-back, took the ball down the wing past Bresciano and into our penalty area.

Lucas Neill closed down the space to challenge him one-on-one. Anticipating a move to the touchline, Lucas lunged at him and fell and Grosso jinked to the right before tumbling over Neill's prostrate body. There was no intention on Neill's part to foul or even obstruct—he had just fallen. In my view, Grosso made himself trip over Lucas and, as he went down, made a meal of it. Very soft call, to my eyes—obvious diving—but the referee didn't agree. He immediately pointed to the spot.

Up stepped Francesco Totti and, with a little smirk, he smashed it past Schwarzer. Last play of the match. We were gutted. They'd done it the Italian way. Down a man, yet somehow they'd stolen a goal to knock us out of the competition.

*

To me it seemed cruel and unfair. We'd dominated for long periods of the match and didn't deserve to lose that way. I was angry with the referee, angry with Grosso for the dive. After the match, I couldn't keep my anger bottled up for the press who crowded around us, wanting comment.

"We're in disbelief because anyone who watched the game could see that it was not a penalty," I told some reporters. "I'm furious. It's unbelievable. Everyone says, 'Well done, Australia's played well, a pat on the back, you've proved everyone wrong'— but we should still be in this World Cup. I respect Italy. They're a good team, but so are we."

We were out of the competition, but we knew we hadn't let our supporters down. We'd lost to the team that would eventually go on to win the 2006 World Cup and there's no shame in going out to the eventual champions.

Looking back, I actually have a lot of admiration for that Italian squad. They had quality players, but the difference was in how well they were coached. Under Marcello Lippi, they were more than a collection of talented individuals. That was a rock-solid team. They often won ugly, scrapping and clawing through, as they did against us with that penalty—right at the death of the match. Cynical tackles. Taunts. Winding the opposition up. But it's called *winning*.

Today I have no hard feelings. Pinching late goals, winning through mental gamesmanship. That's still part of the art, if not the beauty, of football.

ROLLING BACK
THE YEARS

LOOKING BACK AT MY EIGHT years at Everton—as both a Blue and a Socceroo—so many big moments flash in my mind like scenes from a movie. Lifelong friendships made. Furious tackles. Special goals. But also the darker times—coping with personal trials, family crises, controversy. During those years as a Blue, I really came into my own—matured both as a player and as a man.

Everyone is familiar with the off-the-park glamour that comes with professional football. The spotlight of playing for your club and country. The trappings of fame and celebrity. The Ferraris and Lamborghinis. Holidays in Barbados, Greece, and the south of France. None of that ever meant much to me. That wasn't the reason I fell in love with the game.

Few people see the amount of gritty—and unglamorous— on-the-park work that comes with the *job* of being a footballer.

Behind every single match at Everton were countless hours in the freezing cold and pelting rain, walking through pattern-of-play sequences set up by David Moyes. At home, our pressing game was excellent; but only because we worked at it endlessly. I close my eyes and can still see the boss out there on the field, holding the ball in the air, shouting "Over here!", and we'd shuffle into position, then "Over here!", and we'd shuffle to our new spot. It's how we learned to hold our shape as a team, how to move as a well-oiled machine. Discipline, drill, repetition. Set plays, defending corners, defending free kicks. Freezing, shivering, wet, tired, but it's how we became who we were. One year I can recall we barely conceded a goal from set plays.

For David Moyes the Monday-to-Friday work was *everything*. If we conceded a soft goal—if you didn't follow the man you were supposed to mark and he beat you, ran and scored—you wanted to be *invisible* in that week's video session. As well you should. We'd spent two hours running through patterns of play, defending set pieces, only for one of us to switch off for two seconds and we'd conceded a goal.

One great thing that David Moyes did was instil a sense of accountability throughout the team. If I'd lost my marker in the midfield and we'd conceded a goal, I was just as responsible as any of the defenders or the keeper who'd been beaten three or four passes later in the play. And he applied it often to himself. He'd come into the changing room after a loss and say, "Boys, you know, tough to take—but this is entirely on me."

*

As I'd found out so early in my career at Millwall, almost every professional athlete at some point has to deal with the mental toll of getting hurt. When I tally up the injuries I sustained and played with at Everton alone, it's mind-boggling. My ACL, ankles, numerous muscle tears and more breaks to my fifth metatarsal requiring radical surgery. I was sure that after Everton, I'd be in a wheelchair.

If the team doctor said, "Tim, you can't play," I'd stare back at him and ask, "Why?" "Because you've got a two-centimetre tear." "Well, I don't *feel* like I've got a two-centimetre tear." Then I'd tell David Moyes: "Boss, disregard what the physio says—I can start."

Before I played in the 2011 Asian Cup in Qatar for Australia, I was in great form with Everton. I was nursing a slight injury, but I'd still scored eight goals in the Premier League. I was in the top five of the Premiership scoring charts before I left to go into camp with the Socceroos. David Moyes and the guys at Everton weren't thrilled as I left for Qatar, but I told them that the Asian Cup was Australia's best chance to win our first trophy in a major international tournament. For all the Socceroos' development, for all our growth as a team since my first call-up, we had yet to win an international competition.

We played well in Qatar, though I took some serious punishment as we progressed to the final game against Japan. Before that game, I remember wrapping my back up, strapping my knee and ankle. My body was in bits. I was probably at seventy per cent to play in that final. There were three or four other players in the same situation, doing our best but in obvious pain.

We played hard, but Japan scored an amazing volley and we lost 1–0.

When I headed back to Everton I was in bad shape: my knee was killing me, my ankle had worsened and I'd also been diagnosed with plantar fasciitis, a stabbing pain in the deepest part of the sole of my left foot. It felt like I had a shard of glass embedded in my foot and I couldn't put even the lightest pressure on it without wincing.

On top of my already banged-up knee and ankle, the plantar fasciitis meant I was playing matches for Everton in excruciating pain. One of the physiotherapists would come and stick this long needle deep into the tissue of the foot, and jolt it with an electrical charge—this little explosion of voltage. That was by far the worst pain I'd ever experienced in my life. But I took it, because it meant I could train and play in the next game.

Much of that season I didn't train from Monday to Wednesday because of the pain. I could barely hobble around, but the physiotherapists would get the foot just right enough that I could make it onto the pitch by the weekend. On Thursday I'd get the injection, on Friday I'd train lightly, on Saturday I'd play, then on Sunday and Monday I couldn't even walk.

It's not my style to complain, and I owed my club every ounce I could wring out of myself. I just kept repeating the process—excruciating treatments, hobbling around, playing as best I could. I wasn't playing to the best of my ability, but I was doing as much as I could to contribute.

After my fine form immediately before the Asian Cup, my scoring went to pieces. I couldn't score to save my life. With an injury that radically affects your play, you start to wonder if your career might be finished, if you've done permanent damage and will never be yourself again.

There was other fallout. Some staff and team-mates were even less happy now about my decision to play in the Asian Cup. "What a waste, Cahill," they'd say. "You flew halfway around the world, you didn't win any silverware, and you got badly injured. What was the bloody point?"

After the season and the summer break I came back to training camp still not fully fit. I continued getting radical treatments. In my mind, I was contributing—linking up well, making unselfish runs to open up play, challenging hard on every tackle. But, as it turned out, I had gone an entire calendar year—factoring the break for the Asian Cup and the off-season—without scoring for Everton. I hadn't been keeping close track of the dates, but the media sure had. Now people were asking all these questions: "Is Tim Cahill washed up? Finished as an Everton marksman?"

The Premiership is absolutely brutal that way—a fishbowl as intense as any professional football league in the world. What people failed to see was the contribution I continued to make as a team player. True, I wasn't scoring, but I was starting plays, laying off passes to players who were in space, sparking scoring sequences. Despite my lack of goals, Everton was still playing brilliant football, and I was doing my bit to make that happen.

Was it hard to take it on the chin when people kept writing, "What's wrong with Cahill? He hasn't scored in a year."? The only thing that was hard was knowing that people weren't seeing the entire game, the full team dynamic. They weren't looking at Everton as a whole, weren't seeing us as more than just a collection of individual players.

It reminded me of something I'd learned as a kid from my dad and from Johnny Doyle: it doesn't matter what anyone thinks as long as you know you're doing your job properly. Let them talk, make assumptions, jump to conclusions—all you need to do is focus on your role. Commit to playing as well as you can for the good of the team. The only time it's a problem is when you know in your own heart that you're slacking off, not putting in the work.

Today, at age thirty-five, having played with world-class players like Phil Neville, Mikel Arteta and Thierry Henry, I understand it's not always the final touch that matters. The finisher—the person on the end of the play—is the one who gets the glory. I've been fortunate enough to be there and have scored some wonderful goals. But without the build-up play, there would be no glory for the scorer.

Being injured and going through that year-long scoring drought actually helped my game. It made me understand what it means to be a leader and it gave me a more comprehensive view of the game. It taught me how to take a step back from the weekly grind and the focus on scoring to think more about the overall arc of the team's season. I started asking different questions: "Where do you want to be at the end of the season? Is it more important for Everton to be up there in the top three or four places on the table, or for me to score twenty times?"

Any really mature footballer will always choose the team over himself.

That season of injuries and the scoring drought taught me to see the game more completely—more maturely. Now when I watch a match I see the full picture. I don't think I did when I was in my early-to-mid-twenties. I still love watching players like Leo Messi and Cristiano Ronaldo on scoring runs— sometimes averaging a goal a match—but I also pay attention to the runs that other players make out wide, carrying defenders with them to create the space for Messi or Ronaldo to be man on man at the edge of the box and curl in a beautiful strike to the top corner of the net. The unselfish run isn't quantifiable, isn't measured by statistics, and there's no obvious glory in doing it, but if you're a complete footballer, or an educated fan, you know how important it is in creating those moments of individual brilliance.

During that year-long dry spell, I remember going into David Moyes' office. We never discussed my lack of scoring. "How does your body feel, Tim?" he'd ask. "How's the knee? How's the foot today?"

We'd talk about the team, what we could do better as a group, the three points we needed to pick up that coming week, or how big the month ahead was going to be. We talked about what was important to Everton Football Club—not what individually mattered to David Moyes or Tim Cahill as manager and midfielder. I consider that tough year among the most valuable learning experiences of all my time as a Blue.

*

By far the most difficult personal challenge during my Everton years was when my older brother Sean was sent to jail for injuring a man in a fight in London. Sean has acknowledged making a massive mistake—one he deeply regrets—and at this point he's paid his debt. But at the time, what he and my family went through actually had me considering quitting football. His trial and sentencing were covered relentlessly in the British and Australian press—because Sean's my brother. There were days I'd wake to find that the story was on the front page, back page and middle pages of the papers. Had Sean not been the brother of a well-known Premier League footballer, his case would never have received such heavy media coverage.

Back home in Sydney, it was tearing up my mum and dad. It was a difficult time for all of us, but especially my mum. I rang my parents and said, "I love football, but what's the point? I don't want to drag all of you guys through all this."

I knew I didn't need the fame and money that come with football. I've lived with nothing and been happy. I knew I could go back to a simple life and be happy. Maybe my mum and dad needed my moral support back home more than Everton needed me as a footballer.

Before Sean was sentenced, I told him: "Look, my whole life you've protected me. You've been my rock. Now I want you to know that during these next three or four years, I'll be here for you."

Then, when I heard the news of his conviction, I couldn't leave my room. The press were calling, wanting me to comment. Those days were some of the darkest times. I didn't want to talk to anyone. I just wanted to be alone. It was only out on the football pitch that I felt better. I could stay on the training ground for ages. I guess it gave me an emotional outlet.

Between matches, I'd go see Sean in jail and, regardless of whether things were good, bad or worse for him, he'd always say the same thing. "No worries, Tim. Just concentrate on your football."

At the jail, it was tough love. We never got soft or teary-eyed or said things like "I miss you."

"You've got to do this," I'd say. "Stay strong, man. You've got to do this time."

In fact, he was putting his time to good use. He was studying and writing in jail.

I'm much more emotional than Sean. Frequently, on the

pitch, my emotions take over. Even in the heat of a match, my feelings are always very close to the surface.

I remember we had a match against Portsmouth. Sean was in my head the whole time out on the pitch because I'd seen him in prison the day before. He'd told me he'd be watching. I scored a nice goal—a well-timed header. As soon as the ball hit the back of the net, I wheeled away. My only thoughts were of Sean. You could see the raw emotion in my eyes. I was hiding nothing.

Instead of boxing the corner flag, I crossed my wrists, gesturing like a man in handcuffs. It was spontaneous. From the heart. The image went round the world and was immediately the cause of some controversy. Let me be clear—that gesture was purely an expression of *love* for my brother. I was sharing a moment with Sean, not making excuses for what he'd done, not making a statement of any kind—other than to let him know I'd scored that goal for him. There was no disrespect intended. I was simply showing my brother Sean in prison that I loved him and that I would always be there to support him.

*

In a long playing career, any footballer is going to meet with his fair share of setbacks and adversity. Sometimes it's injuries, or a family crisis—like the situation with Sean. Or those moments on the pitch when you've got to measure up and accept unfairness.

For the 2010 World Cup in South Africa, after a hard-fought qualifying campaign, Australia was placed in a very tough group. We faced Serbia, Ghana and Germany. We had all the right attributes as a team and we felt we had a decent shot at progressing.

But no one gave us much of a chance for our opening match against Germany in Durban. Germany's always one of the powerhouses of world football, but we had hope in the days leading up to the match that we might pull off an upset. Maybe we could play them tight, hold them to a draw, or possibly sneak a win. After twenty minutes, it was clear that it wasn't on the cards. Podolski scored after just eight minutes, then Klose at twenty-six. Not even thirty minutes played and we were under the pump.

Then in the fifty-sixth minute, a fifty-fifty ball came my way. I went into a tackle with the German midfielder Bastian Schweinsteiger. As always, I was fully committed to winning the ball, but when I saw I couldn't get it cleanly, I pulled out of the challenge. Schweinsteiger rode the challenge, went down and made a lot of noise, rolling around and making it look like I'd intentionally pinned his leg back.

In that split second, the referee had to make a decision.

Straightaway, he went into his pocket and pulled out a card.

I was expecting a yellow, but the card he waved in my face was red.

I was standing next to Brett Holman and he said, "How the hell is this a straight red?"

I was too shocked to react. A *red*? It meant I was out of the match. Australia would be chasing a 2–0 game with only ten men. It also meant I would sit out the next game against Serbia.

There was an audible groan among our fans in the stadium. Most knew that Bastian had made high drama of the challenge. He stayed on the floor, rolling around. I knew the contact we made wasn't that severe. If you see the video or still pictures, you can see my legs are bent; I clearly wasn't trying to injure him. If I was lunging in to injure him, my legs would have been straight, studs up, and I could have seriously hurt him.

But that's never been my game. A hard challenge, yes—but setting out to deliberately injure another player? Never.

Instead of arguing with the referee, I took a deep breath and tried to gather my thoughts. I bent over to see that Schweinsteiger was okay, I had some words with Podolski, and I walked off, saying to myself, "You've got to take this on the chin, Tim."

There were three reasons. First, I knew the referee wasn't going to change his mind. Second, I also knew there was no intent to injure and that anyone watching on TV would likely see that. Third, and most importantly, I knew there were *millions* of kids watching at home in Australia. I didn't want to be seen as the guy in the green and gold complaining, arguing, pleading my case or flapping my arms in protest.

The most honourable thing to do, I felt—as unjust as that red card seemed in the moment—was to walk off in silence.

That was the longest walk to the touchline I've made in my career.

I was more upset with myself than anything. I knew I'd tried to pull out of the challenge, but could I have done more? The red card meant my depleted team would have to hold the fort against a hugely talented and disciplined German side. It was looking like an impossible task.

I walked through the tunnel with security trying to escort me. I said, "You're not going to get any problems from me, mate. I know where the changing room is."

In the changing room I took my shirt off and sat down. It was an eerie feeling. There were tens of thousands of people outside, shouting, cheering, and I was alone with my thoughts. Was this really happening? What the hell? Had I really just been sent off in the very first game of the World Cup?

I checked my phone and saw a text message from Rebecca. She said how sorry she was to see me sent off and that my son Shae was watching, and he was devastated. "He wants to come to see you to give you a hug," she wrote. I could just picture it: Shae—my shadow, my second son, then aged five—taking it hard, crying his eyes out. That felt like a second sucker punch.

We lost the match. Afterward, I spoke to Schweinsteiger.

"I didn't go to kick you," I said. "I was going for the ball and tried to pull out of the challenge." He acknowledged as much.

But that's life. That's football. I learned my lesson. Walk off, take it on the chin, and speak to the other player afterward— even if you think it's unfair. For me, that's a sign of true professionalism.

As upsetting as it was, I can see it more clearly now that I'm a few years removed from it. The referee only had one angle on the play. He didn't have the benefit of replays and slow motion. And Schweinsteiger had only one thought—win the match. Sometimes, whether you're right or wrong, it's best to take the punishment in silence.

*

The day after the loss to Germany was a family day. All my closest family were there. My parents, Bek and the kids, as well as a bunch of my mates—trying to cheer me up.

"Don't worry about it," I said. "It'll be fine. I'll be back against Serbia and you know I'll be on that pitch with one objective—to score."

For the next three days I worked the hardest I have ever worked in my life as a footballer. I did extra sessions. Focussed with such intensity during training. There was nothing I could do for our upcoming match against Ghana except cheer the guys on, so I worked to prepare myself for our last group-stage match against Serbia.

We played Ghana in Rostenberg. The worst part for me was having to watch with the crowd. I felt powerless. Ghana are always tough—physical and fast—but it was still a winnable game for us. Most days we could have taken them. But Harry Kewell got a red card and we were down to ten men. Holman scored, but Ghana equalized, and that was the result. A loss and a draw made our chances of getting out of the group look pretty bleak.

Would the score have been different had I been out there? Watching it unfold, powerless, only added to the frustration I felt about the red card in the Germany game. Still, I tried to keep my focus. All I could do was be professional and get into the right frame of mind for our final match of the group stages.

We were now in the position where we had to win the Serbia game if we were going to advance to the knockout round.

On 3 June 2010 we lined up against the Serbs. Talk about battles! I had to push my way through Branislav Ivanovic of Chelsea and Nemanja Vidic of Manchester United, both top defenders. I knew them both from our time in the Premiership. The whole time, Vidic and I, every ball, we were in each other's pocket. Elbows, pushing, fouls, arguing, grappling—we went at each other *hard*.

I knew a lot about Vidic, a very dangerous player, exceptional at marking you tight. I also knew his psychological make-up. Vidic doesn't like being harassed, doesn't like someone on his shoulder all game long.

For the first forty-five minutes I gave him hell. Still, neither team scored. During the second half, our side was fluid and attacking, and we took control of the match.

Luke Wilkshire crossed the ball from deep, a beauty with his right foot, a good thirty- or forty-metre pass, put it into a perfect area for me. Ivanovic was there, as was Vidic, and Chipperfield was in the mix, too. Four of us jumped at once. I knew there would only be one winner. My timing and vertical leap was exceptional and, as the ball came over, I got some great contact.

Split second, off my head, on the grass, back of the goal.

It was one of the best headers I've scored as a Socceroo, having to fend off such top-class defenders, attain such height, contact and direction on the ball.

I ran over to the corner and boxed the flag—jab, cross, hook, duck, hook—then looked over to my family, blowing a kiss at my mum, dad, Bek and the kids. I was nodding, as if to say, *I told you I'd come out and score ...*

We won 2–1, but unfortunately, as things played out in the group, it wasn't enough to allow us to advance. But we all felt we'd played with conviction and made Australia proud.

To have made it to two consecutive World Cups was a new landmark for the Socceroos and to have scored in two consecutive World Cups was a new milestone for me. I'd taken the red card on the chin, sat there and watched the team play a tough match without me, then got my chance to show I could still contribute, netting one of the best headers I've ever scored. Despite that rocky path and our early exit, I look back on the South Africa World Cup as another of the great learning experiences of my career.

*

For any player seriously devoted to the game, the mental aspect eventually becomes as important as the physical one. You can train your body as hard as possible, but, in the end, if you want longevity in football—or any sport, really—you need to develop and strengthen your mind and your spirit as well.

The path to fully developing my inner strength as a player started where I least expected it: deep in my past. When we were kids in Sydney, living in Annandale, my brother Sean and I used to be driven to school. One day, for some reason, Mum and Dad said it would be okay for us to walk the whole way. Before class, we'd buy cheese-and-bacon rolls at the bread shop, then walk the rest of the way to school. That day, as we came out of the shop with food, we noticed a mentally disturbed guy standing outside. Without warning, he started lashing out, kicking and throwing punches at us. Sean, being the protective big brother, stepped into the guy's path, and got hit with some punches and kicks.

I was terrified and remember the man's face, wild-eyed, screaming and full of such rage. Sean managed to defend us long enough to allow us to run off. There was a police station right in front of us, but we weren't thinking straight—adrenaline and fear taking hold—and we ran all the way to school.

Though neither of us was hurt, it was extremely traumatic. Only later did I realize how much the incident had affected me. It came on as a very delayed reaction. Months later I started having nightmares, reliving the man's punches and kicks, seeing his angry eyes. I'd wake up in the middle of the night shouting and soaked in sweat. Sometimes I wouldn't even remember these terrors, but my mum would tell me in the morning that I'd been screaming.

When I wasn't having night terrors, I'd often find myself stricken with insomnia. I used to lie there rethinking everything, asking myself all kinds of questions. The one question I kept asking myself was, "Why?"

"Why were we attacked? Why did he choose us?" Those first questions led to bigger questions—like "Why are we alive?" and "Why are *any* of us here?" I was a young kid but the attack made me aware of my own mortality for the first time.

Years later, at Everton, I formed a close bond with the physio, Danny Donachie. I've never needed someone to inspire me as an athlete—I've always had plenty of self-drive and motivation. But, off the pitch, I was looking for someone to stimulate my mind when it came to conversations other than football. Danny and I often spent hours talking in the physio room.

One afternoon, Danny had a visitor come to speak to the Everton team, a well-known Indian mystic called Sadhguru. He's a small man, with a long white beard and a soft-spoken demeanour, a spiritual teacher to hundreds of thousands of people throughout the world.

I was immediately impressed when I heard how Sadhguru helps his followers take anxiety and negativity out of their minds. One of the things he told us was that we should stop creating mental obstacles that simply aren't there. He talked to us about proper breathing—through the nose, deep into the lungs, out through mouth—classic yoga breath work that helps with relaxation, balance and mental clarity.

I'd never explored any Eastern philosophies, though I always felt myself to be very spiritual. I get that from my grandmother and my mum. The three of us would often have premonitions about each other. My mum and grandmother were also the ones to pass along certain beliefs from our Samoan culture, such as "You should never do an act of kindness expecting something in return."

Despite that, when Danny introduced me to Sadghuru I initially was a bit of a sceptic.

"Why should I believe you?"

"You don't have to," he said. "I'm just giving you my ideas about the world. Take what you want and leave what you don't want."

He had a warm demeanour, a good sense of humour, and after chatting a bit about my family and playing career, he smiled at me.

"Tim, what do you fear?"

I took a long moment to think before answering.

"I'm scared of dying," I said. "I suppose that's the only thing I fear."

"And why do you fear dying?"

I told him I feared dying because it would mean leaving my children, Bek, my parents, my brothers and my sister. "I'd never again see all the people I love," I said.

He smiled and reassured me that Bek and I had instilled the proper values in our kids and that I shouldn't worry about how the rest of my family would carry on if I wasn't physically present in their lives.

The talk with Sadhguru about my fear of dying was one of the most enlightening moments of my life.

That night, I had the longest and deepest night's sleep I'd had in years.

There's an expression of Sadhguru's that I really like. "I'm not the body. I'm not even the mind." I started to say it over and over, as a part of my mental preparations each day. For me, it's about understanding how much of life is beyond your control and that the best thing you can do is let go—to free yourself from worry and self-doubt. I now believe that mental training, including the kind that Sadhguru teaches, can help you cope with thoughts and anxious feelings that may be irrational and at times overwhelming.

You might not even be aware of them. I wasn't aware of how that attack when I was a kid played a role in the way I feared death and was concerned for my family as an adult, but it was there. I can't say I've never had a nightmare since I met Sadhguru, or that I've never had a sleepless night—we all do from time to time—but I learned something very important from him, and I repeat that simple mantra often, both on and off the pitch.

I'm not the body. I'm not even the mind.

Some of Sadhguru's devotees say it aloud, sitting in lotus position—that's traditional yoga. I just put on one of Sadhguru's CDs—a guided meditation—lie down in bed and listen for fifteen minutes either before I go to sleep or when I first wake up.

It's a difficult meditation to grasp but, in a nutshell, it simplifies life. Once you have this awareness, you start to recognize that thinking is a conscious process. Thoughts are things you can control; you can *choose* to set them aside. If you want to have a thought, you let yourself think it—otherwise it's almost as if there's nothing but stillness and calm in your head. That's what Sadghuru calls "the beauty of emptiness". It takes many hours—some say years—to achieve, but you can train yourself to reach a state of inner calm. What I love about this type of meditation is that you can do it almost anywhere— at the gym, in the swimming pool, even driving a car—and you simply become aware that while *you* are "here", your mind is somewhere out "there". Once you realize and accept the distance, whatever stray thoughts, distractions and anxieties are firing around in your brain actually have little effect on you.

I'll often repeat these simple words silently on the football pitch—*I'm not the body, I'm not even the mind*—and feel liberated. It actually makes you feel free of some of the constraints of the physical world. It can help you, in an anxious or pressure-filled situation—a Premier League or World Cup match being watched by millions—to see yourself in a more detached way. Almost in the third person. In the heat of a football match, a bit of detachment and distance—calming your senses, freeing your mind from the constraints of fear— can make all the difference.

*

I made another important spiritual journey during my Everton years—and again, this one took me deep back into my own past. My grandfather, the chief of the village of Tufuiopa in Samoa, had a tattoo from his neck all the way down to his knees. It was done by tapping, the traditional way, with a shark's tooth and a steel bit: slowly, dipping it in ink, wiping away the blood. That traditional Samoan technique dates back thousands of years. Doing even a small tattoo by tapping can take forever, so you can imagine how many hours it took to tattoo my grandfather from neck to knees.

Samoans are considered inventors of the art of tattooing. In the Pacific islands, it's not something taken lightly. Tattoos aren't fashion. It's a deeply spiritual ritual. In fact, for Samoans, every mark and symbol in a tattoo has a special meaning and the ceremony itself has the power of tradition, culture and religion. Every single man in my family has a marking of some kind. My older brother Sean started with a captain's armband as a sign of respect for my late grandfather. He'd asked my mother and grandmother for permission first and gave the appropriate reason—said he was getting tattooed as a sign of respect to our country, village and family.

I was young at the time and said to Sean, "What? You're crazy! How can you do that, man? *Needles* in your arm? And it's going to be sore for weeks ..." I hate needles. To this day, I can't even stand getting the blood tests required during routine medicals.

I was still too immature to understand the meaning. Sean connected with the passion and pride of our Samoan culture long before I did.

My grandmother was always the spiritual head of the family. As I said, my nan, my mum and I had an unspoken three-way connection. Throughout my childhood, I could tell my grandmother stories about things on a football pitch, on a playground, at school, and she would often act as if she knew about them already.

In May 2005, my grandmother died during a visit to Australia. She was surrounded by family and, in her final moments, I know she was at peace. Her death hit me hard, but it also brought everyone in the family a bit closer together.

I never thought I would get a tattoo, but after Nan passed away, I decided it was time to pay tribute to her. During the off-season of 2008, I organized a large party of fourteen family members to travel to Samoa—my parents, Bek and the kids, and my three siblings.

We first went to spend time at my grandmother's house then paid tribute at the graves where the family are buried. We were staying at a resort called Aggie Grey's on the water. I arranged to have Junior Suluape, a renowned tattoo artist on the island, come do my entire left arm. I'd left Everton with no ink anywhere on my body and would return with an entire sleeve.

Junior set up his equipment in the hotel room, starting at about six in the evening. He kept asking me questions as he drew freehand lines on my arm. I explained that every inch of my tattoo had to have meaning. It had to start with my grandmother, to whom I was paying homage, and include every single family member as well as Bek and the kids, leaving space to add more children—my own, my nephews and nieces—in the years to come.

He started on one patch, which was my grandmother's lifeline, working in the traditional style, though done with a modern tattoo-gun, not the shark's-tooth tapping of my grandfather's era. Still, the work is as traditionally Samoan as we could make it. My grandmother's lifeline turns into my lifeline, and next to my lifeline are my mum's and dad's. Next to that is what gives me my livelihood: my football career. Junior carefully lettered in Millwall Football Club and Everton Football Club. I have my sons and my grandfather, each with his own unique symbol. My daughter, Sienna, is represented by a diamond, my wife by a flower, and so on. My two brothers, my sister and all my nephews and nieces and many cousins are also included.

Any Samoan can look at my arm and read it, just like an autobiography, and see the entire story of my life going back to my grandparents.

I sat there, watching Junior at work—the tattoo-gun buzzing, his hand carefully wiping away blood—for fourteen hours nonstop. Throughout, I had my mum and dad come in, my sister, then my kids. The process went on all night, into the dawn, Junior asking me if I needed a break, but we kept going without stopping.

Honestly, I was never fully *aware* of the pain. I was in a kind of trance. I can only describe it as feeling fearless, the way my brother Sean always seemed. I knew this was all a tribute to my grandmother, so I willed myself to not feel the pain. During parts of the tattooing, I ran through the whole range of emotions: sometimes laughing, sometimes melancholy, sometimes ecstatic. At times I was even singing.

Fourteen hours later, after the tattoo was done, all the family members came in to see me. Someone had a bottle of Jack Daniel's. We started saying "Cheers!" and "To Nan!" and eventually drank to all members of the family.

For some reason, I didn't bleed much. The general rule when you get a tattoo is to be very careful in the days and weeks afterward, and maintain proper hygiene. This is especially important with a full sleeve tattoo because they're easily infected. You're supposed to smooth it over with antibiotic ointment and cover it in plastic wrap for showering. But after my celebration with my family, I was so happy I ran into the ocean, had a wash in the salt water and then carefully dried my arm.

I'd begun a new chapter in my journey.

I felt that it was time to attack life refreshed, to take on new challenges. Most importantly, after getting the tattoo, I felt *safe*. According to our Samoan belief system, everywhere I go—on and off the pitch—I am forever protected by my grandmother.

*

But, of course, there are no *saints* on a football pitch. There are no spiritually enlightened mystics either. It doesn't matter how emotionally centred and mentally focussed you are most of the time, there are always moments on the park, or in real life, when you simply lose your mental clarity. You slip up. You let another player get under your skin. It happens to the best of us.

It happened to me, famously, in May 2012—one of the most controversial moments of my Everton years. It was when I was sent off in a game against Newcastle after getting into a confrontation on the pitch with Yohan Cabaye, the French international who was then a central midfielder with the Magpies. Much was written about that incident, including wild speculation in press commentary and on the Internet, but until now I've never publicly told anyone the whole story behind that pretty notorious red card.

It was our last match of the season. I was on the bench to start. Beautiful day at Goodison Park, the fans were out in force, everyone was buzzing.

The game was feisty, on and off the pitch. In the first half Cabaye had shoved one of the Everton ball boys, and that created quite a ruckus. He apologized for it, but I was shocked. I'd been a ball boy myself as a youth player with Sydney Olympic, so I couldn't imagine why any professional footballer—any adult man, for that matter—would feel the need to shove a young kid. When I saw it, I was angry. It upset a lot of us on the Everton side. But Cabaye apologized, so I let it go. In general, I try not to take things personally on the pitch.

I'd played against Cabaye a few times and I knew it wasn't out of character for him to do that sort of thing. I'd always found him to be one of those players who liked provoking situations just for the hell of it—talking a lot in your ear, winding you up, trying to get a reaction. Call it gamesmanship, but with him it was usually of a pretty ugly nature.

In the second half, the boss called me over and said: "Tim, get ready. Time to go on. Go in the midfield, protect the back four. Be disciplined. Make the box if you can."

The Magpies were playing with great energy. Bullying us in the middle, staying strong at the back. Going in trying to win a challenge, I caught one of the Newcastle players; I mistimed the tackle a bit, came in late and fouled him, but nothing malicious. I helped him up to his feet, he shook it off, then he ran off into position. Out of the blue, Cabaye came up to me and started screaming in my face. I knew French was his first language, so at first I thought I might have misheard him.

"Excuse me, mate?" I said.

"Fuck your mum!"

He shouted it again.

"Fuck your mum!"

"Listen, I don't know you," I said, "and you definitely don't know me …

"Fuck your mum!" It was ludicrous the way the words kept coming out of his mouth—almost like his tongue was on autopilot.

"Do you even *understand* what you're saying? I know you don't speak English, but still—you'd better watch your mouth."

He was looking at me more aggressively, squinting his eyes, and saying it with more force. "*Fuck* your mum!"

I turned to two of his team-mates, Ameobi and Coloccini.

"You let him know," I said. "Tell him he'd better watch what he's saying." Then to Cabaye: "Players like you don't understand the game of football."

Then he said it again.

Cabaye and I were separated, but now my Samoan temper was getting the better of me. Whether or not Cabaye understood English, just from the way he was glaring at me and the aggression in his voice, it was evident he intended to be really offensive.

The whistle blew for the restart. All my team-mates knew what was up. Even the boss, from the touchline, knew something bad was brewing.

At this point, the game became completely irrelevant to me. I flashed angrier than I've ever been on a football pitch.

My eyes were only for Cabaye.

"You're finished," I said, when I got within earshot.

Now I was the aggressive one, tracking him everywhere, ready to clatter him in a challenge if I got half a chance. Cabaye's tone changed, he was now running scared. He did everything he could to steer away from me.

Everyone knew my head was *gone*. The boss could see it from the touchline. Our players were trying to settle me down. Cabaye's team-mates were trying to settle me down. The referee was trying to settle me down.

I didn't want to hear any of them. I didn't care if he was a fluent English speaker or not. I wanted to hear an apology. That was my mum he was talking about—the woman who'd sacrificed so much of her life to make it possible for me to be out there on that football pitch.

As soon as the final whistle blew, I made straight for Cabaye. I told him now to say those same words again, to my face, in front of all his team-mates. He kept talking at me, angrily, and then I grabbed his throat. Hard. He was struggling. Serious business.

Rarely do I see red mist, but I was seeing it then.

I drew a straight red card. The referee showed Cabaye a yellow.

Highly unusual scene, especially after the final whistle of a football match.

To be honest, only by later watching the video did I understand how incensed I looked to the crowd at Goodison and the fans watching at home.

For me, this had gone beyond a football game; we'd crossed over into something personal. All I expected from Cabaye was an apology. I've made bad mistakes on the pitch—been sent off loads of times. The rule of thumb among footballers is this: apologize straightaway if you've done something stupid. I wanted Cabaye to know that when you make such an offensive remark about another player's mother, grandmother or sister, over and over, looking them squarely in the eyes—at least the way I was brought up as a Samoan—there are *always* going to be consequences.

On my way off the pitch, I walked past David Moyes and offered my own apology. "Sorry, boss," I said. He wasn't annoyed, just wanted me to cool off. "Go inside, son. See you in a minute."

I knew you should never take to heart what other players say on the pitch. Never. That's always been my rule. People say unbelievably nasty things on the pitch—just winding you up. Looking back now, should I have been the bigger man and walked away? Yeah, maybe. Fair enough, I'll take that criticism.

After the match, Cabaye issued a statement on the Newcastle website, clearly written by the club's publicist: "I would like to apologise for the cross words I exchanged with Tim Cahill which resulted in his red card and my booking on the final whistle". I made my own statement, saying that his language had "no place on or off the football pitch".

Speculation was rampant. Most Everton and Newcastle fans were thinking I was still angry with Cabaye for shoving our ball boy.

My dad, however, knew better.

After the match we got straight on the phone.

"Tim, I know just what happened."

"What? No, you don't," I said.

"Yeah, he said something about your mother."

Then we both laughed. Truth be told, if Cabaye had said something about my *dad*—fine, whatever, I'd probably have shrugged it off. As soon as I hung up, I got a call from my brother Sean. He was laughing as well.

"Cabaye said something about Mum, right?" he said.

*

For me, as a kid back in the inner-west suburbs of Sydney, it all started with dreams in the back garden, dreams of playing in World Cups and at Old Trafford and Stamford Bridge, dreams of crazy bicycle-kick goals and left-footed volleys and furious last-minute comebacks.

I was lucky enough during my days at Everton to turn many of my dreams into reality.

In 2010, Manchester United were a devastating team, loaded with talented individuals who could cut you to ribbons if you had just a momentary lapse. In our October match at Goodison we went up 1–0 with Steven Pienaar's goal just before half-time. We had the momentum and then—as happens to even the best teams—the wheels simply fell off. Darren Fletcher scored the equalizer for United within four minutes, then Nemanja Vidic and Dimitar Berbatov added goals to put them up 3–1.

United looked like they were blowing past us—Goodison Park went quiet. Rarely does Goodison go that quiet. Soon the fans were grumbling. We heard some booing. I looked over at David Moyes and could see he was restless. Players on the bench had their heads dropped. That wasn't like us at all.

One thing I'd learned—at Everton, if you're going to lose 3–1, you had better lose *fighting*. No hanging of the heads, no throwing in the towel. If we lost badly to a visiting powerhouse like Manchester United but still gave it everything, lunging into the last challenges, then we'd likely be clapped off the park. The Everton fans only turn on you if they think you're not giving your all for that badge.

It was nearing the final minutes and I was muttering under my breath. I didn't want to go home, watch the highlights on *Match of the Day*, eating a takeaway, and feel miserable that we hadn't performed.

Enough of this rubbish, I thought. *We need to start winning the hard challenges. We need to bloody well get in their faces …*

It was the ninetieth minute and the game looked out of reach. We knew we'd only have, at most, two or three minutes of injury time. I decided to take the weight on my shoulders: something needed to happen. Right now. To get off to a 1–0 start, then fall down to three straight goals, was just not *acceptable*. It was not *Everton*.

I started shouting to the boys behind me:

"If we can claw just one goal back, lads, we're still in this!"

I took on Cristiano Ronaldo in a tackle; that seemed to lend the match a new-found tone of scrappiness. One thing I knew for sure. Manchester United had brilliant, skilled players, but they weren't as hard as us. After we won a few good challenges, our players had an added spring in their step.

The first minute of injury time: we made a break forward, the cross came in from Baines on the left—I leaped and got great contact on a header. It was one of those near-perfect moments: time froze, the keeper scrambled, the defenders leaped, but I knew I had the edge on them. The ball left my forehead and ripped into the net.

I ran into the goalmouth and grabbed the ball, leading the charge back to the halfway line, ready for the kick-off. We probably only had another minute, maybe only seconds, but it didn't matter as long as we made a final charge.

All of a sudden, the mood of the match had changed. My fire had become infectious. Goodison was roaring. When someone sparks something, everyone wants to be a part of it. The gaffer was on the sideline, screaming out orders.

"Keep your heads! Keep your discipline—but let's get another one!"

In the second minute of injury time, another ball came over and I could see where Mikel Arteta was positioned at the edge of the box.

Normally, I'd have gone for another header on goal, but in this instance there were too many defenders swarming around me. There wasn't much chance of getting enough purchase for a strong header on target. Instead, I leaped and used my forehead, not for *power*—just gently cushioning the ball down into the path of Mikel who was tearing forward and shouting.

I'd set the table perfectly. Mickey ran up and smashed it through the forest of defenders.

Back of the net!

Somehow or other, at the death of the game, we'd tied things up. To claw back from 3–1 down to draw 3–3 felt like we'd carried the day. Not in terms of points in the table, of course, but as a moral victory, a major comeback against, of all teams, Manchester United. It was a draw that felt like a victory.

Normally, when you play United and they're on a tear, scoring three goals, it's impossible to stop them, but somehow— through grit, belief and heart—we'd managed to do it. At the final whistle, I had my arm draped around Mikel's shoulder, both our jerseys soaking wet. We were whacked, ready to collapse. We'd been running like madmen, probably each covering twelve or thirteen kilometres during the match.

*

Another favourite Everton memory was an away match in November 2007 at Stamford Bridge. That's such a beautiful stadium to play at; many of our fans would travel to London for those matches. They'd be in the top left-hand corner of the stand as you walk up out of the tunnel. They never stopped chanting and singing the whole match.

One thing about Chelsea—they'd always allow us good possession; they'd give us space to play football. But when they won the ball back—man, they could ping it about quickly and punish you on the counter.

In the seventy-first minute, Didier Drogba scored to give them the lead. We pressed on but couldn't equalize. In the final ten minutes we had to throw everything we had at them. James McFadden ran down the line and unleashed a shot-cross. As Faddy's ball swung over into the goal area, it took this strange bounce.

Should I swivel and try to hook into the goal? Tough play. Their defender, the Brazilian Juliano Belletti, was right up my back.

I squared my shoulders—back to the goal—took my stance, the ball popped up, hanging there in mid-air. It was one of those moments when you think: *Why not? Take a shot at the title. Either it hits the back of the net—or goes in Row Z. If it goes in Row Z—so what? At least I tried to grab that moment ...*

I positioned myself for an overhead scissor kick, planted my left leg, leaped up off the ground. From that point, it's pure chain reaction. You're no longer consciously thinking. When I struck the ball with my right boot I knew that I couldn't have made any better contact. Once again, the keeper had no chance. The ball whipped past Peter Cech and hit the back of the net with power. On my back, popping my head round, I could see the net rippling, the away fans going mad up in the top left-hand corner of the stand.

I ran over and did my boxing celebration against the corner flag. I looked over at the gaffer—man, David Moyes was happy! For me, the best part of that moment was knowing we'd provided value for money: a bicycle-kick goal in the dying minutes of the game makes the away journey worthwhile for the fans. It's a weekend trip for them, costs them a few hundred pounds.

I tried to give them their money's worth and also left them a priceless memory. Any kid there at Stamford Bridge with his dad will remember that goal for years to come. A goal like that also reminds you that, even though football's a high-pressure business at times, at the most fundamental level it's also fun and spontaneous. Scoring an overhead scissor-kick goal reminds you of all the reasons you fell in love with the sport as a kid.

*

When you've been a Blue, nothing reverberates in your memory like those Merseyside derbies. Rolling back the years, one of the most fantastic moments at Everton was my third derby.

It was September 2006. I'd scored in two prior matches against the Reds, but both were Everton losses. Still, I was gaining a reputation among our fans for being one of the Blues who could be counted on to step up big against Liverpool.

I remember it being a hot, brilliantly sunny day in Liverpool. Hours before kick-off, the fans outside and inside the park were already in full voice. The changing room was buzzing. The boss was confident, telling us in the pre-match talk that we needed to seize this moment and show our growth as a team.

We were champing at the bit to get out there on the pitch. As we came out to the strains of "Z-Cars", the Goodison grounds never looked more stunning in that blinding sunlight. The groundsmen had just run the sprinklers—ensuring that the ball would zip around the park quicker—and the tips of the freshly mowed grass were glistening.

I was sure the game would be decided by the midfield battle. I had my own strategy: focus on their two playmakers: Xabi Alonso, the spectacular Spanish international, and Stevie Gerrard, always the inspirational captain of their team. Anytime you could stop their two playmakers from getting into a rhythm, Liverpool would no longer be a dynamic force.

As always, I said to the boys: "Don't let them win the first tackle." In the seconds before kick-off, I could see a similar passion in Gerrard's eyes: he was thinking, just like me, that the tone would be set by the early challenges.

Right before the whistle, I glanced back at Tony Hibbert, our right-back, shouting:

"Hibber! You're the man!"

Tony, like me, loved getting in that first heavy lunge.

At kick-off, our fans were roaring. Liverpool's fans in the away corner were roaring almost as loud. But it wasn't Hibbert or me who set the tone. Lee Carsley got in the first proper tackle, hard but clean, winning us the ball. Nothing vicious. Just English football. You could hear our fans shouting their appreciation.

Man, the tempo was quick—the ball zipping about—not much dribbling from anyone. No one *wanted* to hold the ball because the tackles from both sides were getting vicious.

As I expected, the main battle on the pitch was in the midfield and before too long I was getting into some physical exchanges with Xabi Alonso. That's funny, too, because Xabi is a friend of mine—we were both best men at Mikel Arteta's wedding.

But in the derby you don't have friends.

The ball broke out to the flank, Xabi and I charged for it and we both went down, his body sliding under me. The way I shifted my weight, and the way my arm fell, I had him in a headlock, something you don't often see in football. And, of course, someone snapped a great image. Just like the photo of me on top of the dog pile when Lee Carsley scored in my first-ever derby, this one has also become a favourite. Honestly, it looks like I'm trying to remove Xabi's head from his neck.

The whistle didn't blow and I was laughing. "Don't even try moving, mate," I said, glancing down to Xabi. I held him there like I had him pinned on a wrestling mat and was waiting for him to tap out. I wanted to give our guys some time to break free with the ball. "Nah, don't bother, mate—you're staying *here* ..."

Those psychological battles help you in any match, but especially during the Merseyside derby. It's not mean spirited, you just want to give your opposite number a reminder that you're there on his shoulder. As the game went on, we took control of the run of play. The only thing we were lacking was a goal.

After twenty-three minutes, we broke forward. Mikel Arteta passed to Lee Carsley; Leon Osman out-muscled Steve Finnan, and somehow out of that mix the ball popped loose into the box. I had broken free of my marker, down the right, and saw the ball bouncing free. No time to settle it with a first touch. I met it on the half-volley, hooked it with my right foot, beating Pepe Reina at the near post.

Game on! I boxed the corner flag, ran to the edge of the pitch and jumped all over the Everton fans. My team-mates were trying to hug me, but I kept shoving them way.

I don't even know what I'm doing when I celebrate some of my goals. I'm in a state bordering on frenzy. The lads used to call me a crazy Samoan the way I ran about. Only seeing the highlights later on *Match of the Day* did I realize how manic I looked.

From the moment I scored we took absolute control. Liverpool had us under pressure for moments, but we went on a romp. Our striker Andy Johnson scored twelve minutes after my opener. In the second half, Andy got his brace to make it a 3–0 drubbing at the final whistle.

You don't know it as a player in the thick of the match, but afterward you hear a game being described as *historic*. All the reporters, all the old-timers at the club—the guys like Jimmy Comer and Danny Donachie—have those records in the back of their heads. We quickly learned that this was the first time

Everton had scored three goals in a derby since 1966 and the first time at Goodison Park since 1904.

I'm not sure there was ever a happier moment to be a Blue. In the changing room, we were shouting nonstop. Banging the walls. Making sure Liverpool could hear us in their adjacent changing room. A bit of payback: they'd always do that to us when we lost derbies at Anfield.

We didn't win many of the derbies during my time as a Blue, and 3–0 at home had us singing and laughing, arms round each other's shoulders. It was a match that seemed to capture everything that made Everton a great football club.

We slapped the walls of the changing room until our palms hurt—*nobody* was going to tell us to shut up. And it was sweeter still when we heard that Everton were top of the Premier League table. The parties in the Blue half of Merseyside went on for a week.

PART
04

GLORY

AMERICA

WHILE EVERTON WERE IN SCOTLAND on a pre-season tour in the late summer of 2012, I got a call from my agent, Paul Martin, with a surprising offer: to fly to America and play immediately that summer—starting mid-season—with the New York Red Bulls of the Major League Soccer (MLS).

I'd now spent eight years at Everton, things were still going well and the camaraderie with the boys was as strong as ever. So I was very unsure. I still loved English football, but after fifteen years in the Second Division, the First Division and the Premier League, I was *spent*. If you want to talk strictly about the pace and intensity and the toll the sport takes on your body, for me there's no debate. The Premiership is the fastest, toughest and most physical league in the world— bar none.

Many top players have to juggle the demands of playing for both club and country, but for those of us from Australia playing in the Premiership, the travelling logistics were simply brutal. There were times I'd play a match at Goodison Park on a Saturday, fly all day Sunday to Australia for a World Cup qualifier, train on Monday with the Socceroos, play the international match on Wednesday, fly back to Liverpool on Thursday, get in one day's training on Friday, and play the Saturday match for Everton again. It was unrelenting. Some of my Everton team-mates said I must be some kind of machine—and I suppose I was. They used to refer to me as The Robot.

I'd learned so much living in Liverpool. Part of what makes Liverpool such a great city is that its heart beats to the tempo of two football clubs, the Blues and the Reds. Coming from Australia, I'd never seen anything like it. Playing at Everton for years and years, you had no choice: you get a bit of Merseyside in your blood. We'd all—even those of us with no family connection to Merseyside—picked up the Scouse flavour. For example, we'd all add "Laa"—that's Liverpool slang for "lad"—to our names. I'd be "Tim-Laa." Tony Hibbert would be "Hib-Laa," Leon Osman "Oz-Laa."

I wasn't sure I was ready to leave Liverpool—my wife and I had a beautiful home, and were raising our four kids—in addition to Kyah, Shae and Sienna, by this time we had a baby boy called Cruz—in a pleasant neighbourhood. Still, I've always liked the challenge of trying something radically new. And I knew a bit about the MLS. Every other year Everton would travel to the US for exhibition games against MLS teams. I'd talked to David Beckham about playing with the LA Galaxy, I'd met Landon Donovan, and of course I'd played alongside keeper Tim Howard at Everton, who had many years' experience in the MLS.

Those trips to the US were always a lot of fun. There'd be fireworks and live music before the games, and to those of us more familiar with the pressure-cooker atmosphere of the Premiership, it was a nice change of pace.

The MLS promised to be a major departure, and a crucial factor in my decision was the fact that Gérard Houllier was the Red Bulls' international sporting director for football. Houllier and I had history together in various World Cups and in the Premiership when he was at the helm at Liverpool. We shared a vision: he knew I had an eye for the goal, was now a veteran leader and made all my decisions with a long-range strategy in mind.

In addition to Gérard Houllier, there was the chance to team up with Thierry Henry, one of the true Arsenal greats. I'd played against him in the Premiership and found him to be one of the smartest, most skilful players I'd ever seen. To be able to link up with a finisher like that—me as an attacking-midfielder, supplying him with service—would be fantastic.

I was torn, thinking of leaving Everton. But by now the team was evolving and I wasn't honestly sure how much of a role I'd have there in the coming years. Already, in that final season, my playing minutes had drastically diminished. I was in the dugout, subbing in for the final fifteen or twenty minutes, sometimes not at all.

Now I had five or six days to make a very quick decision about leaving the world I knew. I'd have loved nothing more than to play out my entire career with Everton—I still had two years on my contract—but I knew in my heart that it was time to leave, for two reasons: my country and my family.

I knew if I wanted to keep playing with the Socceroos, I had to say farewell to Goodison Park. By 2012–13, my match time had dwindled so much that I knew it could be the death knell of my career as an international. I had to go to a competitive league that still gave me enough high-level playing time so that I could be selected by the national team manager. I had my eyes on the two biggest tournaments on the horizon: the 2014 World Cup and the 2015 Asian Cup. I felt my country needed me; certainly the Socceroos could use my services—and my leadership role—more than Everton.

A move to the New York Red Bulls seemed the perfect solution. I'd be a starter, getting enough playing time to satisfy the Socceroos' manager, but it would be at the much less harried pace of the MLS, allowing my body time to recover for international duty. After that initial phone call from Paul Martin, we did the deal remarkably quickly—in less than a week.

As it unfolded, I went to talk to only one person in the Blues family.

"You're not leaving," David Moyes said. "You're not done here yet, lad. You've got some good years left here at Everton."

I told him my vision for my final years in football: to go overseas and to enjoy myself, play in a league where the pace was less frenetic and less stressful, so that I could have a bit of a private life again and still represent my country.

In the end, David respected my decision. We finished the meeting with a hug. I laughed at the memory of that *other* hug—on the touchline after I'd scored my first-ever goal for Everton and got teased mercilessly by the lads about being *Son-of-the-Gaffer.*

David Moyes had believed in me from the start and I hoped I'd repaid his faith in my potential. In those eight years at Everton, I'd played 256 matches and scored sixty-eight goals— quite a decent haul for a midfield player—making me one of the highest-scoring Blues in recent history. Most importantly, David knew I'd given everything I had, both mentally and physically, to being a Blue.

The one thing I asked David was not to tell any of my team-mates. I wanted to do that myself.

I rounded up all the physios and the old-timers—guys like Jimmy Martin, Tony Sage, Danny Donachie, Jimmy Comer, Dave Billows—and called them all to the medical treatment room. Throughout my years as a Blue, that's where we'd always congregate, where we went to recover and heal our wounds. I always said, "That's where the magic happens."

I brought together the people who were most important to me: Osman, Hibbert, Pienaar, Jagielka; the staff who had been with me since Day One, the players who'd been with me for so many moments on and off the park. They crowded into the treatment room, around the six medical beds.

"What's up, Tim-Laa?" Ozzy laughed.

"I've got something I need to tell you," I said.

"What's this? Tim-Laa suddenly getting serious?"

"Listen," I said. "I didn't want you to read about it or hear it anywhere else. I wanted to be the one to tell you. I'm leaving Everton."

They still thought I was pissing about.

"Yeah, right, you leaving? You're a Blue through and through."

"Spoke to the gaffer—I won't be playing this weekend and I leave for New York in four days."

"For where?"

"I'm signing with the New York Red Bulls."

"New York—what?"

They knew very little about the club other than that Thierry Henry was now there. Some were in disbelief, some thought I was still clowning around. There had been rumours in the press about a possible transfer to the Middle East or China.

But New York? MLS? That surprised them. Of course, they all wished me the best with my decision. I told them I'd always love the club and my team-mates. Even without wearing the badge, I'd always be an Everton supporter.

I had a private chat with Danny Donachie, the physio who'd become something of a life coach for me. "You never cease to amaze me, son," Danny said. "There are always so many surprises."

"Danny, I've *jumped* now. This is going to be one of the hardest tests I've ever faced." I told him I would be going to the Red Bulls as a high-profile overseas player and joining a club that had never won a trophy. "They're basically telling me, 'Cahill, you're coming here to win the Red Bulls some silverware,'" I said.

"Ah, come on, Tim," Danny said, smiling, "you love nothing better than pressure."

*

The other major reason to choose New York was my wife and kids. I'd already decided in my final year at Everton that I had to give back to my family.

I'd dedicated the whole of my twenties and now the start of my thirties to being selfish. Just being a full-time player. As far as my home life was concerned, it was non-existent. I was there physically, but I was often miles away emotionally. Sometimes we'd have three matches a week—Premiership fixtures, FA Cup ties, European tours, and then I'd go flying off for international duty with the Socceroos. There was no room for real quality time with the family. When I had the opportunity to leave Everton for New York, a large part of the decision had *nothing* to do with football. I saw it as a reward to my wife and kids.

While all the negotiations were unfolding, Rebecca was on holiday with the kids in Florida. On the phone I could hear they were having a fantastic time and I didn't want to tell her anything until I was sure the deal was rock solid. After four days of negotiations and coming to final terms, I called her up and told her to get ready for a new adventure.

"I'm signing a three-year contract," I said. "Leaving Everton."

"You're what?" Bek said.

"How do you feel about New York?" I said.

She knew I'd been contemplating a move somewhere, but it had all just been talk and speculation. But by that time all that was left was for me to get on a flight and pass an eight-hour medical.

As always, Bek was behind me all the way, especially once I explained that the demands on me as a footballer in the MLS would be much less than in the Premier League, and I'd be home to be a father and a husband a lot more. We'd experience a different culture, not as tourists to New York but as residents.

"Imagine that, nugget," I said. "I'll still get to play football but not at that crazy level where I've got *zero* time for a private life."

"Yeah," I heard Bek laugh. "Imagine that."

Bek had always been there to support my all-consuming passion, through injuries, the weeks and months of my absence, the long hours and hardships of air travel with the kids when she travelled with the family to see me play. My career in football had occupied centre stage in our life since we had met. Even to the extent that, after I'd proposed to her in Liverpool, it had taken us fully four years—until after the 2010 World Cup—to get married, in a beautiful ceremony in Las Vegas.

Without Bek, without my kids, there was no way I'd have made it this far and I felt a move to New York was one of best ways I could say thank you to her and my four children.

*

When I arrived at the Red Bulls headquarters in Harrison, New Jersey, my first impression was of how gorgeous the stadium was. I hadn't expected anywhere in the US to have a $250-million development just for football. During our Everton tours of the US, I'd noticed many of the pitches in the MLS weren't up to scratch—some were still made of older Astroturf—but the grass in the Red Bulls park was as good as any in the Premiership.

I'd watched a lot of Red Bulls games on video where the results were 5–2, 4–3, 6–2. What sport was I watching? Seemed like cricket or tennis scores at first. Ridiculously high-scoring, free-flowing play to a guy coming from the Premiership. And tactically, the play seemed very naive. It was clear that a massive financial investment by MLS was being made in football, but it was equally clear that the quality of play still left something to be desired.

Chemistry makes any club. As two of the big foreign stars in the Red Bulls, it was important that Thierry Henry and I connected. Building the sort of off-the-park and on-the-park connection I'd had with Mikel Arteta or Fizzer doesn't come quickly, of course. Those things can take *years*.

But Thierry and I immediately hit it off. His warmth and openness were a revelation. For a guy who's among the top strikers in football history—the leading all-time goal-scorer for *both* Arsenal and the French national team—Thierry's one of the most down-to-earth and soft-spoken players in the game.

In those early days we were both living in Manhattan. I was in the Crosby Hotel waiting for Rebecca and the kids to come over and get settled in America, so Thierry and I used to hang out a lot, having breakfasts and dinners.

One night, eating in a SoHo restaurant, I started laughing, remembering a match I'd played against him in the Premiership. Arsenal had come to play us at Goodison, wearing not their familiar red kit but a third kit in bright canary-yellow. Thierry had this wicked move where he stood on the left of the pitch, called for the ball, controlled the pass with his left, dragged it with his right and then—like a neon sign over his head reading GOODBYE—pure jet propulsion. His explosive pace and close control left you gasping. I reminded him of the Gunners' January 2006 visit to Goodison Park, where none of us—no midfielders or defenders—could mark him.

"You were *killing* us that day, mate," I said. Throughout the match, Thierry was running down the touchline, using that slick little drag and burst of explosive pace. Three or four times in succession, I was left for dead. The next time round was different. I lunged at him with full intent to trip him. My sliding tackle was nowhere near the ball, my studs up, attempting to sweep him off his feet—what footballers politely call a "professional" or "tactical" foul.

Someone at Goodison snapped a perfectly timed photograph and the image is on the Web, so I pulled it up on my phone to show him. He took my phone and stared at it for a long time, shaking his head. I'm so late on the challenge, it looks ludicrous.

"Man, that's *disgusting*," Thierry said. "Why didn't you get a red card?"

"I probably should have," I said. "But what did you want me to do? Let you run down the line again and score another goal? No fucking chance."

Sipping his coffee, he squinted at me in momentary disbelief, then shrugged his shoulders.

"But you know what?" I said. "After the game, you swapped jerseys with me."

"Yeah, that I *do* remember."

Luckily, I didn't have to mark Thierry anymore. Now we would be working in tandem and I could watch as Thierry— still, at the age of thirty-six—beat MLS defenders regularly with that right-footed drag and burst of pace. He'd have a smile on his face too, as if he knew he was unstoppable and was just taking the piss.

*

Coming in halfway through that season with the Red Bulls I knew we had a big problem with conceding goals. Our defensive position was, to put it mildly, atrocious. We'd concede in the first minute, then score, then concede in the twentieth minute. Our defensive midfielders were overcommitted; our back four were porous. It was as if we were leaking goals for fun.

I was signed as an attacking player but, on my own initiative, I often ended up playing defensive midfield, which is not my natural position by any means, but I'd learned my trade well at Everton. If there was one thing we knew how to do it was hold our shape and not concede.

Thierry would ask me: "Tim, why aren't you making it into the box?"

After all, that had been my natural role—I'm most comfortable as a box-to-box midfielder—arriving late, behind the strikers, poised for heading a cross or mopping up a loose ball to score.

"Look, Thierry," I said. "First and foremost, I've got to help us keep a tight ship." We had Rafa Marquez, the Mexican international, anchoring our back four and we had a world-class striker in Thierry up front.

As long as we gave the ball to Thierry, he had so much creativity, ingenuity and pace, he could always be counted on to score. The guy could make something out of nothing—all in the blink of an eye. If I could arrive late in the box to mop things up, catch a rebound, be ready for a back pass—great. But I knew the team was better served if I was a deadbolt in the midfield. In fact, I was playing the way Lee Carsley would at Everton. My primary job, I told Thierry, was to do all the graft, to destroy and disrupt the other teams' attacks, to shout my lungs out at the boys to keep in formation.

My analysis of the MLS was that the style of play was very exciting for the fans: you attack, we attack; you attack, we attack … all match long. It reminded me of the end-to-end action of the National Basketball Association, but it wasn't the style of football I was used to at Everton. I sat for hours studying videos of Red Bulls matches, honing in on the problem. There seemed to be little structure and no basic communication between the midfielders and the defenders.

At Everton, if we were up 1–0, we shut up shop and very few teams could break us down. Once we had a lead, we'd set up in two banks of four, with our two forwards, who were always high-pressing, defending from the front. Sometimes, in fact, David Moyes would have us shifting into a 4–6–0 formation, playing with no forwards at all—an almost impossible tactical formation to break down.

That was all I knew. I tried to bring that sense of order and discipline to the Red Bulls. I talked to Mike Petke, the Red

Bulls' manager, and to Thierry. "For me it's simple," I said. "4–4–2. End of argument. Two banks of four, solid, disciplined."

The 4–4–2 formation may no longer be fashionable, but it bloody well works. Keep a tight back four and four midfielders who know how to hold their shape and track back, and you won't be letting in a bucket-load of soft goals.

We formed a good midfield partnership and up front we'd play Thierry Henry and Bradley Wright-Philips. By the start of my first full season with New York, we could see great improvement. But because I wasn't coming forward much in attack—wasn't playing box-to-box—I was getting hammered by some very opinionated ex-players and commentators. I was on a sizable yearly contract—they never missed a chance to point out that I'd signed for $3.5 million—and I wasn't scoring many goals. I actually got into a bit of humorous banter with former US national team player, now ESPN soccer analyst, Taylor Twellman.

Twellman went on ESPN and his social media, repeatedly focussing on my high salary and lack of goals. The faithful Red Bulls supporters were coming to my defence on Twitter, but I finally sent out a message:

"Please don't entertain this Muppet," I wrote. "Let him keep sucking on that lemon."

I private-messaged Taylor and we had a long phone chat, man to man—I said my piece; he said his. Then we actually settled our little war of words amicably. From my perspective, analysts like Taylor—in fact much of the MLS coverage—

dwelled too much on obvious statistics: goals scored and assists. They never spoke about how well the defenders or goalkeepers played. The US is quite unlike England or Europe that way. What they failed to realize was the unexpected role I was assuming, doing the graft, the often tedious work of keeping the team shape. Focussing on my lack of goals, they'd not noticed how few goals we'd *conceded* since I'd arrived. They didn't appreciate how a low-scoring game, like a 1–1 draw away from home, was a tactical and moral victory—as it had been at Everton.

I've found that the best way to respond to criticism is on the park. When I scored both our goals in a 2–1 win over Toronto on 28 April 2013, in a moment of light-hearted banter I Tweeted, "Hey Taylor, how do you like dem apples?" and, all credit to him, he replied by posting a hilarious picture of himself on Instagram staring, straight-faced, at a big pile of Granny Smith apples. That had a lot of us in the Red Bulls dressing room laughing.

*

The MLS matches may not have been played at the level of football I'd been used to, week in and week out in England, but the entertainment value Commissioner Don Garber had instilled in the league was superb. Just brilliant. In the short time I'd been with the Red Bulls, I'd developed the highest regard for Commissioner Garber. He had an all-consuming passion for developing the league and his players, and ensuring that soccer gained a higher profile in the crowded and competitive American sports market. And the owners throughout the league—at Portland, the LA Galaxy, Columbus, and now the newest and most high-profile club, New York FC—are visionary businessmen. Fireworks, DJs at half-time: for me that was a massive eye-opener. It was so different from the Premier League—so family-oriented, so kid-friendly. In the MLS, it's about the total sport–entertainment *experience*—like going to a football match mixed with a live-music event and a taste of carnival thrown in.

Our manager, Mike Petke, was a youthful, enthusiastic, passionate American. Mike's a former player with the Red Bulls, actually a couple of years younger than me. Andy Roxburgh, the world-renowned sporting director of the Red Bulls, had brought in some new players, too, probably the most high-profile being the English striker, Bradley Wright-Philips. We now had something to work with and we had Thierry and me as proven veterans, well into our thirties, to lead the team in the years ahead.

We worked hard in camp, doing double sessions, with the conditioning trainers raising our fitness levels. Thierry and I talked a lot to Mike Petke about tactics and formations.

Both Mike and Andy Roxburgh understood my vision for remaking the tactics: now it was my job to get the rest of the team to follow suit. As much as possible, I wanted to bring the Everton atmosphere and ethics to the Red Bulls. I felt I could take us from a freewheeling and entertaining but defensively porous club to a solid, battling team.

By the time my first season with the Red Bulls was in full swing, we had tightened up our game. We began picking up some great early results, winning games 1–0, 1–0, 2–1. I believed that Thierry and Mike Petke were vital to making this happen, but the reason it happened at all was down to what I'd learned from David Moyes—and from players like Carsley, Stubbsy, Weir, Hibbert. It was all of those years of my apprenticeship and maturation as a Blue.

After those early games I started banging in a few goals, and the midfield partnership I had with Dax McCarty, Jonny Steele, Lloyd Sam and Eric Alexander was suddenly on fire. All I'd ever ask of my fellow midfielders was, "If you go forward, guys, make sure you track back."

I remember a few particularly big moments in the season. We played Seattle away, without Thierry. Throughout the season, he'd never play away games on Astroturf because of his sore Achilles tendon, which was understandable. After playing on certain Astroturf fields, I could barely walk for three days myself. But, without our star striker, I knew we would be pushed to get a result. Seattle scored, but I got the equalizer and that was a great moment of self-belief for the team.

Another fantastic memory of that 2013 season was when I scored the quickest goal ever recorded in the history of the MLS, in October, against the Houston Dynamo. Straight from the kick-off, Thierry played the ball back to Dax McCarty, I made a fast run directly downfield, took the long ball from Dax on my chest, one bounce, and whacked it with fury into the back of the net. Only eight seconds from kick-off—it's a record that still stands today. Funnily enough, that same season, I scored the latest goal ever recorded in the MLS—a header against Chicago to equalize in the ninety-sixth minute, stealing a point for us.

One of the best things for me as a Bull was the warm connection we developed with the fans at the Red Bulls Arena. It's not a huge stadium, but it's gorgeous, it's always filled and the fans were so appreciative of our improved level of play.

Late in the season, we went on a two-month undefeated run. In our final eleven games, I was in top form, scoring seven goals and adding two assists.

On 27 October 2013, beating the Chicago Fire at home in New Jersey, we won the Supporters' Shield, which is given to the team with the most points in the league at the end of the season.

Riding high on the Supporters' Shield honour, we entered the MLS Cup play-offs. We were knocked out, unfortunately, but we had achieved a lot, and I had made good on my signing promise to bring the club some silverware for the first time in its eighteen-year history. I was also named the Red Bulls' Most Valuable Player and as a member of the MLS All-Star team.

I was delighted that I was able to play a fantastic season of club football and still have my body in shape for the Australian national team duties. That's something I'd made clear from the moment I signed: that this was a strategic decision for me, at the age of thirty-two, to keep myself fit for a call-up to the Socceroos. Throughout it all, internationally, I was flying—I kept scoring goals for the Socceroos in friendlies and World Cup qualifiers—and looked forward to some potentially big matches wearing the green and gold.

BRAZIL AND BEYOND

QUALIFYING FOR THE 2014 WORLD CUP was our hardest campaign yet. Parity in the world game has made every match you play in qualifying—especially away games in the far-flung nations of Asia—potentially perilous.

Our manager now was Holger Osieck, a smart German tactician, who really had only one mandate: to get Australia to the Brazil 2014 tournament. We travelled all over the Middle East and Asia, playing in the brutal heat and in politically volatile countries such as Lebanon, Jordan, Oman and Iraq. Some of the conditions, even setting aside the desert heat, were extremely challenging. I remember our qualification game in Jordan—there wasn't even a proper changing area.

We just weren't in good form on the road, dropping valuable points against teams we should have beaten. The Socceroos could only draw 0–0 and then 2–2 against Oman, and we actually lost 2–1 to Jordan, which is unacceptable for a team of Australia's pedigree. Osieck got us through. Rocky road or not, he fulfilled his mandate and we booked our place in Brazil 2014, though not without considerable grumbling in the press back home about our inconsistent level of play.

Then, after qualifying, we found ourselves booked to play a couple of tough friendlies. There was one match against Brazil in September 2013; I had commitments to the Red Bulls and didn't travel with the team to Brasilia. We lost 6–0 and the press back home called it a total "humiliation".

The next friendly we played was away to France, in the Parc des Princes in Paris; I played in that match and again we were ripped apart, right from the opening kick-off, losing 6–0.

Friendlies or not, conceding twelve goals and scoring none was not a good omen on the eve of the World Cup. In the past we'd proven we could give a good account of ourselves against the likes of Uruguay and Italy. We were true Aussies that way, known for having that fighting spirit and pride in wearing the colours. We could play tight games and beat some of the world powers, but now we'd lost two games, one after the other. And not close ones, either; these had been proper thrashings.

While holding a team meeting after the game in France, we were told that Holger Osieck had been sacked by Football Federation Australia. I was upset and made no bones about telling the rest of the team in some very blunt language. As a player you should always own up to the fact that you've contributed, in some way or other, to any manager's firing.

Let's get one thing straight: Holger and I had our differences, some of which were well publicized in Australia, but, whatever our issues, we were always professional. I sought out Holger, and we sat and talked for a long time. I was telling him that, regardless of what anyone on the outside said, it had been the hardest of the three World Cup campaigns I'd been involved in, and I was grateful to him for the crucial role he'd played in getting us through.

*

On 23 October 2013, eight months before the World Cup in Brazil, the Socceroos made the bold decision to bring in Ange Postecoglou to coach the national team. Born in Athens, Greece, but raised in Australia, Ange had an impressive résumé as a manager—he was highly experienced at coaching at the club level in both Europe and the A-League.

But now everything was suddenly in flux. A major reshuffling was in the works: staff, players, tactics; nothing was fixed in stone. Day after day the media talked about the shake-ups. Big players were being dropped. Some of the best-known names weren't selected for camps; others were choosing to retire rather than risk being dropped. One by one, many of the faces I'd played with in the Socceroos were gone, falling by the wayside: Mark Schwarzer, Brett Everton, Bret Holman, Harry Kewell, Lucas Neill …

These were Australia's major football stars—players with whom I'd shared so many fantastic moments, both on and off the park, guys who'd been the backbone of the national squad for over a decade—and they had either to step aside or be left behind. Ange Postecoglou made no secret of the fact that the new face of the Socceroos was going to be fast, fired up and youthful.

Where did that leave guys like Mark Bresciano and me? Did I still have a role to play in the squad? Did Bresh? The media kept writing about it: *Will Tim Cahill be kept? Will Mark Bresciano be kept? Will the old guard go to yet another World Cup?*

I hadn't been dropped, but I also had no guarantee I would be picked. I spoke to my mum and dad and asked, with all these players falling by the wayside, should I perhaps do the safe thing: rule myself out, announce my retirement from the Socceroos? I talked it over with Rebecca as well. I thought back to the long legal battle with FIFA for my eligibility, Frank Farina's first call-up for that friendly against South Africa at Loftus Road. Seemed like a lifetime ago …

But why would I step back from something I'd fought so hard for? That FIFA eligibility legal battle had drawn out for years and years. I'd never fought for anything as diligently as I had fought for the honour of representing Australia as an international. I wouldn't be retiring because I felt I couldn't *contribute* to the Socceroos. I'd be retiring out of *fear*.

I let it be known that I would continue my national career, as long as the manager saw fit to call me into camp. I'd structured my entire life—coming to New York, playing for the Red Bulls—in order to be able to play for the Socceroos. Finally, word came through: I'd been selected for the squad and would go into my first camp run by Ange Postecoglou. At our first meeting, we exchanged minimal words. Throughout the whole camp—minimal words. I couldn't read him at all. But again, I never needed to be mates with my manager. I just needed to work hard and play for the team.

I'd been an international footballer long enough to know that I was now being tested again. Every single move I made was being watched, on and off the park. Your résumé and your past history meant nothing. At my age—entering my mid-thirties now—they would let me go at the first opportunity. No question—I'd be dropped in a heart beat. Same with Bresh. We'd be dropped from the selection if we didn't hold our own with the young lads, so we knew we had to prove ourselves all over again.

It was a nervous time, but I thrive on nervous energy. Under pressure on the football pitch, I've always thought the best players show up. The first camp we had was in Costa Rica and I impressed Ange. As with every national team camp, I came in ready. He had us under a microscope, watching our play, even noting the meals we ate, the hours we slept. The data from our club career too—in my case, all my statistics with the New York Red Bulls—were analysed. Everyone was on a level playing field. So long as I performed, regardless of my age, I'd be selected.

In March 2014, we played a friendly in London against Ecuador. We lost 4–3, but I scored a brace, making me the

Australian national team's all-time leading scorer. In the post-match meeting, Ange stood up and spoke about my work ethic. "Timmy comes into every camp and trains harder than anyone. He treats every game in the Socceroos' shirt like it's his last."

For my part, I could now see what made Ange tick. He wanted Australia to be fearless and courageous, play fast, transition smoothly, not hold the ball long. He was scientific. We could be one of the fittest national teams in the world. When we won games he wanted to know why we won; when we lost, he wanted to look at why. His knowledge of the game and his belief in Australia's potential were impressive. He was a great motivator and man manager, a lot like David Moyes. He knew how to get the best out of a group of individuals.

Ange fully believed that whenever you put eleven Australians on the pitch, they can hold their own against just about any country. We may not always be the most technically gifted eleven, but we'll fight to the final whistle.

"For the first time ever," I said, "I've found someone who loves the Socceroos more than I do."

As we went through the qualifiers, I started to reward his belief in me, scoring loads of goals. No one was sugar-coating the fact that I was getting older, but Ange also knew I was a true professional, always took care of my body, and was fully devoted to the Socceroos.

In his selection for camp, he went with youth, but he strategically called up Bresh, Mile Jedinak and me, Mile as captain, the three of us as unquestioned team leaders. It was a subtle use of the old and young. Ange knew he needed us for our experience, for our calming influence, because we'd been there before for the high-pressure matches.

*

Heading into the World Cup in Brazil, we were prepared to face three of the toughest teams in the entire sport. Australia had been tossed into the infamous Group of Death. It almost made you laugh. Every single World Cup—now three in a row for me—we seemed always to be facing teams who made it next to impossible for us to advance to the knockout rounds. This time it was the Netherlands, Spain and Chile ... everyone rated us rock bottom out of that lot.

Yet we were in good spirits; we had the best camp we'd ever had, hours and hours of preparation, working hard on our passing triangles, on our set plays, on our tactical discipline. Group of Death or not, we went into that World Cup with the intent to win. Never were we going to play negative football, never put ten or eleven men behind the ball—no matter who we were facing. Ange's philosophy was to play fearlessly in our first group-stage match against Chile.

Mile, Bresh and I made sure we had all the younger boys up for it. As the Cup was being played in South America, Chile were rated in the top five or six to win it. Alexis Sánchez, Arturo Vidal—these guys were budding young superstars—but the entire Chilean team was loaded with some awesome talent.

At the start of the game, Chile were playing loads of short balls, great possession football, then they switched direction, catching us on the back foot. They scored two goals very quickly. I looked at Mile, saying, "We're too deep! We're too far away from each other!" We needed to high-press them. We needed to rattle them a bit more.

"Step the fuck up!" I shouted. "All of us! Fuck it! 2–0 down—so what? We can do this!"

Mile was shouting too: "Play with some fucking pride!"

Something clicked in all the Socceroos: it was remarkable, because for the next fifteen minutes, I don't think Chile *touched* the ball. Not only were we playing faster, we were also playing *smarter*: longer balls, knowing we'd have the aerial advantage against their undersized defenders. I knew I could physically overpower any of my markers.

Mile started getting some crosses to me. I told our right-back, Ivan Franjic, if he was switching to attack, making an overlapping run down the right wing, "Just cross the ball into good areas, Cheech. Don't worry about putting it perfectly on my head. These guys can't cover me. You just worry about putting it over the first man. If it's me against the second defender, he's got no bloody chance in the air against me."

And, just like clockwork, Franjic put in a great cross over the first defender. I jumped a bit early, the defender tried to nudge me, but my shoulder was too high for him. As the ball came over, I felt as if I was hanging in midair for ages: I could see the whole goal laid out before me. Beautiful! My eyes were wide open. There was only one place the ball was going—across the grain, back in the direction from which it came. I said *good morning* to the ball and my technique was spot-on. I used the ball's natural pace, guided it back across the goalkeeper, who was glued in place, and hit the back of the net, exactly as Johnny Doyle had taught me so many years ago—in fact, I could almost hear Johnny's voice as it rippled the net.

I didn't celebrate—didn't run to box the corner flag—but dashed straight into the net and grabbed the ball. I could see fear in the Chileans' eyes. I turned to Mile and Bresh. "They're shitting themselves now," I said. "Any more crosses into this box, I've got them on toast."

We dominated the rest of that half and should have scored again, but we came out of that first half down 2–1. In the changing room, the boss clapped his hands loudly.

"Okay, not the best of starts, but you kept your composure, played good football, and got the goal back. Now let's go out and win it."

We came out after the break with real confidence. Our football was great. Now every man stood up to be counted. Mathew Leckie, in particular, had a cracker of a match. Early in the second half, I got a cross in from the right, I lost my marker, made a run for the near post and headed it nicely into the net—the tying goal!

But I groaned when I turned to see the linesman's flag was up. Disallowed! I was offside by literally the length of one size-eight football boot.

In the end, we couldn't manufacture another goal, but the 2–1 loss wasn't a fair reflection of the quality of our play. We looked at the match afterward and were proud. We gained a lot of respect from the footballing world and took confidence from that loss, knowing we'd turned the game around completely and played with heart.

*

In the Chile game, I'd picked up a yellow card—as I almost always to do in tournaments. But Ange wasn't exaggerating when he said I played every match in the green and gold as if it might be my last. All my challenges are physical and I'm often in the referee's book. No worries. Comes with the territory.

In the next game, against the Netherlands, the atmosphere was just incredible. The whole stadium was divided between our Green-and-Gold Army and their equally passionate orange-clad supporters. The day was hot, the crowd buzzing. I jogged around during warm-ups, found out just where my family were sitting.

No one rated us. No one gave us a chance in hell of winning the match, because the Netherlands had just spanked Spain, the reigning world champions, 5–1. And if they can beat Spain 5–1, all the commentators and supposed football experts thought, we'd be run off the park.

Ange didn't agree.

"Fellas," he said, before the match. "This is a winnable game for us."

We'd studied the Dutch for hours in video sessions. We'd seen the way they'd played Spain. We knew if you high-pressed the Netherlands they'd kick the ball long. We also knew that if we pressured their midfield, they'd play the ball back to the centre-backs. Their goalkeeper was relatively young and inexperienced. He might be rattled under the pressure of the big occasion.

Right before the game, I was in the changing room and, for some reason, started spewing up. Not nerves, but something wasn't right with me and I kept vomiting. Everyone wondered if was too sick to start.

"Just an upset stomach, no worries."

I hydrated, got my mind into the zone. We walked onto the field and belted out the national anthem; I glanced down the line and saw so many faces I'd played against and held in respect: Robin van Persie, Nigel de Jong, Arjen Robben, Wesley Sneijder. Some of them, in fact, were personal friends. Quality players throughout that Dutch line-up.

In the moments before kick-off I spread the word with the boys: "Let's get stuck into these guys. Straightaway. Take it to them physically. They're not going to want to *mix* it with us. De Jong might—but the rest of them won't."

The game started fast. The one thing I'll never forget is Mathew Leckie and I pressing really high: as we expected, the Dutch couldn't play it out from the back with our high-press tactics. I said to Mile: "I've never seen the Dutch kick the ball away so easily. Normally, they are such a possession and finesse team."

But again, as those young Socceroos often did early in matches, we shut off mentally for just a moment and were made to pay. In the twentieth minute, Robben went on a mazy run and scored a great goal—against the run of play, I'd say. It was just a moment of individual brilliance and we found ourselves down 1–0. Ange was shouting at us from the touchline, trying to make sure we kept our tactical shape.

"Stay calm, boys," he said.

I did.

In spite of the furious pace and the heat, and the fact that we were chasing the game, I remained in such a relaxed mental state. My body was churning. I was in the zone.

*

When it happened, there was a brilliant team build-up, with perfect understanding among the players. The ball started from the left and came out to our right-back, Ryan McGowan, deep in our half. The Dutch centre-backs were close to me—De Vrij and Vlaar. I made a run into empty space, arcing around them. I watched as Ryan McGowan struck the ball, curling it with his right foot, from a good forty metres. The only reason Ryan would even send such a searching ball to me is because he knows what I'm capable of. I never ask for the ball to be fizzed along the pitch to my feet. Send it into space—I'll make something out of nothing ...

The ball came curling over the top and I wondered if it would be best to head it, try to loop it—almost like a lob—over the keeper. Or should I bring it down on my chest, settle it with one touch, then shoot? But that would give their centre-halves too much time to close down the space. In that calm, trance-like state, I said to myself, No—*hit this first time. Don't let fear hold you back ...*

That's the method in my madness—it has been my whole career. I always tell myself: *What does it matter if I miss?* I've always done things that were spontaneous, and might seem a bit crazy to others. *Take the risk. No one's going to bloody care if it sails into Row Z. Why the hell not? Take another shot at the title.*

The ball came looping over my shoulder and I knew exactly where the goalkeeper was, where the defenders were. As the ball dropped, all conscious thoughts left my mind. There was just a Zen-like focus on technique: my timing and proper contact.

My left boot met the ball—immaculate contact. I drove my laces through it and it shot off like a rocket. For a fraction of a second, I thought the contact might almost be *too* good, that the ball would hit the crossbar and pop over. But it struck the bar precisely on the underside, bounced down and settled in the back of the net.

I stared at the goalkeeper and the defenders. Everyone was in complete shock.

I knew instantly that volley was one of the best goals of the tournament and my team-mates, as they surrounded me, were saying as much.

"What a strike!"

I ran off, boxed the corner flag, hugging all the boys, screaming at the top of my lungs.

As I ran back to our own half for the Dutch kick-off, it was one of those moments where you say to yourself, *You know what? I could retire now, never play another minute of football. That's the pinnacle—the greatest goal I will ever score ...*

*

In a perfect world, the game would have ended with us scoring another goal, winning the match and walking off the pitch in celebration. But this was a real-life World Cup match, not a Disney movie. We won a penalty on a Dutch handball and Mile Jedinak scored to put us in front. After that, however, we lost mental focus, then conceded a goal to Robin van Persie in the fifty-eighth minute. Just ten minutes later, Memphis Depay struck from twenty metres out to give the Netherlands a 3–2 lead. We chased the game hard, ran ourselves ragged, but were simply unable to equalize.

It was a game with a bit of everything—a back-and-forth slugfest—the most entertaining match of the Cup so far. For me the situation was even more bittersweet. In the forty-third minute, I'd gone into a challenge with the Dutch left-back Bruno Martins Indi—it was a bit reckless, on my part, but there was no intent to injure. He did get the worst of it, though, hit the ground hard and was stretchered off, and I picked up a yellow card. Now I had two bookings in the Group Stage, meaning I'd miss our final match against Spain.

Such a strange crush of media after the match. People were buzzing about the first half volley I'd hit, but also a lot of reporters, especially from Australia and the UK, asking me about my booking. The truth is, I never play a match—certainly not in an international tournament—thinking about the game to follow in three or four days. It's just not in my mental make-up.

When I go out onto the pitch, I play every match wholeheartedly for the team, I go hard and give every ounce of my passion. We *needed* to beat the Netherlands. The next match against Spain wasn't even on my mind. I honestly had no regrets about the two bookings. If I was holding back my play—in any way—to save myself from a yellow card, then I shouldn't have been on the pitch for the Socceroos.

It was tough to be on the bench watching the players go out there for the national anthem against Spain, the reigning World Cup holders. I had a couple of good mates in the opposition, including Pepe Reina and Xabi Alonso, my fellow best man at Mikel's wedding. And the Spanish were already knocked out of the tournament, so they were playing solely for pride. They'd lost both their matches and did not want the embarrassment of going from champions to finishing at the bottom of Group B. They got off to a nervy start in the opening half-hour, then soon caught their slick passing rhythm and gave us a thorough thrashing with goals from David Villa, Fernando Torres and Juan Mata. The final score was 3–0.

*

We'd failed to advance out of the Group of Death, but for me—and I think for a lot of Australian fans—Brazil 2014 will be remembered for that one goal, for that one special moment. No one ever talks about the Spain or Chile matches any more—they simply talk about that one unexpected strike against the Dutch.

A lot was later written and said about the so-called "wonder goal." It ended up being a finalist—though not the ultimate winner—for FIFA's 2014 Puskas Award, which honours the "most beautiful" goal of the year.

Those awards and rankings are so subjective that for me they're a bit pointless. What that goal represented was the culmination of years of hard slog, from the parks and pitches of Sydney to my years scrambling up through the ranks in England.

"I've always fought against adversity in football," I remember telling the press after the match. "When you have a heart that you learned from Millwall and Everton and a knowledge of how to play English-style football, you produce moments like that today. I score goals like that every day in the garden, so to do it on the biggest stage in the world, for Australia, makes me very proud."

From a technical aspect alone, true football people know what it took to score that goal: the ball travelled such a long distance. I chose not to trap it, but to hit it calmly and with power, with my *weaker* foot, and made perfect contact, beating the keeper with tremendous velocity.

Of course, I also heard some people calling it "a fluke". But I know the years of work that went into acquiring the technical ability, mental discipline, confidence and, most importantly, calmness to be able even to attempt that left-footed volley.

Leaving Brazil in 2014 was a bit emotional because I knew I'd likely played in my last World Cup. I'll continue to help the Socceroos in qualifying games, as Ange Postecoglou sees fit to call me up. But, by the 2018 tournament, I'll be thirty-eight years old, and I have to be honest with myself about my chances of being called up for the national team at that age.

Whatever happens, I can look back with pride at how far the Socceroos have come during my time wearing the green and gold: from not appearing in football's biggest tournament since 1974, we've now qualified—earning some fantastic, spirited results and scoring some memorable goals—in three consecutive World Cups.

And the truth is, almost from the final whistle against Spain, we were looking *forward,* not back. All of the Socceroos were already setting their eyes on the next big opportunity— the Asian Cup in 2015, when we'd have another opportunity to make history, this time back home in Australia.

GREEN AND GOLD

DURING MY SECOND SEASON WITH the Red Bulls in 2014, I'd missed quite a few regular-season games in order to help Australia qualify for our third consecutive World Cup. I'd helped the Red Bulls make it to the play-offs, beating Sporting Kansas City and DC United, and making it to the Eastern Conference final, falling only at the final hurdle to the New England Revolution.

That was a bit of a heartbreaker, because we all felt we had the talent to make a run all the way through the play-offs. And then at the end of the season, Thierry Henry announced his retirement from football. I left for the Asian Cup camp not sure where I stood with the Red Bulls. I knew I'd made an impact in the MLS—the most important thing for me with any club I'm signed to—and had been selected for the MLS All-Star team in both my seasons. But once again, my future was in a state of flux.

I could only focus, though, on my duties with the national team. The build-up to the Asian Cup of 2015 was the culmination of my strategy to be able to represent Australia at the highest level while still giving my all for my club. Finishing that season in New York, I went into another zone, mentally and physically. I trained furiously, improving my muscle-to-fat ratio, and can honestly say that, though I was thirty-four years old, I was in the best physical condition of my entire career.

The Socceroos were spirited—but we were also young and relatively untested. Still, I remember one team meeting, six months out from the Asian Cup, when Ange Postecoglou got up and said: "You might not believe it *now*, but come the Asian Cup, that guy sitting there with the armband"—he gestured to the skipper, Mile Jedinak—"*will* be lifting the trophy."

Like Ange, I always had faith in us. I knew that the only things that could stop us winning the Asian Cup were our own egos, overconfidence and lack of discipline.

After our first training camp in Australia, the boss was purposefully making us play some rough games on the road. Very few of the players in our team, apart from Bresh and me, had had the experience of playing in the scorching heat of Qatar, for example. As in the World Cup qualifiers, playing in those Middle Eastern countries was incredibly challenging. It was often hard to breathe, the game slowing to a crawl at times. In that desert heat, in the full ninety-odd minutes of the match, the ball would often be in play for some fifty-two or fifty-four minutes at the most. There was so much time wasting, just to catch our breath, to conserve our energy.

I'd played in two previous Asian Football Confederation Cups, so I could offer some valuable leadership advice to the younger guys. My first had been in 2007 in Thailand; I came into that nursing a bunch of injuries, but I'd still managed to score the first-ever goal for the Socceroos in that tournament. But as a team that year, I don't believe we were properly prepared. We weren't as fit as we should have been and we weren't acclimatized to the heat and humidity in Thailand. We had come in much fitter to my second Asian Cup, in 2011 in Qatar, and made it all the way to the final. Though we had lost 1-0 to Japan, we could see progression in our form.

But now, during our preparation for the 2015 Asian Cup— in spite of Ange's utter faith in our abilities—our form became increasingly worrisome. We lost 2–0 to Belgium, barely defeated Saudi Arabia 3–2 at Craven Cottage in London, then travelled to the Middle East for some truly dismal showings: held 0–0 by the United Arab Emirates, beaten 1–0 by Qatar.

I was now the oldest player in the team. I could see that if I didn't say something after those miserable results, I wouldn't be doing my job as one of the leaders of the Socceroos. In a team meeting after the Qatar loss, Ange said his piece—he was angry with us as a squad—and then I got up.

"It's unacceptable," I said. "Bloody unacceptable. Frankly, we need a kick in the arse. Don't bother looking at each other, expecting the *next* man to step up. It's not about our technical ability. We know we've got quality in this team. This is about what we're made of *inside*. Do we have the appetite to take our game to the next level? Do we have the discipline to finish teams off? Do we have the *belief* that we can win the Asian Cup?" I closed off by telling the team that, in my view, fear was the only thing standing between us being a good team and a great team.

We went off to play an away match against Japan—18 November 2014—and were beaten 2–1 in a tough, scrappy encounter. Yasuyuki Konno and Shinji Okazaki, in a seven-minute period in the second half, gave them the lead, 2-0, before I scored a header in stoppage time.

It wasn't enough. Our rankings in the FIFA global standings were plummeting. The fans and press back home were grumbling.

*

Before the final camp in Australia, the Asian Cup Socceroos team was selected. I was already being scientific about my body—even back in my training with the Red Bulls in New Jersey—making sure my weight was precisely 75.5 kilograms, charting how much I slept, watching my diet in the most precise way. The camp, as a whole, was the most scientifically advanced I'd ever been a part of.

I spoke to the boss and I was clear: "Five minutes, ten minutes, ninety-five minutes," I said. "Play me whenever you want. However much you want. I'll help lead these players, on and off the park. Any problems with the young lads, boss, you just let Mile, Bresh and me know and we'll sort them out."

As in our Brazil campaign, Mile was the captain. It was an obvious choice. He was playing in the Premiership, with Crystal Palace, and would start every match. Bresh was in the twilight of his career, playing in Qatar. Mile was a great, vocal leader. Bresh never said much, but when he did, it was usually about a serious problem with some of the younger players. Bresh would take me aside and tell me, I'd talk to Mile, and we'd sort it out internally. All three of us knew our roles as veterans. It was an excellent three-headed leadership dynamic.

In the camp, I told the younger guys: "Think carefully about *every* decision you make." Because we were the host nation, the players had more options away from camp, more chances for distraction. "If you feel that having coffee or a meal with your family is going to help with your play, then go and do it," I said, "If you think hanging out on our day off with some mates— having a few laughs, going shopping or to a restaurant—is going to help us win the Asian Cup, I have no problems with that."

I also had long chats with the players about being careful about what they posted on social media during that tournament. Nowadays, just a momentary mental lapse—the wrong sort of picture on Instagram or an ill-advised Tweet—can land you in a world of trouble with the media or the boss. Again, I believed that talking to them was part of my leadership role. If one of the young guys slipped up and put something controversial on social media, there'd be a stink about it, and his mind wouldn't be right: he'd suddenly be distracted on the pitch.

This developed such a sense of trust. We generally ate dinners together, even went out shopping as a team. That sort of bonding is critical, I've found, for the sake of team camaraderie. Again, that's more of the same spirit I'd learned back at Everton.

Though I was the oldest player in the team, I always hung out with the youngsters. Bresh wouldn't. Mile wouldn't. But I'd be there in the hotel and we'd have FIFA15 Xbox and PlayStation tournaments and, if I didn't win the game, I'd chuck the remote or smash it on the table. It got to be a joke: no one wanted to use the remote after me because it'd always be defective and rattling. It got to the point where we had to have extra remotes on hand, because I was known for busting them up nightly.

But we weren't pissing about for the sake of it. I knew the pressures of big tournaments. If I sensed any fear or anxiety in the younger players, I'd spend time with them, have some laughs. Sometimes I would create a bit of a ruckus—all with the objective of alleviating stress. One night, Mat Ryan was banging the walls in my room while playing FIFA15 and the next morning Mile took me aside to ask me, "Tim, who the bloody *hell* was in your room screaming at half past eleven last night?"

I took the blame because, for me, that was part of leadership, too—not always being a disciplinarian but putting young guys in a situation where they have something else to think of besides football.

I'd seen the other side of the fence. I remembered how Guus Hiddink, at my first World Cup in Germany, wouldn't let us have PlayStation in the rooms, wouldn't let us horse around. Everything was so strict. It kept you focussed, yes—but it also kept you thinking about nothing else *but* football. You'd go to bed thinking about the last match, your brain wound up, preparing for the next. Sometimes that's not good for the psyche. It's not sensible to have football on the brain to the exclusion of everything else, especially for younger guys, especially at big tournaments. You need to let your mind wander, piss about during the evening, have some laughs.

At our Asian Cup camp, even nights before a game, I'd let the guys play games until nearly midnight. I didn't give a damn about how many hours they slept. All that mattered was how the players looked on the pitch. We'd have FIFA15 going on in one room and Mario Kart in another. Our floor of the hotel was almost like a video arcade. But the team was bonding, hanging out, building camaraderie. And it worked.

*

We played the first match against Kuwait to a full house in Melbourne. The game had hardly started when we suffered yet another mental lapse. In the opening minutes, we went down 1–0. The ball came in to the near post and someone lost their runner—I scrambled back, trying to make a last-ditch block, but I couldn't get there in time.

We needed someone to rally us and it was young Massimo Luongo who stepped up. Mass created something out of nothing, coming down the line, dribbling past a few players, passed the ball to me and I headed it home. Fantastic interplay leading to that goal. I ran to the corner flag, throwing punches, hugged Mass and thanked him for the brilliant service.

Now it was clear to me: every team has its unique rhythm and with that 2015 Socceroos squad, we were definitely slow starters. It could take us a while to get going, but once we scored, watch out—we could catch fire. Massimo played brilliantly. From 1–0 we came back to dominate with goals from Mass, Mile and James Troisi. We won 4–1 in the end.

We'd set the tone: great team performance, four different goal-scorers. But the media was still accentuating the negatives after the game. They were more focussed on our shaky start. There were question marks about how far we could progress if we continued to concede early goals as we'd done in the first match.

*

Our next match was against Oman. Mile was out injured and I was named captain. That was one of the highest honours of my career, the privilege of strapping on the captain's armband for the Socceroos. We were well prepared and thrashed Oman 4–0. I was substituted in the fiftieth minute, and it was just a fantastic feeling to pass the armband on to Mark Bresciano. Who in history deserved the captaincy more than Bresh?

South Korea was our next opponent and Ange decided I should be rested. I came on late as a substitute with twenty minutes left, along with Robbie Kruse. Against the run of play, we lost 1–0. The South Koreans were the strongest team we'd played in the competition to that point.

In hindsight, it was probably the kick up the arse we needed. Maybe we'd have become complacent if we'd breezed through the group stages, racking up big wins. In fact, we'd only needed a draw to finish on top of our group, and now we'd finished in second slot. That result further unsettled a lot of the fans and the Australian press.

In the wake of the loss to South Korea, the coach asked all of us to get up at a team meeting and say what it meant to be a Socceroo. It was the first time in my international career any boss had asked us to do this. We all had our turn—Mile, Bresh, all the younger players, too—and there was a common theme to what a lot of the guys talked about: we'd all taken similar paths, following a dream, many of us coming from humble beginnings.

When I got up, I told them about how I'd been supremely focussed since my childhood in Sydney, constantly told that I wouldn't make it as a youth player in Australia: that I wasn't big enough, quick enough or strong enough—sometimes simply that "my face didn't fit". I told them that my parents had taken out a loan so that I could go to Millwall—without even a guarantee of a trial. I also told them about my first call-up to the Socceroos, Frank Farina fighting to clear my complicated eligibility with FIFA, and my relationship with that brilliant tactician Guus Hiddink—purely business, no emotions ... But my main message was that we all had to feel our own special purpose in why we were here in this moment, representing our country. That all of us—all of our families—had made sacrifices and it was now our time to show what we were made of.

*

Finishing second in our group surprised a lot of people. The media were saying that Ange needed to shake things up, go completely with youth up front, dropping Bresh and me. Ange didn't listen. In our knockout-stage match against China, I was sure I'd be able to perform. In training, doing pattern-of-play sequences, crosses were coming in and I was finishing. I was finishing as well as I'd ever done in my life.

As we approached Brisbane Stadium, I spoke to Bresh, Mile and Ange, and told them we needed to push our young players. We needed to keep them hungry and focussed. No more mental lapses. No more giving away soft early goals. Mile was playing in great pain. He was badly banged up for that match. His ankle was so swollen, I don't even know how he made it onto the pitch. That's how badly Mile wanted to play for Australia.

In the first half, we played well and had a few chances, but we could see China were a strong team. I touched the ball only four or five times during the entire first forty-five minutes—the defenders were all over me. They weren't getting tired. They were supremely fit. They were shutting me down, tugging on my jersey and grabbing my arms when the referee wasn't looking. They were playing me tight. Going into half-time, I said to the boys, "Look, I'm not getting any breathing space. These two guys are all over me. Here's what I'll do: if they're going to mark me with two players, I'll take them into space. Someone else can score."

I set that as my second-half job: to hold the two centre-backs deep, to make space for our midfielders. I was getting frustrated, and I thought the boss might take me off at half-time.

Ange gave me the chance to come out after the interval and, in the forty-ninth minute, we won a corner. Bresciano took it. I finally made some space for myself, made my run to the near post. As I jumped, the Chinese captain and I clashed heads. He went down and stayed down. The ball popped out. Franjic, outside the penalty area, headed it back into the mix.

I was on the left-hand side of the goal as the ball looped toward me. I could have brought it down on my chest and swivelled, but there was no chance in hell I was going to have the time or space: the Chinese defenders had been draped over me all day.

The only thing to do was an overhead scissor kick as I'd done for Everton against Chelsea. But in that Chelsea match, I'd been in a great position: squarely in front of the net. This time the angle was completely wrong. I could sense the goal to my right, but there were also defenders between the keeper and me.

I set with my left foot and went into the chain-reaction of the overhead scissor kick. I hit the kick sweetly with the outside of my boot. Even with my back to the goal, in my peripheral vision I could sense the ball had gone to the right of the goalkeeper, hitting the grass and skipping past him. He stood glued to the ground. I turned in time to see the ball had bulged the netting and was settling in the right-hand corner.

I ran off and, for the first time in my life, I slid through the grass on my knees. I jumped up, boxing the corner flag—screaming—and was buried by my team-mates.

Normally, my mind-set would be to defend at that point, but the momentum was with us and I could smell another goal coming. In the sixty-fifth minute, the ball went out to the left, outside the penalty area. Jason Davidson took a touch, crossed it beautifully, just like I'd often said to the guys: "Miss the first man, don't worry about the second man, I'll deal with him."

It was a very soft cross, almost no pace on the ball at all. I knew I had to do more than say *good morning* to this one. I had to twist my neck and generate the power to beat the keeper from ten metres. I also had to use the dew on the grass to make the ball skim along the ground.

It was technically a very tough header to execute, but the way I angled the ball, it bounced outside the goalkeeper's reach and into the bottom right-hand corner of the net.

We won 2–0 and I was named Man of the Match. I spoke to Ange in the changing room. "Thanks for not subbing me at the half," I laughed.

I had now scored thirty-nine goals in my international career. After the match, I read one hilarious Tweet from "Mr Football", SBS broadcaster Les Murray: "Timmy not happy with just a Pele goal. He had to score a Cahill goal."

We had booked a place in the semi-final against Qatar. Japan had been knocked out of the tournament in a major upset, a penalty shoot-out loss to the UAE. I was disappointed by that, actually. Steel sharpens steel. I'd wanted to face Japan, which had long been the powerhouse of the Asian nations, just to prove that we could outplay them; also as payback for the 2–1 loss they'd handed us in the months before the Asian Cup.

We dealt with the UAE at Newcastle very professionally, clinically—two great goals from Sainsbury and Davidson. Done and dusted. We'd booked ourselves into the final in Sydney.

*

Now we were going to play in my hometown. Man, there was never a sweeter feeling! We were playing South Korea, at Stadium Australia, in a rematch of our first-round game. We were ready. Mentally, we were focussed. Physically—on *another* level. I don't know that there's ever been a football team as scientifically prepared for fitness as that Socceroos side was.

It was a match between a fiery attack and a solid defence. We had banged in twelve goals in our five games, while South Korea had yet to concede one.

I was in the centre circle for the opening whistle. I took the kick-off, side-footing it gently to Mark Milligan. In the opening minutes I ran to the left edge of the box, shaped up to cross, but instead I shot straight to the keeper—not my best effort. But we were coming forward, with positive intent, hungry for goals. I was also racing back to defend. In the fifth minute, we gave away a free kick outside the goal area, but we handled it well and I headed clear. South Korea kept pushing up again and again. They were not letting our back four play it out. I didn't mind the high-press, because I knew we had the speed to hit them on the counter.

And that's what we did. In the twenty-fourth minute Leckie fed Kruse out wide with a well-weighted inside ball. I found space on the edge of the box, then I took a quick angled shot, saved by the Korean keeper, Kim Jin-hyeon. Still, the South Koreans kept flying at us. In the thirty-seventh minute, they found space and Son Heung-min beat Franjic, then got in a deep cross that Son volleyed with his left—luckily, just wide of Mat Ryan's right-hand post.

Finally, it came, just seconds before the end of the first half. Mass Luongo, stepping up big time, made a quick complete turn in a tight space off a pass from Sainsbury, then left his marker for dead before unleashing an unstoppable twenty-metre shot to beat Kim Jin-hyeon.

It was 1–0 for Australia!

We'd been holding the ball well, with some nice passing between the back four, the midfield and the forwards. We felt confident we could hold the lead after the interval, though South Korea had a lot of fire and were surging, constantly coming forward with pace.

Early in the second half, Lecks blasted one straight into the keeper's hands. From the resulting corner, I rose well to get a header in, but the ball went wide to the right.

In the first half I'd been kicked hard on my Achilles tendon—I was struggling quite a bit. In the second half, one of their centre-backs raked his studs down the back of my sore Achilles. The pain was excruciating. I couldn't turn. I could barely run. I jogged on, but clearly I was hurting. Ange could see it and in the sixty-second minute he took me off. I gave way to Tomi Juric. Coming off, I heard a huge ovation, nodded and waved to our fans. On the touchline I gave Ange a big hug.

As the match progressed, we looked assured of victory. We held that 1–0 lead past the ninetieth minute. Then in the second minute of injury time, in probably our only major lapse of the match, South Korea got the ball to Son Heung-min, who broke toward the goal and beat Mat Ryan.

Conceding a goal in the ninety-second minute, we were all gutted. Shell-shocked. I was on the bench next to Bresh. With all our home supporters behind us, Stadium Australia had now gone from a mood of elation, so near to claiming the trophy, to palpable nervousness.

The final whistle blew: extra time.

We felt like the better side; our confidence was high, but in extra time anything can happen. And what if those extra thirty minutes ended in a stalemate and it came to penalties? Then all bets were off. We couldn't count on Schwarzie's heroics anymore, as we'd done ten years earlier in the World Cup qualification shoot-out against Uruguay.

When the players came out for extra time, we were shouting at them. Confidence swelling even more now. One thing we knew for sure—we had the edge in fitness. All that scientific technique in our training camps, all the monitoring of our diet and sleep, the remarkable amount of time we'd put into our training—on the pitch and in the gym—was about to pay off.

I stood face to face with Tomi Juric, holding him by the shoulders. "This is made for you, Tomi," I said. "Go out and *grab* it."

He did. In the fourteenth minute of extra time, on the right-hand side of the goal, Tomi beat his marker with a wicked backheel nutmeg, then sent in a low cross. After the goalkeeper made the initial save, there was James Troisi.

And what a great finish—roof of the net!

South Korea refused to lie down, kept pressing and pressing. As the minutes ticked down, things got increasingly frantic. We were holding the fort, though, blocking shots, defending beautifully. To a man, every Socceroo was throwing his body on the line.

The final whistle blew .... the stadium erupted ... and the realization hit us:

We were the champions!

We'd captured our first-ever cup.

The crowd at Stadium Australia hadn't looked like this since November 2005—nearly a decade earlier, during the moments after the penalty shoot-out against Uruguay . . . but this eclipsed even that special night.

Back then I was twenty-five, a fresh young face in the Socceroos. Now I was the oldest man in the team. I was shaking my head at the wild, crazy journey my years on the national team had been ...

Watching Mile as he was handed the Asian Cup, lifting it skyward, it fully sank in. We'd *done* it. The biggest achievement in the country's footballing history. The confetti was fluttering, sticking to our sweaty faces and arms ... Queen's "We Are the Champions" blared from the stadium speakers as we passed the Asian Cup from hand to hand.

I could scarcely hear myself think for the roar in that stadium. I smiled at Ange and nodded. He'd called it, six months earlier, hadn't he? Looking at Mile, "That man right there with the armband will be lifting the Asian Cup ..."

We'd had that greatest attribute possible in a team: *belief.* We'd played so well as a unit, each man contributing to the collective, but there were some fantastic individual achievements, too. My midfield partner Mass Luongo was named player of the tournament and Mat Ryan best keeper.

It is hard for me to put into words the swirl of emotions that hit me at the end of that match. The presentation was euphoric. I took a selfie with all the players, immediately putting it up on Instagram. At the time I felt this could be my *last* moment with these lads—at least the special group we had assembled.

Yet even in that moment, in all that happiness and shouting, you couldn't help but feel some sadness, too. I looked at Bresh—thought about ten years earlier, right here: Bresh lashing home that great goal against Uruguay. We'd just been kids. Now I thought this might be our final match together. Last time for Bresh putting on a Socceroos jersey—and, in fact, it was.

My injured Achilles tendon had me hobbling a bit, but the pain didn't matter at that moment. I soon had all my kids with me on the pitch—Sienna, Shae, Kyah, Cruz—snapping photos, making memories. Little Cruz was wearing a replica Socceroos jersey as I carried him and gave him a big kiss—such a tender moment.

Waving to the fans, walking around the pitch with my kids, I kept thinking back to all my youth clubs, from Balmain Tigers and Marrickville Red Devils to my days with Sydney Olympic and Belmore Hercules. To the visionary coaches and mentors, like Johnny Doyle, who'd always believed I could hit the green door and win those golden bicycles. But also to the coaches who'd told me I was too small and not fast or strong enough to make it to the highest level, or the school career counsellor who thought I was daft for setting out with such a single-minded vision of my future …

I took my turn holding the cup. Millions of Australian kids would always have this picture locked in their memory. A long way from *wogball*, weren't we? The sport I'd loved so dearly from the age of four had cemented its place in Australian culture and history.

Most of my family were in the stadium, except my father, who was ill and watching on TV back home. As soon as I got a spare moment, I rang Dad up.

"Job done," I said, smiling.

NEW HORIZONS

WE WERE STILL IN THE post-celebratory glow of that Asian Cup win when my whole life turned upside-down again. At the end of my second season with the New York Red Bulls, before I left for the Asian Cup, I knew we were in transition. New staff were bringing in their own philosophies—new players, a new vision. My agent, Paul Martin, and the Red Bulls management agreed I was unlikely to have a future that was satisfactory at the Red Bulls. We announced that the decision to part ways was both mutual and amicable, and during the winter 2015 transfer window I suddenly had a number of offers to play in England, Europe, the Middle East and China.

The conditions I set for my agent were pretty high. "I want some sort of guarantee that I'll have an input in the grassroots program of the club." Going back to the Premiership, or Europe, felt like I'd be retracing my steps, and now at a much older age. The Middle East, though financially lucrative, meant living and playing in a brutal climate—which wouldn't be fair to my wife and kids.

Researching what was out there, I realized more than anything else, I wanted another big project, another test. Another massive adventure. I'd done fifteen years in England, two in America—was it time to look toward Asia? The Asian Cup match against China, when I'd scored twice, was seen by an estimated one hundred million people in China alone. I started seriously to consider opportunities I'd received from a few clubs based in the most populous country on Earth. In truth, I'd always felt that someday, when the time was right, I might end up playing in Asia.

Now I had to strategize as a businessman—not just a footballer. The Chinese Super League was growing, the owners spending big money on development and infrastructure. The crowds were passionate and it was the best-attended football league in Asia. Football may not be the most popular sport in China yet, but for hard-core fans it has become a full way of life as much as it is for fans of Everton or the best clubs in Spain, Italy, Germany and France.

I sought the counsel of a lot of more experienced business minds and saw that, at the age of thirty-five, this was likely my last club-playing experience, so I had to factor into my decision things that made the most sense for me, not just as an athlete but as a father and a husband looking to provide a long-term financial legacy for his family. What would be the best move that allowed me to play football and continue my transition into a future as a businessman and builder of grassroots youth football programs, both back home in Australia and around the world?

I signed with Shanghai Shenhua for one year, with an option to extend it longer. I relocated my wife and kids to this booming metropolis of more than twenty-four million people—roughly the same number of people who live in all of Australia—with plans to be here for a considerable time. As always, I had done plenty of research into the club I was joining. I knew the owners, the Greenland Group, were one of the biggest real-estate developers in Asia and now had a huge presence building up the skyline in cities like Sydney. I knew the history of the club as well—two superstars, Didier Drogba and Nicolas Anelka, had played at Shanghai Shenhua before me. I researched their training ground, the French manager, Francis Gillot, and the staff.

What I didn't fully realize until I got to Shanghai was the scope of the Chinese market. I don't think it's actually possible to grasp it until you relocate to a city as vast and thriving as Shanghai. I thought New York was a major market, but the economic opportunities in Shanghai are *staggering*.

The day I landed at Shanghai's Pudong International Airport in February 2015, I thought a handful of reporters and perhaps a few die-hard fans might be there. I couldn't have been more wrong. There were more than a thousand people waiting as I came through customs and immigration, mostly Shanghai Shenhua supporters, chanting, bedecked in the blue and white team jerseys, and waving club scarves. Some 300 officers were detailed to provide security for my arrival. I had no idea what I was stepping into. The crew of my flight had actually presented me with a Shenhua jersey and scarf during the flight, so that I could arrive fully dressed for the occasion.

As soon as I stepped through the double doors with my suitcases, the fans were snapping photos, waving their iPhones, screaming and singing club songs, chanting my first name: "Tim! Tim! Tim! Tim!" No club I'd ever played for—Millwall, Everton, the Red Bulls—had ever laid out a welcome mat like this. Before I could even leave the airport, I spent forty-five minutes in a waiting room signing team shirts and posing for cell-phone photos.

It was humbling and actually, at one point, it got a little *too* intense. After a quick interview with a group from the Chinese press, people started grabbing at me—someone shoved a bouquet of flowers in my face—and the coppers whisked me out of the airport immediately. If anything, the fans' level of enthusiasm wasn't quietening down; it was becoming mayhem and more than a little overwhelming.

I thought I'd go to the hotel to shower and sleep, but the translator told me, "No, the President of Shenhua has a special dinner planned for you." I was taken to a huge banqueting hall where I joined the president, the coaches and some of my new team-mates, like Colombian captain Giovanni Moreno, Brazilian striker Paulo Henrique and Greek defender Avraam Papadopoulos. We were served a seven-course meal, and every person at the table made a speech at the microphone. I was dog-tired, but I managed to get up and say something. I knew the club had quality and talent but had been underperforming. The previous season they'd only won one away game. They hadn't managed to win two games in a row. I knew I was being brought on board to shake things up. I told the room I saw Shenhua as a sleeping giant and that I hoped I could help wake it up.

At ten the next morning, we trained, and it was *not* a light session. This was strictly business. I did eighteen training sessions in my first two weeks in Shanghai—double sessions some days. I don't speak Mandarin, of course, but I immediately made a connection with the Chinese players. They could see that, even at thirty-five years of age—most of them are ten years younger—I was as fit as any man on that team.

In my debut game, we won 6–2 at home, and my teammates saw that I wasn't some high-priced foreign prima donna who was going to wait for the ball to be delivered to his feet. I was playing like I'd always played: hard challenges, tracking back, doing the graft. Someone told me that Shenhua had never before scored six goals at home. I didn't get on the score sheet that first match, but I worked as hard as I've ever worked for any club in my career. The next game we played away, and we won 1–0.

Once again, as in New York, I got the guys to play like Everton. Nick a goal early on, then shut up shop defensively. After we got our goal, I got behind the ball, ran my arse off and kept yelling to my team-mates, "Defend! Track back! Hold your shape!" All I did was shift back to being a defensive-midfielder, protecting the back four, scrapping for every loose ball, and we held on for a tough win away from home. I felt right at home now. We followed that with a win the next game at home—making it three straight wins, two clean sheets. Most importantly, in the changing room, you could see we now had a real sense of belief.

Some Australians were a bit disappointed that I didn't choose to come home and finish my career in the A-League. The A-League is fantastic, but for me there was still so much out there in the world to explore. I weighed all the pros and cons, but in the Shenhua offer all the boxes I needed were ticked. China is this sprawling global economic superpower, with a culture I knew so little about, and millions of people were incredibly receptive to my coming to play in their growing league.

Part of my requirement for the deal was that I would be involved in the youth academy set-up for Shenhua. No club can thrive in the long term just by buying up big-name players; it needs a grassroots program to develop home-grown talent.

Five years from now, I predict, football in China is going to reach a new level. Ten or fifteen years from now, it may be one of the world powers. The President of China, Xi Jinping, is a huge football fan and has spoken about wanting to host a future World Cup.

Having settled now in Shanghai, I've seen the cultural difference at work. The first priority among almost all Chinese parents is education. Sport comes a distant second. I see this not as a stumbling block but as an opportunity. How can we merge the two? Give the kids a vision where they can see themselves both as academically proficient *and* fine athletes?

There is no doubt in my mind that China, given the proper organization and development, will emerge on the global football stage in the next five to ten years. Why? The numbers speak for themselves. If you want to build a club team to challenge on the world stage, China is the place to do it. With a billion people to draw on, and with proper youth training through academies like those I'm helping put in place, China is the future.

Football changed my world. Now, in Shanghai, I have a chance to play a part in changing the world of football.

LEGACY

WHEN I FIRST STARTED ON this journey, I wasn't the least bit interested in the commercial aspect of being a footballer. I was focussed solely on learning my trade. Then I was fully committed to doing my job. As the years progressed, I started seeing more and more players become ambassadors for some of the biggest companies in the world.

One player I've always held in high regard is David Beckham. He was the first guy I'd met personally, and played against, who was intensely focussed on becoming a global brand. And from his time with Manchester United through the Real Madrid and LA Galaxy years, David more than fulfilled that ambition.

My first foray into the commercial side of football was pretty funny, actually—it happened during the build-up to Australia's appearance at the 2006 World Cup in Germany. I got asked to do an endorsement deal for Weet-Bix. When my agent rang me about the offer, I said, "Are you serious? Weet-Bix? Of course

I'll do it!" I even started singing the song: "Aussie kids are Weet-Bix kids, Aussie kids are Weet-Bix kids ..."

My brothers and sisters and I all grew up with that jingle. My mum and dad ate Weet-Bix in the mornings. We kids ate it. I suppose any kid of a certain age who grew up in Australia has eaten soggy Weet-Bix with milk before school.

"It's a pretty small offer actually," my agent said.

"I don't care how much money it is," I said. "I loved Weet-Bix as a kid. Take the deal. If I do it well, who knows what other avenues will open up?"

I signed the contract for very basic money, did the commercials and suddenly had my face on millions of Weet-Bix boxes. When I scored the first-ever Socceroos' World Cup goal, Simon Hill, the commentator, shouted that, yes, I'd eaten my Weet-Bix. That was unscripted, but everyone in Australia watching the game heard it, which is a perfect example of how an athlete and brand can help each other in unplanned ways.

Three years later, I did another popular Weet-Bix TV advertisement, with me, in the Socceroos jersey, bending a free kick around a wall of Italian defenders who are singing, operatically:

"He's not tall enough—he's not strong enough—he's too small ..."

I sat in the meetings planning that advertisement, because the content was personal—that song told the entire story of my childhood. By using something relevant to my life, we'd also sent a message, I felt, to everyday kids in Australia who might be hearing the same thing from their coaches, teachers, even parents.

An unexpected turn from doing the Weet-Bix advertisements was the close friendship I formed with cricketer Brett Lee, one of the best fast-bowlers in the world. We didn't know each other before Weet-Bix put us together for some promotions, but we soon found out we had so much in common—especially with our clear vision of helping inspire young kids in Australia.

Normally when working with a brand, athletes do exactly what they're told; they turn up and read the script, stand in front of the camera, and leave. Brett ("Binga" to his mates) and I would take the script and flip it on its head. I'd read it and say, "No, that's not me." Binga would say the same and we'd put our heads together and collaborate to make the ad better. In the end Weet-Bix got something more natural and powerful, because it was true to our real-life stories.

When I scored Australia's first-ever goal in the Asian Cup in Thailand, I did my version of Binga's famous chainsaw celebration. Soon after, Brett took a wicket in a cricket match and did a version of my boxing celebration. We've been through so much together—on and off the park; when we've both suffered injuries, we've been there to help each other deal with it. And we give each other advice, not just about our respective sports, but about life in general. Brett and I continue to bang ideas off each other constantly, but these days it's less about sport and business and more about helping kids at a grassroots level.

Through Brett I was lucky enough to build yet another important relationship when he introduced me to the 2GB radio host Alan Jones. Alan's a guy who always speaks his mind. That makes him a pretty controversial figure in Australia—people either like his style or they don't—but very few people know all the hard work Alan does behind the scenes. Out of the spotlight, he spends time mentoring athletes from a wide array of sports. He's hosted most of my charity events, and done loads of charitable work with Brett as well. Alan's got a background in coaching rugby and is a powerful speaker and motivator. He's somebody who's been there for me, through thick and thin, always offering up solid and straightforward advice.

Just as I'd said to my agent years before, that first Weet-Bix deal wasn't about the money: it did open up whole new avenues I'd never envisaged, most importantly my relationships with Brett Lee and Alan Jones.

And after Weet-Bix, more business opportunities continued to come my way. I've always tried to be selective, to choose things that matter to me on a personal level. For the last seven years I've been lucky enough to be on the cover of the world's best-selling football video game, EA Sports FIFA—next to Wayne Rooney, Messi, Benzema and Kaká. But that's not just some random endorsement—during my free time, I'm constantly playing FIFA with my kids and, as I mentioned, I played it with the younger players in the Socceroos while we were in the camps for the 2014 World Cup and the Asian Cup in 2015.

As I watched players like David Beckham become innovators, with endorsements and even forays into fashion, I realized the importance of having a business strategy. I saw that it could make a difference for my family in the long term and give me a way to stay involved in the sport well beyond my career as a player. I had received a few offers after the 2010 World Cup in South Africa to do some clothing photo shoots, but I said no; one-off shoots made no sense to me. But later I thought, *Why not think long-range here?*

I had worn Armani suits for eight years. I had always treated my career as a job, and wearing smart, tailored clothes off the park was part of that attitude. It was a way of showing respect to the work, to my career, team and club, and to football itself. I got to know the designer, Giorgio Armani, and we developed a strong relationship. I even went to Milan for his fashion shows and met other designers like Ted Baker, and struck up friendships with them as well. Then I thought, *Why not build a brand of clothes that I like to wear?*

I've recently teamed up with Shoreditch International to create CAHILL+, a line of menswear. It's tasteful—I don't put my branding all over it because I know that not *everyone* likes Tim Cahill. What matters most is the quality of the garments. They're understated, fresh, youth-oriented, with relaxed tailoring—smart jumpers, no loud colours, things I myself would wear out in Sydney or London or New York.

As I began heading in this direction, I told myself I needed to be strategic and smart. I didn't want to saturate the market.

Today I turn a lot of endorsements down because they don't seem like *me*. I have to feel a personal connection to the brand. An example is New Balance boots and clothes. I'd wear them regardless of whether I had a deal or not. The New Balance Furons I wear in league and international play are, to my mind, cutting-edge and offer me better ball control than any other boot.

In truth, the business projects closest to my heart are always about kids. I'm creating a phone app for coaching kids, where children can log on and keep track of healthy eating, sleeping and training. It gives the kids a taste of professionalism, a chance to train scientifically the way I've done. I'm also doing a line of children's books because I remember how amazing and exciting it was as a kid to belong to Book Club in school. We'd get stickers and feel like we'd accomplished something—and it made reading both a challenge and great fun.

*

For years, since my Everton days, I'd always had this dream of remaking grassroots football back home in Australia. That's a lot more complicated than it sounds, but understanding the power of branding and commercialism has helped me now achieve this goal.

I brought in Robbie Anderson from the youth academy at Everton to help me develop a program improving kids' fundamental skills and hand–eye coordination, using tests like

SAQ (speed, agility and quickness), as well as training with ladders and hurdles. I'd never used ladders and hurdles as a kid, but at Everton I'd watched Robbie Anderson and his fellow youth coaches working with kids as young as five years old. Ladders and hurdles are a wonderful drill to develop agility, coordination and quick footwork.

Robbie knows how to coach kids better than *anyone* I've ever seen. He's a native of Liverpool and as True Blue as they come: a lifelong Evertonian, going back several generations. He coached Wayne Rooney at eight years old and brought up a whole generation of guys who eventually made it into the Everton first team.

He used to come over to my house in Liverpool and coach my own children: Kyah was six, Shae was four and Sienna was three. Kyah was extremely enthusiastic but needed to work on his coordination; Shae was always a little hard nut like me, would run through brick walls; Sienna was so small, but she'd join in and try anything just because she loved being part of the group with her brothers.

I used to watch from my upstairs bedroom balcony. I had turned part of the back garden into a mini football pitch with proper goals and lines. People may wonder why I wasn't out there coaching my two sons and daughter, teaching them the fundamentals. I've found that it's best, as a father, to step back and let someone else coach your kids. As any parent reading this knows, sometimes your kids just won't listen to you. They'll get frustrated and boot the ball over the fence, huff and puff, and go inside. My kids respected Robbie's time—he'd come over for private lessons at least twice a week—and it was disciplined, structured learning, no different from being in school.

He practised techniques I'd never seen in my life. For hours, he'd have the kids just bouncing the football with the palms of their hands—basketball-style—switching from right hand to left. They had to do it inside a square, repetitively: left, right, left, right. When I first saw it, I was bemused. It made no obvious sense in a sport where it's forbidden to handle the ball, excepting on throw-ins or if you're the keeper. I went down and spoke to Robbie after I saw that.

"What's that all about then—the *bouncing* business?"

"Basic coordination."

Some kids, he explained, can't even bounce the ball ten times consecutively in a square. So he'd work on hand–eye coordination, the mental wiring of kids' brains, before he'd ever get them started with passing, shooting or dribbling with their feet. Then he eventually worked out the ladders and hurdles, which work on similar elements of coordination in footwork. Really simple things, having nothing to do with kicking a football.

In a little over a year, I saw the difference in my kids—my eldest son especially. After two years, the improvement in all of them was remarkable. A lightbulb went off one afternoon when I was watching Robbie down in the garden with my kids.

I looked at my wife. "You know what, Bek? This is exactly what I want to do in Australia. I want to take someone like

Robbie back home and help me teach kids fundamental skills using the Everton system."

"So do it," Bek said. "And why '*someone* like Robbie?' Why not just bring Robbie?"

I wanted to teach Aussie kids at this sophisticated level—employing proven, scientific training—and give them something I never had as a kid. I'd had excellent coaches and private teachers like Johnny Doyle, but this was really cutting-edge training. What if I could bring this to hundreds, maybe thousands of kids? Robbie and the other Everton youth coaches taught football with an actual syllabus and curriculum—just like schoolroom studies.

I went back to Australia with Robbie in tow and set up a pilot program. First day, we'd have a talk, show the kids videos, then move on to ladders and hurdles, passing, dribbling, shooting, loads of touches. Then have a nice lunch. Then a similar session all afternoon. The second day, we'd already see a progression: many of them would have improved noticeably in their footwork and fundamental ball skills. More than a few of the kids were unrecognizable: there was so much more confidence in them.

We also set up a seminar system to coach new coaches. Robbie handled that—and we trained eight or ten new coaches to help us run the course. A lot of these coaches were guys like David James, with whom I'd done private training as a kid and played alongside at Sydney United—good personal friends. I had so many old mates in Sydney, who'd played at a high level and now wanted to give back to the game. We gave them a crash course in Robbie's knowledge based on the Everton youth model.

When it came to the kids, I felt it was important to have both boys and girls, so we brought in girls and trained women coaches as well.

We did our first kids' camp at a football stadium in Homebush, in the inner-west suburbs of Sydney. We had fifteen coaches and 800 kids, divided into two groups: six to eight years old and nine to eleven years old. Those are the most crucial years, when you really have a chance to change kids' lives. By the time they're teenagers, they've already developed more of a fixed personality. If you start with them young enough, you can have maximum impact. We made sure the clinic was good fun, and each kid went away with an individual football and a gift bag.

Our first-ever training camp was one of the most exhausting two weeks of my life. I was involved at every level: organizing, coaching and keeping both the parents and kids happy. By the end, I was worn out, but it was incredibly rewarding.

After paying out all the costs—salaries to coaches, insurance and taxes, renting the stadium—we had a profit of $80,000. I immediately took that $80,000 and reinvested it in running more camps. These would be in outlying cities in Australia where few people would have expected us to operate. It would have been easy to keep running the same sort of camp right in Sydney, but we went to Newcastle, Canberra, Townsville. It cost a lot—the entire profit from the first camp, and then some, went into shipping the equipment and setting up shop in all these other cities. But the expense hardly mattered. I was getting a footprint across the country. It felt good investing my time and my own money into the program.

At our first pilot camp, we'd charged the kids $200 for three days. When we were done, that bothered me a lot, even though I personally never took one cent in profit and reinvested it all into the program. Some kids' families could afford to pay for a camp, but what about all the families like mine when I was growing up? What about kids with parents living on a razor-thin line each week paying the rent and bills? I remembered how hard it was when I was a kid for my family to scrape together the funds just for kit and registration. I started to look about for a partner, a sponsor, so that we could make these camps free for kids who couldn't afford them.

When I'd signed with the New York Red Bulls, I'd had the chance to meet Robert Thomson, the Chief Executive of NewsCorp, at the offices of *The Wall Street Journal*. Robert had invited me to an interview about my arrival in the MLS and we sat with a bunch of reporters. Later, when we were alone in his office, he asked me:

"How's the state of Australian football, Tim? What would you like to see happen there?"

I told him about the academies.

"If I was to leave one legacy behind for Australian football," I said, "it would be to completely remake the grassroots level of the sport back home."

He was nodding as I spoke, then said, "Why don't we make it happen, Tim?"

It was a perfect alignment. Robert is Australian. Like me, everything he does is with clear intent and a long-term vision. He very quickly put me in touch with Foxtel, the Australian cable network, and I sat down with Richard Freudenstein and Patrick Delany, the CEOs of Foxtel and Fox Sports, respectively. In a matter of a few short months, we came up with the Foxtel All-Stars Tim Cahill Academy. Foxtel was willing to invest millions in delivering a free program to kids around Australia.

New Balance have since come on board, making fantastic uniforms, boots and balls expressly for us. Kids get free kit, balls, plus this fantastic experience. We even created our own Disney television program and took two of our teams to tournaments in Disneyland. They were fantastic youth teams and we won both tournaments.

When you want to be innovative and try something completely new, you often run into bureaucratic roadblocks, and I found myself—once again—fighting elements in the Australian footballing establishment. For example, we had a syllabus that the Football Federation Australia (FFA) didn't approve of, which meant I couldn't use any Australian coaches with FFA badges; I had to train new coaches myself. It was very political. But I was willing to jump through hoops to develop the program according to my vision for it.

This, after all, was my dream: to give kids the best experience, top-notch coaching, and to make the camps completely free.

As I write this, we've just launched Ambitions Tours. With Foxtel and New Balance backing us, we select twenty kids from throughout Australia and give them the experience of a lifetime. Many come from difficult backgrounds. I read all their portfolios myself. Their football experience is of secondary importance to their *life* experience.

There was a boy named Chai I remember really well. He'd had a difficult start in life and was smaller than anyone else in his age group. That really struck a chord with me. Chai was not naturally a footballer—but our academies aren't about that. We wanted to help his confidence. Chai's experience was about feeling better about his life and leaving the Ambitions Tour with a new sense of pride.

That's one of the great things about the program: one of its core goals is to teach more than football. Living like a footballer, eating correctly and training your body help with all sorts of things outside sport. We unlock something inside these kids so that, we hope, they go back to school and to their home lives with more confidence. As I always say, confidence is everything. That applies both on and off the park.

I remember one fifteen-year-old girl called Alannah. In her previous teams, they had always made her play goalkeeper. She hated it. So during our clinic, we let her play outfield. Over the course of the three days, she banged in an unbelievable number of goals. She was always poised to score. It was immediately obvious to Robbie, the other coaches and me that Alannah had something you can't teach: an instinct for goals.

I remember her coming to us at the end of the camp in tears. She was telling Robbie and me that we'd changed her life. "No one ever gave me the chance to try to score goals," she said.

"Well, now you're playing to your strengths," I told her. "When the ball is played out you're always ready to shoot. You're poaching goals. We have sixteen- and seventeen-year-old boys—very athletic, playing at the highest level—but over these three days, not *one* of them has scored as many goals as you."

She seemed uncertain at first, then started to smile. "When I leave here I'll tell my coach I want to play striker," she said. Then we heard her on the phone with her mother: "I'm not playing keeper anymore. My new name's Poacher."

As Johnny Doyle had taught me decades before, you need to teach attitudes and emotions. It's not enough to coach technical skills, such as ball control, heading, dribbling and passing. Your job is to find that kid who always stands at the back, uncertain and shy, and make her want to take her place at the front the next day.

*

As I write this I will soon be thirty-six years old: still a young man, but in my final years as a full-time footballer. I'm still as fit as I've ever been, proud still to be playing for Shanghai

Shenhua and still wearing the green and gold. Qualifying for four straight World Cup tournaments would mean yet another milestone for Australian football. The Socceroos will continue to evolve. I know Ange Postecoglou well at this point—we're both really straightforward guys. I won't take it hard if he rings me up and says, "Tim, I think it's time." And I don't think he'd take it hard if I told him I'd decided to hang up my boots as an international player.

As an athlete, you've got to know when you're done. I've always said that I don't need to be the main man. I don't need to be the number-one figure in any team. But, of course, I can see retirement from international football on the horizon.

Probably the question I'm asked most frequently by fans is: "Tim, when will you come back to Australian football?"

I definitely plan to return to Australia, but only when the time and conditions are right. I can see myself owning an A-League club in the future. But I'd have to do it on my terms, make sure I could do it according to a long-range vision: that I'd have control right across the board—from the babies all the way through to the first team. I wouldn't be reinventing the wheel, just trying to bring over the Everton youth system.

The Everton method is designed so that every *single* year one player comes up from the academy to play in the first team. That's a tough ask—taking kids up to the level where they can quickly move from the Under-18s to the reserves to the first team. But you have to set the bar high. If not, you're settling for mediocrity. It means you're not training the youth well enough—not expecting enough of them. If I do have the opportunity to run an A-League club, it would have to be from the grassroots level up to the top professionals, the way I learned it in England.

As for my other business ventures, I'll be working for the rest of my life—not because I need to work, but because I *want* to. My strongest memory as a kid was of getting up in the morning and not seeing my mum because she'd already left for work; then coming home from school and going to training and not seeing Mum because she was off at her second job. The very fact that I'm still thinking about it—still writing about it today—means that her sacrifices made a deep imprint on me for life. But they also made me who I am.

My youngest son, Cruz, is three at the time I'm writing this and I'll often sit with him on my lap, watching World Cups and Premiership matches the same way I did with my father. I'll have all my kids with me on the sofa: Kyah and Shae and Sienna, as well. Little Cruz may not understand the finer points of football, but he certainly lights up when I show him some of the goals I've scored for my clubs and for my country. He can see the sheer joy in my eyes after I've scored; sometimes he'll even do his own version of my corner-flag boxing celebration.

My life has been about moments. I've missed some *chances*—everyone does—but those pinnacle moments, I can honestly say, I've seized almost all of them. All I've done is stay consistent: year in and year out I've worked hard and positioned myself to be ready to take my opportunities as they come. Most importantly, I've never internalized anyone's lack of belief in me. On the contrary, people's doubts only fuelled me to succeed, fired up my desire to prove that they were wrong.

I often tell my kids, and kids I meet throughout Australia and across the world, that just because someone says you can't reach your dream—that you're too small, not strong enough, not fast enough, or whatever mental obstacle is placed in front of you—it doesn't mean you have to *believe* them.

Barriers, in the end, are there to be broken.

ACKNOWLEDGMENTS

I'VE BEEN ASKED ABOUT WRITING my autobiography regularly over the years but the timing had never seemed right. It wasn't until the end of 2014 that I was able to see the vision of what I wanted to achieve with it, and to me that was always the most important thing. I knew that I wanted my book to be different from other sports books, something that football fans and non-football fans could all enjoy and get something out of.

The other thing that I wanted to be clear about was that I wasn't writing a retirement or end-of-career book. It was important to me that I wasn't doing this for the sake of it, but rather because now was the time when I really wanted to share my story.

Firstly and above all, I want to thank my wife and best friend Rebecca for her constant support of everything I do.

Since high school you've helped define me as a father, partner and footballer and still to this day keep me focussed on that. We both know that without your support through the challenging times, none of this would have been possible. I know that we have done a lot together in our career, but I'm sorry to say the adventure is just beginning! Love you all the world. I know how proud Lou and Ada Barnett would be of you and the person you have become. Thank you also to my four beautiful kids, Kyah, Shae, Sienna and Cruz. To put it simply, you are my world and make me the happiest I can be.

To my mum and dad, as well as Opa, Sean and Chris and your families, thank you for sharing my journey with me from the beginning. You've all lived my ups and downs as your own and your unwavering support at every point has made this possible.

Thanks to Uti and Taua, my mother's sisters, and their families, for their endless support and love throughout my career.

To Paul Martin, my agent throughout my professional career in England, we could probably write a book about my contracts that would be longer than this one! Our journey together has been amazing and has carved out careers for us in football together, on and off the park. From your wedding day, when you were interrupted walking down the aisle by an issue with my contract, to the support through the tough times, I can't thank you enough for being a close friend and someone I will always stay in contact with. Football hasn't just been about money for us, it's been about making decisions together to support our families and projects outside of the game. As you know, you'll always be my Jerry Maguire and I'm Rod Tidwell screaming "Show me the money!" while you think I'm crazy. Thank you to Cathy and your beautiful children for putting up with both of us. Now that I'm my own man and can take care of myself, your workload is much lighter, so hopefully you, Mikel, Phil and I can take that trip to Vegas that we always planned! Thanks also to Tania Shaw, the brains behind Paul and I, and the person who kept our lives in order through all the madness in England.

This book couldn't have happened without Richard Abate and Douglas Century embracing my vision. For Richard to understand what I was hoping to achieve and to suggest that a non-sportswriter would help me approach this from a different angle was especially important. For Douglas, who flew over to Shanghai and spoke with me for hours until we couldn't stand the sight of each other, then did it all over again and again, you've both helped me create something I'm really proud of.

To my publishing team at HarperCollins, thank you for buying into my wish to do everything differently! You've helped me truly make this 'my' book, even when you didn't always agree with my decisions. A huge team of people has made this possible and I appreciate your professionalism and trust in me.

There are so many people I want to thank over the course of my career and life for their guidance, advice and support.

The life of a professional sportsperson is made possible by the people around them and my career is a testament to every one of these people and more.

To my friends, team-mates, clubs and coaches when I was growing up in Australia, thank you for believing in me and most of all for making football fun! If it wasn't for those experiences on cold, early Saturday mornings – frozen oranges at half time and begging my mum and dad for a treat from the canteen after the game – I wouldn't have grown to love the game the way I do.

So many people were a part of that early stage but, in no particular order, I want to thank John Doyle, George Pseroudis, Nick Theodorakopoulos, Nick Tsevares, the Panzarino, Xipolitas, Frenkel and Hansimikali families, Huss Joma, Con Tsolkos, David James and Phil Pavleva, and so many more – you have all gotten me to where I am today.

Moving overseas as a teenager was incredibly difficult for a kid whose life revolved around his family. Firstly I need to thank Bob Pierson and Alan Batsford for taking me to England. I have Glen, Lindsey, Ben, Michael, Sam and Olivia Stanley to thank for taking me in. You were my second family and treated me as your own. Later on, Chris, Debbie, William and Grace Grey would take over that role when I moved into digs at Millwall, and I'll never forget their care, kindness and generosity.

Millwall was my 'apprenticeship' as a footballer and shaped me more than anything – if you can play in front of the Millwall fans at the Den, you can play anywhere. This apprenticeship has been priceless in my success as a footballer. Thanks to Keith

Stevens, Joe Dolan, Mark Magee, Dennis Wise, Paul Ifill, Roy Putt and every other team-mate and staff member for teaching me those lessons.

The staff at football clubs never receive the plaudits that the players and managers do but in many cases make just as many sacrifices for the team. The physios, masseurs, kit-men, secretaries and everyone else are the ones that get the players in a position to be able to perform come match day. I've been lucky enough to build some amazing friendships with the staff at clubs I've played at. I want to thank especially Sue Palmer, Tony Sage, Jimmy Martin, Jimmy Comer and Danny Donachie, and everyone else I have had the privilege of meeting and working with.

Making the move up to the Premier League was a big jump for me. Every player at Everton over my time there deserves a mention but in particular I want to thank Duncan Ferguson, Tony Hibbert, Lee Carsley, Nick Chadwick, Alan Stubbs, Leon Osman, Tommy Graveson, Steve Watson, Kevin Kilbane and the squad from my first season. These were the guys who made the biggest and longest-lasting impression on me as a footballer. All of the hours spent after training playing darts, pool and anything else we could make into a competition were bonding experiences that made our fourth-place finish that season possible.

From later years at Everton, I want to thank Phil Jagielka, Louis Saha, Joleon Lescott and Marouane Fellaini, as well as every single team-mate. It would be a chapter in itself to give all of you the credit you deserve. Phil Neville and Mikel Arteta became two of my closest friends away from the game and really influenced me as a player and person. In professional football, team-mates can come and go so regularly that forming long-term friendships can be difficult, but in Phil and Mikel I know I have two mates for life.

David Moyes, Bill Kenwright and their families were among the biggest influences on me, on and off the park. These two men took a chance on me and taught me a lot about the game of football. I can't say enough about the respect I will always have for them.

Having positive influences, mentors and friends away from football has always been important to open my eyes to the wider world. It can be so easy to become a 'machine' as a footballer and live in a world where football is the only thing that exists. Spending time with people like Robert Earl, Alan Jones and Robert Thomson has allowed me to find and explore my passions away from the game, which has no doubt helped my football career in a roundabout way.

Post Everton, I want to thank Thierry Henry, Andy Roxburgh, Gérard Houllier, Don Garber, Mike Petke, Nate Camili and the squad and staff at the New York Red Bulls for showing me a whole new world of football away from the UK. My time spent in New York will be something that I will always look back on with great memories.

Playing for my country has always been one of my favourite footballing experiences and I firstly need to thank the tireless efforts of Frank Farina and Bonita Mersaides in making that possible in the first place. Without them, many of my greatest moments as a footballer could never have occurred. To Craig Johnston, Lucas Neill, Charlie Yankos, Phil Wolanski, Marco Bresciano, Mark Schwarzer, Graham Arnold, Archie Thompson, David Carney and Ange Postecoglou and all of my team-mates over the years, you have been my biggest influences in the Australian football community.

Dominic Rabsch, the Socceroos' kit-man, is a close friend who has been there since my first international. He's looked after me countless times and we've shared a journey over three World Cups, three Asian Cups and over 80 internationals. Dominic is a true example of how it isn't always about the players, and individuals such as Dom, Gary Moretti and Joel Freeme and all of the other Socceroos staff work tirelessly for the team behind the scenes.

I want to thank the team at Sanitarium, my first and longest-serving partners. To have formed enduring friendships away from business with Rick Wilson, Brett Lee and Neil Maxwell is a testament to that relationship that is still going strong today. Thanks also to Angelo Nicholson and family; Angelo has been a loyal friend to me and to my family.

Some other people I want to thank include Liz Leatherbarrow, who has done so much for my family and been an amazing friend and support for Bek and myself, and Mary Chiew from Armani, who taught me so much and helped develop my love of fashion.

To Chris Elder, thank you for being someone I can totally trust. Your guidance has been integral to me and you are someone I know will give me an honest answer about anything I ask. I want to acknowledge you as the ten-pin bowling champion and most importantly for always being there through thick and thin. I regard you as family and someone who will always be by my side, on and off the park, in everything I do.

Following on to Jake Elder, the mastermind behind my business, someone who is ambitious, driven and motivated to help me be as successful as possible on and off the park. Behind every sportsman there are important people supporting them on a day-to-day basis. Chris and Jake are my team and are pivotal to everything to do with the Cahill brand in Australia and Asia.

Thank you to Robbie Anderson for showing me how to put my passion for grassroots football into action, coaching my kids and flying around the world to run my academies. Robbie is important to me because of his appetite for the game, his love for his family and the support he has given to me and to my family. Robbie has shown me how to develop kids on and off the park, not just by teaching football but also by instilling the right attitudes and emotions. He is a close friend and a fellow die-hard blue. His son, also called Robbie, has been a great support and friend to my family in Australia as well.

To my extended family, the Mariners, Opetaias, Roberts, Stanleys, and all of my other cousins and relatives, I love every one of you and appreciate all of your love, support and company over the years, especially all the times as I was growing up that we spent at barbecues, kicking a ball around in the garden and playing video games together.

Lastly, thank you to every Millwall, Everton, New York Red Bulls, Shanghai Shenhua, Socceroos and football fan. It is your passion and love for the game that have given me a life beyond anything I could have dreamed of. To every person who has cheered their team on in a stadium, at a local oval, at a bar or at home, you are what makes football the beautiful game.

HarperCollins*Publishers*

First published in Australia in 2015
by HarperCollins*Publishers* Australia Pty Limited
ABN 36 009 913 517
harpercollins.com.au

HarperCollins*Publishers*
Level 13, 201 Elizabeth Street, Sydney NSW 2000, Australia
Unit D1, 63 Apollo Drive, Rosedale, Auckland 0632, New Zealand
A 53, Sector 57, Noida, UP, India
1 London Bridge Street, London, SE1 9GF, United Kingdom
2 Bloor Street East, 20th floor, Toronto, Ontario M4W 1A8, Canada
195 Broadway, New York NY 10007, USA

National Library of Australia Cataloguing-in-Publication data:

Cahill, Tim, 1979– author.
  Legacy / Tim Cahill.
  ISBN: 978 1 4607 5048 3 (hardback)
  ISBN: 978 1 4607 0504 9 (ebook)
  Subjects: Cahill, Tim, 1979–
  Soccer players – Australia – Biography.
  Soccer – Australia.
796.334092

Cover design by Matt Stanton, HarperCollins Design Studio
Front cover image by Adrian Cook
Back cover image: The Under-8s Balmain PCYC team in 1986, with Tim at right of the goalkeeper (courtesy Fairfax Syndication/Balmain Police Citizens Youth Club)
Inside front cover: Tim scores against Japan in the 2006 World Cup in Germany (Fairfax Syndication/Tim Clayton); celebrating a goal for Millwall against Norwich City in a Nationwide Division One match at the Den, London, 11 August 2001 (Getty Images/Mike Hewitt/ALLSPORT)
Inside back cover: Tim's children join the festivities after Australia's victory over South Korea in the AFC Asian Cup final, in Sydney on 31 January 2015 (Getty Images/AFP/Saeed Khan); Bek and the children on vacation (Tim Cahill); a spectacular scissor-kick goal against Chelsea at Stamford Bridge, London, 11 November 2007 (Getty Images/Richard Heathcote)
Typeset in Sabon by Kirby Jones
Printed and bound in Australia by Griffin Press
The papers used by HarperCollins in the manufacture of this book are a natural, recyclable product made from wood grown in sustainable plantation forests. The fibre source and manufacturing processes meet recognised international environmental standards, and carry certification.